DATE DUE

D1571530

Reading FAULKNER

Reading FAULKNER

Wesley Morris

with

Barbara Alverson Morris

The University of Wisconsin Press

The University of Wisconsin Press
114 North Murray Street
Madison, Wisconsin 53715

3 Henrietta Street
London WC2E 6LU, England

Printed in the United States of America

Library of Congress Cataloging-in-Publication Data
Morris, Wesley.
   Reading Faulkner/Wesley Morris with Barbara Alverson Morris.
   272 pp.   cm. — (The Wisconsin project on American writers)
   Includes bibliographical references and index.
   1. Faulkner, William, 1897–1962—Criticism and interpretation.
2. Social problems in literature.   3. Politics in literature.
I. Morris, Barbara Alverson.   II. Title.   III. Series.
PS3511.A86Z9137   1989
813'.52—dc 19   89-4806
ISBN 0-299-12220-4

For our children
John Wesley Alverson Morris, and
David Nathaniel Alverson Morris

CONTENTS

ACKNOWLEDGMENTS

The scholarly debts of this study are documented in the notes and need no reiteration here, but *Reading Faulkner* is not simply a book about dialogue, about conversation, it continues dialogue throughout and echoes many conversations that mark the true origins of its composition. Those conversations trace back over ten years to talks we had with David Minter about his Faulkner passion. There were conversations with John Irwin and Carolyn Porter which began in Houston and continued long distance to Athens, Georgia, and Berkeley, California. I am particularly indebted to conversations with Frank Lentricchia and to that wondrous Mellon Seminar on Faulkner and modern theory that we co-directed in Houston. Some of the papers of that seminar have appeared in the *New Orleans Review* and remain now as testimony to the energy and inventiveness of those daily discussions. In the several seminars I have taught at Rice University the work of undergraduate and graduate students has continually raised issues and released them into discourse. How much of this book belongs to those half-remembered, deeply influential exchanges I cannot measure, but without them I would not have undertaken to write on Faulkner and modern theory.

There is one debt, however, that is clear and distinct. Barbara Alverson Morris has always been a brilliant participant in these conversations. To her I owe the greatest debt, for it was she who began writing on Faulkner before I took up the challenge. And again, I am certain that were it not for her essays I would not have been inspired to my own poor efforts. Her presence in these pages is pervasive, but in particular Chapters 1 and 2 of Part 2 are substantially her writing. Her love of Faulkner and familiarity with modern theory continually reassured and directed me. Often in casual talks which seemed far from the rude and unrewarding world of academic scholarship she unlocked a bit of a mystery or challenged a complacent opinion in consequence of which this is a better work. She is the best reader of Faulkner.

Houston
June 5, 1988

WESLEY MORRIS

PART I
_____

Reading the Critics

CHAPTER 1

Representation: Theory and Practice

FAULKNER'S POWERFUL representation of the South is the true ground upon which we must measure his achievement as a writer. But representation in Faulkner implies no truth claims. Accuracy, the authenticity of Faulkner's experience as a Southerner, is not an issue. The South of Faulkner's representation has no priority to its narration; there is no original South against which to measure the precision of the copy. What critics usually mean by Faulkner's South, both those who affirm and those who deny the aesthetic significance of the representational dimension of Faulkner's fiction, is a geographical space, a familiar reality displayed in the manner of a road map, a place one might visit because it is defined by its borders, identified by a road sign: "YOU ARE NOW ENTERING . . ." Faulkner's South, for these critics, has a proper name, "Mississippi," which seems to guarantee the objective existence of a place that is displaced into the language of Faulkner's texts as "Yoknapatawpha." It is just this that Howard Odum claims: "I myself have known Yoknapatawpha, and it is no purely imaginary fantasy. . . . I have been close enough to Faulkner's quicksands to sense something of its terrors and have often imagined, behind the cedars and columned houses, that anything could happen there."[1] Yet the power of Faulkner's representation is only indirectly related to such a sense of place. Odum's is a stock response, the recalling of images of a place created by American journalism, history, and art. Faulkner, of course, contributed to this store of images; he helped produce the South he represents for us, a South realized, articulated in discursive practice. And this South, for all its discursivity, is no less a place and a time where people lived and died, loved and hated, listened to the tales told by others who had or had not been there. The telling makes it so.

Reading Faulkner, therefore, disabuses us of the simplistic ontological skepticism of antirepresentation theories. "Reality" has been problematical throughout the history of the philosophy of mimesis, and modern skeptical thinking is merely one version of an old set of issues. The question has always been one of priorities, whether one speaks of what one sees or sees that of which one speaks. The one genuinely new focus added to the history of representation by contemporary thinkers, however, is the displacement of models drawn from the visual arts by those taken from semiotics. Foucault's striking essay on Magritte, *This Is Not a Pipe*, is a case in point. Representational accuracy in Magritte's painting merges the visual and the linguistic; what Foucault emphasizes is the departure of the image from the mechanics of copying into the function of signifying. Representation *says* something about something, but that latter "thing" is the activity of representation itself. The process is circular, although never innocent. Moreover, we must think of semiotic representation as a departure from monologue as well as a departure from the visual. The classical model of imitative art rested on the transaction between an individual artist and reality, whether this latter was conceived of naively or with neo-Kantian skepticism. What this transaction produced was the artist's version of the real, perhaps a revelation of the object of imitation, a representation of something that is known but not present. The crisis of modernist subjectivity, on the other hand, problematized this transaction and produced a postmodern investigation of the act of signification itself. Semiotic representation, consequently, became entangled in the structure of signification. Language emerged as the medium of representing reality but also as the object represented, for the images of language were unable to copy by drawing or outlining; signs were double: they represented diacritically as well as referentially. What was said indicated an object in one's experience of the real world only by way of its prior participation in a collective discursive practice.

Foucault's discussion of "serial representation" emphasizes the secondary status of the object of imitation. His theory issues from the context of a radically secular consumer society where mass production obscures the model; there is no discernible original that is simply reproduced, no first version to be copied. An "original" is an outmoded idea in a society where repetition of "the same" has displaced the quest for the unique. Faulkner resisted the coming of this postmodern world

throughout his career; yet he did so by means of repetition, for he discovered in the representational powers of language a repetition with
difference. This discovery, of course, is the play of what Jacques Derrida terms "differance," and the interpenetration of Derridian presence
and absence in language is a persistent theme in Faulkner's representation of the South. His southern novels reproduce for us the mystery
of lost presences; traces of messages from the past, in many voices, ob-
trude into his narratives, appropriate the narratives at times, and recede
into a hazy background at others. On occasion the author's narrative
voice seems to resign its authority to the discourse of others just as
do the character-narrators; the struggle to speak forms the tensional
undergirding of the novels.

Simply stated, the story Faulkner narrates has been told many times,
and his novels are partly commentaries on these tellings as well as critical interpretations of the act of retelling. There is, after all, a critical
sensibility necessary to commentary. The author's identity is in question; insofar as all writing is immersed in discursive practice, commentary may not legitimately be thought of simply as self-expression.
The Derridian critique of such self-expression is persuasive, and after
his early "aesthetic" novels Faulkner abandoned this particular romantic idea, although he remained, in his self-portrait, always a romantic
figure.

To accept self-expression as an illusion does not, of course, render
the writer a passive conduit for the voices of others. The relationship
between author and discourse, *parole* and *langue,* is adversarial. The
writer is not appropriated by discourse any more than he appropriates
it. His commentary may be designed to set off deconstructive confes-
sion in the writings of others, as it is in the strategic rhetoric of the
early Derrida. Or, in the mode of Harold Bloom, the term "commentary" may be rewritten as "profession," wherein the voices of others are
misappropriated for the purpose of defining the author's different and
superior position. In either case, there is no position outside discourse,
and commentary and profession both involve critical awareness and
interpretation of collective discursive practices. Writing that desires to
say something rather than to be said situates the author for us. It is
here that we find the biographical and psychoanalytical coordinates of
geography and history, the "reality" that is represented in that author's
writing.

Faulkner's narrative genius, like that of Joyce and Dickens but very
few others, moves between two definitive poles of representation. The

discourse of the South is both historical and mythical, the difference between the two being functional and somewhat Aristotelian. Myth is the plot imposed upon history to render logical that which is merely accidental, but, expressed in this manner, this dualism is little more than a formalist tautology. As an element of discursive practice, as commentary and not profession, historical narration is the representation of social practice, of behavior; it is the articulation of an explanation of the hegemonic in the order of events. The characters of history are dispersed according to race, class, and gender, and the method of history is the gathering of scraps of conversation and fragments of texts. History is obsessed with voices in the play of absence and presence, for history is by nature nostalgic and ethical. Mythical narration, as profession and not commentary, is a representation of the unconscious ideology of social action. Ideology is not exterior to discourse or separable from it; its narration as myth is an articulation of an explanation of the universal order of things. Myth is obsessed with power and authority, legitimacy and originality; its methods are parabolic and its nature is moral. For Heidegger the subject matter of myth was the "destiny" of a people,[2] and this is a useful definition as long as we remember that myths are made and not found. What is most interesting is that history and myth, while narrating the past, must be composed, or recomposed, always in the present. As distinctly different narrative functions they reveal to us a distinction that is not clear in social practice and discourse: that between hegemony and ideology.

The reading of Faulkner put forth in the following pages proposes that history and myth, hegemony and ideology are the elements which comprise his life as a writer. His representation of the South contains its own critique of the South, and, as a consequence, his novels are both commentary and profession. They express thematically and structurally the social and historical conditions which form the discursive practice within which he wrote. Yet this implies nothing about his conscious or unconscious intentions with regard to his subject matter; those intentions are not themselves an explanation of literary works but a part of their production, their meanings. Neither is the formalist alternative valid, the reading of texts for what is said, regardless of intention or discursive context. Reading Faulkner will necessarily take us beyond text and intention, for what Faulkner said or intended to say is not all that can be said about the meaning of his literary productions.

The task of any critic is to read the deferred meaningfulness of the text. By such a discursive practice of interpretation, the critic reestablishes the text. Meaning is not recovered or induced or mystified, all of which deny the text its discursive dynamics. It is, therefore, out of respect for the text that the critic will refuse to read it closely and reverently. Pierre Macherey puts the role of the critic, the difficulty of critical practice, very clearly.

> The work must be elaborated, *used,* for without this it will never be a theoretical fact, an object of knowledge; but it must also be *left* as it is, if we are to achieve a theoretical judgment and avoid value judgments. It must be constructed and maintained within its proper limits: that is to say, not used for edification. This double requirement will only really make sense if it corresponds to the nature of the work. The writer's work must be open to displacement, otherwise it will remain an object of consumption rather than an object of knowledge.[3]

No American writer's work opens itself for critical displacement more readily than Faulkner's, yet for many years the critical tradition largely repressed that openness for the purpose of a certain edification that explicitly denied Faulkner's novels their status as objects of knowledge. Recently, however, readings of Faulkner have departed from that tradition of denial and repression and have initiated a critical dialogue with the Faulknerian texts. It should be clear that this reading of Faulkner is implicated in that critical departure. But more than that is at issue here, for the claim will be made that any productive interpretation of Faulkner must henceforth self-consciously acknowledge its participation in this critical departure. Thus the double burden of reading Faulkner is to establish the novels historically and to read them not only against this background as critical representations but also within the context of their critical history. The theoretical and practical concerns of literary criticism merge in such a productive enterprise, and the achievement of that merger may be the most significant problem confronting contemporary literary theory.

CHAPTER 2

Political Writing / Political Interpretation

I T I S R E M A R K A B L E that Maxwell Geismar included Faulkner in his *Writers in Crisis: The American Novel, 1925–1940* given the general opinion in the early forties that Faulkner's novels showed no authorial interest in social or political issues. Faulkner's compatriots in crisis according to Geismar were Lardner, Hemingway, Dos Passos, Wolfe, and Steinbeck, all with strong political credentials. Nonetheless, Geismar recognized Faulkner's place among these writers of the late twenties and thirties even if he found Faulkner's often reactionary politics difficult to stomach. Of this period he claimed that "never before, perhaps, has the American writer been subject to so many changing pressures within so short a period." [1] It is also interesting that this crisis for Geismar is broadly American, although when he comes to Faulkner and Wolfe it is their southern heritage that occupies his attention. Faulkner's southernism is central, of course, but it is necessary to bear in mind that the cultural crisis in the South of the twenties and thirties was not an alien or isolated phenomenon.

It is equally important that Faulkner was, as Warren Beck puts it, a man of ideas with a point of view. [2] Or perhaps it is better to say with Daniel Joseph Singal "We must see Faulkner . . . for what he was— an immensely gifted intellectual living through an experience of intractable cultural change." [3] Singal's fine book focuses on the South, more precisely on the southern mind, which places Singal in the tradition of W. J. Cash, although not in imitation of him. I will call upon Singal often in the following pages, but here the emphasis falls on the characterization of Faulkner as an "intellectual." Faulkner's representation

8

of the South in crisis is too self-consciously critical to be the work of an unreflective primitive, and we will see that his career is structured around a series of carefully orchestrated critical works which are also novels. Yet if Faulkner is not a primitive neither is he a philosopher. His representation of the South is not objective-scientific or speculative; he is not writing documentaries so much as participatory accounts of that crisis of cultural change that swept the South in the twenties and thirties. In this respect Faulkner's writing resembles in crucial ways the sociological work of James Agee and Walker Evans in *Let Us Now Praise Famous Men*, the primary experiences for which occurred in 1936, the year of publication of Faulkner's most ambitious effort at representing the South, *Absalom, Absalom!*

Agee's flamboyant style has Faulknerian character, and Agee shared Faulkner's modernist distrust of language as a representation of the truth. Yet despite the flourishes of Agee's writing, he advocated the avoidance of self-conscious artfulness; it was a lack of art that he admired in Evans' photographs. Richard King notes that the effect of the juxtaposition of Evans' pictures and Agee's writing is like Brechtian "alienation."

> Evans's photographs work against the grain of Agee's prose. In their spare, austere, even classical quality, they come much closer to Agee's aesthetic than do the writer's romantic sensibility and literary style, which is dense, convoluted, and often extremely self-conscious.[4]

Faulkner, of course, openly sought the devices of art and a flamboyant style in his presentation of his southern world, yet here too I would argue that there is an alienating effect that distances the reader from the comfort of programmatic commentary. Neither Agee nor Faulkner does all the work for the reader; neither adopts a realist or naturalist stance toward the objects of his representation. They describe for us their participation in the subject, a generative-interpretive and critical interaction that forces the reader also to participate. One cannot remain passive or neutral toward the worlds they present.

Agee, of course, was obsessed with photographs because he believed words failed more readily than pictures. For Agee photography did not describe so much as it represented its subject in what today would be called unmediated presence. Faulkner was not concerned with such presencing; for him the problem with words lay in the relationships between language, human feelings, and human actions. His most eloquent spokesperson on this subject is Addie Bundren.

I would think how words go straight up in a thin line, quick and harmless, and how terribly doing goes along the earth, clinging to it, so that after a while the two lines are too far apart for the same person to straddle from one to the other; and that sin and love and fear are just sounds that people who have never sinned nor loved nor feared have for what they never had and cannot have until they forget the words.[5]

The distance between doing and saying is most problematic when language represses human experience as it does in mere description or in the egocentrism of mere self-expression. Language represses when it is not shared, when it is not communal, when there is only monologue and no dialogue. Faulkner's concern, therefore, is not classically mimetic, not with the clear articulation of experience through a well-made plot or a realistic description of a setting. Rather, his emphasis falls on the modern issues of narrative voice, expression, and communication. Addie's critique of language springs from her sense of isolation, and her disillusion with words reflects her conviction that in her world the most fundamental of all human emotions, love and fear, as well as the most communal and ritualistic of human actions, sin, are not the focus of shared human sympathies. Talk for Addie is empty of all true exchange of feelings and ideas, of all dialogue. For Addie loneliness is the condition of monologue.

As I Lay Dying is a novel of isolation; in the rigidity of its fragmenting form, which denies dialogue and virtually dismantles social discourse, it is more like *The Sound and the Fury* than any other Faulkner novel. The narrative voice is purified and simplified in these two works; but despite the power of the stories told, this form of narrative presented Faulkner with a dead end. It was suicidally destructive of individual and community and failed to serve Faulkner's primary goal of representing the South. Faulkner's career as a writer is marked by a dialectical participation in a southern discursive practice that is enormously complex, polyvocal, and often filled with contradictory perspectives. This is the South he sought to represent in his novels, and it is both a prison house and a generative power for him, the "old tales and talking"[6] to which he added his own voice, itself comprising many voices not his own. "I listen to the voices, and when I put down what the voices say, it's all right. Sometimes I don't like what they say, but I don't change it."[7]

The dismantling of social discourse and destruction of community expressed in Addie's language theory and in the fragmented form of the narrative do not banish discourse and community altogether from *As I Lay Dying*. The world of the Bundrens clearly represents the social and economic conditions of many poor white farmers in the South in the late twenties, but most critical attention has focused on the experimental nature of the narrative, particularly its formal similarities to *The Sound and the Fury*.[8] The anguish of Addie's monologue, expressed in puzzling stylistic twists, with its powerful political statement concerning a woman's role in the family and rural southern society, has largely been ignored by readers who prefer to discuss style or narrative structure for its own sake. The implication is that politics and aesthetic form are two separate aspects of writing, and with this particular novel the claim is that Faulkner was interested only in the latter. Robert Penn Warren, like many critics, finds Faulkner utterly apolitical and is hard-pressed to understand why.

> It is really strange that in his vast panorama of society in a state where politics is the blood, bone, sinew, and passion of life, and the most popular sport, Faulkner has almost entirely omitted, not only a treatment of the subject, but references to it.[9]

To be sure, Warren's own essay, "Faulkner: The South, the Negro, and Time," appears in his collection of Faulkner criticism along with other politically oriented essays by Edmund Wilson, Elizabeth Hardwick, Andrew Lytle, V. S. Pritchett, and Norman Podhoretz. Yet for the most part, these critics find in Faulkner's fiction a general lack of political commitment and in his public statements an unfortunate but largely irrelevant reactionary temperament. Moreover, and much more unforgivable, there is a tendency to excuse this temperament on the grounds of Faulkner's great talents as an artist.

Faulkner, of course, lends support to the accusation that politics plays no role in his novels in an often-cited passage from *Faulkner in the University*: "If one begins to write about the injustice of society, then one has become a polemicist or a propagandist."[10] This statement alone, however, is out of context; the passage goes on to say that the injustices of society (and the inevitable political implications thereof) are not excluded from his work.

> The fiction writer is not that [a propagandist]; he will use the injustice of society, the inhumanity of people, as a—as any other tool in telling a story, which is about people, not about the injustice or inhumanity of people but of people, with their aspirations and their struggles and

the bizarre, the comic, and the tragic conditions they get themselves into simply coping with themselves and one another and environment.[11]

What we see first in this passage, what was seen by critics like Warren who found Faulkner apolitical, is a simplistic either/or choice between being a fiction writer or a political polemicist. It is in this same spirit that Faulkner proclaimed his amusement at hearing critical discussions "about the sociological picture" presented "in something like *As I Lay Dying.*"[12] But here as elsewhere in Faulkner's comments the terms "propagandist," "polemicist," and "sociological" are to be read narrowly, for surely the recognition of injustice and inhumanity and the writing about a people's aspirations and struggles constitute a fundamentally sociological and propagandistically political act of consciousness. Faulkner tells us, in effect, that social action and issues of social justice inform the very structure of his storytelling.

One must differentiate between political writing as propaganda— a question of genre—and political interpretation which is an action taken with regard to any text. One can refrain, as Faulkner usually did, from making overt political pronouncements, but this does not mean that his novels thereby exclude political readings. No text neutralizes political interpretation; Faulkner's texts invite it, for Faulkner is more sociological than he thinks in his investigations of human behavior and motives, in his interest in the psychology of individuals and groups, and in his observations and recordings of human injustice and aspirations. Critics like Philip Rahv, who charged Faulkner's work with being politically "impotent," and Granville Hicks, who argued that "Faulkner was not 'interested in representative men and women' but only in criminal violence and insanity that cannot lead . . . to any 'constructive analysis,' " are not so much wrong as misfocused, single-mindedly looking for overt polemics.[13] Their error is generic, which prevents them from seeing precisely what they are seeking. Both echo the more famous and formidable charge that Sartre leveled at *The Sound and the Fury*: "In Faulkner's work, there is never any progression, never anything which comes from the future."[14] Implicit in Sartre's sophisticated critique of the concept of time in Faulkner's narratives is the political activist's argument that Faulkner denies the possibility of change and consequently lacks any programmatic approach to reform of those injustices that provide the subject matter of his narrative representations of the South. Faulkner is depicted as all talk and no action; and Sartre's analysis, largely concerned with the suicidal Quentin in *The*

Sound and the Fury, is accurate. But if one views that novel in the context of Faulkner's more "historical" works, Sartre's critique, like Rahv's and Hicks', is misfocused. Faulkner dwells on the past where "everything *was,*" as Sartre puts it, yet he does so from the perspective of the present, that is, from the South of the late twenties and thirties where history reified in myth acts as a barrier to any future projects. The "past," Faulkner wrote, "is never dead. It's not even past."[15] These are the conditions of Faulkner's social being and what he consciously and critically represents to us as cultural obstacles to southern critical thinking.

That myth of a past social order was constantly rewritten, although not often critically, from the twenties to the forties by southern journalists, religious and political leaders, as well as historians, sociologists, and novelists. It is not surprising that Faulkner's Yoknapatawpha novels, produced during that same period, also engage that rewriting process. The fundamental problem for Faulkner was to discover the thin line of demarcation that runs between history as retarding and history as enlightening. Edmund Wilson defends Faulkner on this point, directly countering the Sartrean charge that nothing progressive can come from an investigation of the past.

> I do not sympathize with the line of criticism which deplores Faulkner's obstinate persistence in submerging himself in the mentality of the community where he was born, for his chivalry, which constitutes his morality, is a part of his Southern heritage, and it appears in Faulkner's work as a force more humane and more positive than almost anything one can find in the work of even those writers of our more mechanized societies who have set out to defend human rights.[16]

Wilson suggests that Faulkner's nonpolemical way may be the most effective way of encouraging social and political change. The argument here is a complex one; Faulkner's defense of his heritage must confront the repressive excesses of his culture, and to do so strikes at the very heart of that culture, destroying its value for the present. Yet as a modernist, one not yet suffering the postmodernist's displacement from history, Faulkner believed that one cannot simply deny one's past. His strategy as a writer was to approach the past from a variety of perspectives in the present, to span a broad spectrum of lives as they are absorbed by a past reified in myth. *The Sound and the Fury* approaches this perspective, but critics fail to take much notice of the roughly contemporary novel *As I Lay Dying* which is set in the present and focused

on the immediate future. If the central themes of *Flags in the Dust* and
The Sound and the Fury revolve around the characters' fixations on
southern history, there is no such obsession in *As I Lay Dying*. Faulkner took time out from the rewriting of the past in order to write about
a contemporary poor white family with no discernible genealogy nor
any involvement in the great problematics of the southern cultural past.

   As I Lay Dying was a pivotal work in Faulkner's newly flowering
career. He described it in terms of his sense of a growing mastery of
narrative form, as something of a test case to prove to himself, and
the world, that he was a first-rate writer. But there may have been
other motivating forces. In the same year as he wrote *As I Lay Dying*,
1929, both *Sartoris* (January 31) and *The Sound and the Fury* (October 7) were published with little sales; Faulkner married Estelle Old-
ham (June 20), settled in Oxford, and the Great Depression began with
the stock market crash of October 29. All of these events must have had
an immediate impact on Faulkner's consciousness. The market failures
and general economic tragedy in particular surely made the future of a
writer with new family responsibilities seem unpromising, and it is not
unlikely that this novel about poor rural whites, however bizarre their
actions, reflects some sympathy for those whose material conditions
were much more desperate than his own.

   The most often discussed facts of the writing of *As I Lay Dying*,
however, are the speed with which it was produced and the conditions
of its composition.[17] Faulkner's critics, and even his biographers, take
little notice of the proximity of the novel's writing to the Wall Street
disaster. David Minter, in fact, mentions this only to suggest that there
is no meaningful connection between the two events.

> Late in October, as panic began to signal America's long economic
> nosedive, Faulkner began calmly writing a new novel. This time he knew
> exactly what he was doing and where he was going. Like *Sanctuary*,
> his new novel would be deliberate. But this time his intention was to
> demonstrate his mastery of fiction.[18]

   The circumstances of the writing of *As I Lay Dying*, during night
shift work at an Oxford power plant, have generally led critics to depict the author in a romantic stereotype as isolated and withdrawn
from the world. It is a pose Faulkner rarely affected. Cleanth Brooks
comments on Faulkner's more typical "unwillingness to call himself a
literary man. He was, he said, simply a teller of tales or even more

simply, just a farmer." [19] Clearly there is exaggeration here, but there is also a warning to critics that writing ought not to be romanticized in terms of the purity of creativity and the alienation of the aesthetic from the concerns of the world. Writing under the pressure of economic need while working nights in a power plant is likely to produce an intense awareness of the concrete circumstances of the writer's life; it is certainly no ideal place of withdrawal from which Faulkner could allow his servants to do his living for him. Clearly this novel is, as Minter puts it, "deliberate," an artistic tour de force which supports Minter's contention that Faulkner was out to "demonstrate his mastery of fiction." "It was as though," Minter continues, "he had set out to make *As I Lay Dying* what Conrad Aiken thought *The Sound and the Fury* had become—a novelist's novel, a kind of textbook on the craft of fiction." [20] None of this, however, confronts the choice of subject matter or the possible relation that subject matter had to Faulkner's sense of his own uncertain professional prospects.

There is in Faulkner criticism, even among his biographers at critical junctures, almost a compulsion to split apart Faulkner the artist and Faulkner the public person, to divide art and life, despite the author's extraordinary and consistent efforts at representation of southern society from the perspective of his concrete experiences. André Bleikasten begins his study of *As I Lay Dying* with a discussion of the novel's subject matter, specifically noting that its rural setting and poor white characters constitute a significant departure from Faulkner's earlier Yoknapatawpha works. Bleikasten then turns his attention to possible sources for the Bundren story, finally concluding that it is irrelevant whether or not Faulkner knew such a family because the novel is no roman à clef.

> The primary source . . . , the most obvious and most elusive, is none other than the South itself. There is nothing surprising in that when one knows that almost all Faulkner's books share the same source. [21]

Unfortunately at this level of generalization the fact that *As I Lay Dying* departs in setting and character from Faulkner's earlier novels also seems irrelevant. Bleikasten simply drops his discussion of subject matter altogether, having easily dismissed any notions of the novel's being about a specific Mississippi family. He then proceeds to discuss the novel's artistic sources, its formal and thematic borrowings from Joyce, Eliot, and Hawthorne. These are flattering and deserved comparisons, yet one might also argue that *As I Lay Dying* should be read as a foreshadowing of a host of Depression era novels, the sources of which are rural, southern, and the subjects of which are poor whites, novels from Caldwell's *God's Little Acre* (1933) to Steinbeck's *The Grapes of Wrath* (1939).

We shouldn't dismiss Faulkner's stories as apolitical, therefore, simply because they are not openly polemical. Sylvia Jenkins Cook points out that "in his treatment of poor whites and southern society generally, Faulkner is as acutely class-conscious as any Marxist and as prone to patterns of economic sympathy and class allegiance." [22] Her insightful analysis of a story like "Wash" reveals the centrality of the theme of awakening poor white class-consciousness. Having killed Thomas Sutpen, his landlord and his image of heroic southern masculinity, for the insulting refusal to marry his granddaughter who has borne Sutpen a female child, Wash Jones realizes for the first time the repressiveness of his former relationship with Sutpen. He awaits what he knows will be the inevitable arrival of a posse.

> Now he seemed to sense, feel, the men who would be gathering with horses and guns and dogs—the curious, and the vengeful: men of Sutpen's own kind, who had made the company about Sutpen's table in the time when Wash himself had yet to approach nearer to the house than the scuppernong arbor—men . . . who had also galloped in the old days arrogant and proud on the fine horses across the fine plantations—symbols also of admiration and hope; instruments too of despair and grief.[23]

Cook's reading of this story emphasizes the ideological functioning of these "symbols of admiration and hope," figures of a world of ease and power that made Wash's poverty seem less bitter. More significant, however, Wash's flickering insight into this repressive system is signaled by the contrasting phrase "instruments too of despair and grief." This is, of course, merely a shadowing of a genuine class-consciousness, for Wash's despair focuses on nothing beyond the destruction of admiration and hope that marks the collapse of a deeply felt symbolic system, the loss of a personal, albeit class-representative, ideal of achieved wealth and power that Wash was permitted to enjoy, if only at a distance through occasional associations. It is an almost incomprehensible discovery for him.

> Maybe if he had gone to the war with them he would have discovered them sooner. But if he had discovered them sooner, what would he have

done with his life since? How could he have borne to remember for five years what his life had been before?

("Wash," CS, 547)

The fall of an idol, by his own hands, leaves Wash tragically with no future as well as no past, but the reader has no difficulty in grasping that Faulkner understood that such idols, regardless of personal despair, must be brought down if progress in deconstructing social injustice is to be made. Interpolated into *Absalom, Absalom!* the story of Wash Jones, set after the defeat of the South, ironically repeats a very different awakening to the repressiveness of antebellum southern class structure on the part of the young, lower-class Sutpen himself and brings into focus the distinction between the establishing of a myth of social order (in Sutpen's antebellum rise to power and wealth) and that myth's death (in Wash's desperate and disillusioned act of vengeance) after the Civil War.

Thus the critical gap between fiction and fact, which lies at the heart of the either/or choice between art and life fostered by a naive reading of Faulkner, confounds the very language of literary interpretation. Terms like "sociological" and "political" and "representational" do not mean the same thing, nor does the term "political" describe only one sort of human activity, yet these terms do overlap and modify one another. The representation of society has sociological implications because the activity of representing involves choice, judgment, and accentuation, and through its sociological implications and historical representations it merges into the realm of political action. The simplicity of either/or has no place here, and, it will become clear, no place in reading Faulkner's novels.

Nevertheless, the critical language of either/or is difficult to avoid. The challenge to political interpretation always comes in that simplistic form. Louis Rubin, specifically attacking Richard King but deliberately misreading him, provides a remarkably instructive example of the blindness of the art-versus-politics position.

In demanding that Faulkner's presentation of his community's heritage of racial injustice "lead to or suggest a way of translating moral gesture into political action," he [King] is asking that literature become, in effect, the agency of action. But the novelist's responsibility to truth is through and in art; and the morality, racial or otherwise, of a work of fiction must lie not in a prescription for action but in exploration, in language, of the human experience it recreates.[24]

Rubin's argument may seem at many points persuasive, but it is an uncritical version of the traditional defense of art against the impurities of politics. Rubin conflates King's statement on the failure of Ike McCaslin to translate moral gesture into political action with what he hopes we will see as an outrageous suggestion that all literature become the agency of political action. King's reading of Ike's repudiation of his inheritance and withdrawal from society, however, makes no such demand. King is merely interested in the apolitical context of Ike's actions in the narrative itself, and he goes out of his way to give Ike credit for the difficulty and critical awareness of his decision. King finally expresses a judgment very similar to that voiced by Warren: "For all the richness of Faulkner's world, it is one which presents no political 'space' within which collective, public action can be taken seriously."[25]

Of course, this lack of political space is central to Faulkner's representation of the southern critical dilemma, of the difficulty of isolating oneself from the community and the terrible force of cultural myths and social solidarity. Ike's actions are presented as futile, misdirected, and tragically noble. In Ike, Faulkner saw the limitations of his own romantic sensibility, his attachment to the heroic gesture of a lonely but morally superior individual, and he could never see beyond such a gesture to any truly collective action. Nevertheless, the devastating moment in "Delta Autumn" when Ike seems to realize that his individual moral gesture has made no impact on the world of social injustice stands as a repudiation of such moral gesturing. Faulkner may not have grasped, or he may have repressed, the idea that a collective response was necessary to bringing about social and political reform, but the reader is made vividly aware of that repression of any space for political action in southern society.

Moral gesture, written into the plot of a narrative that centrally depicts social injustice, invites political interpretation. In this sense the novel is an agent for political activity. Rubin's fears are realized in Macherey's description of what must be the elaboration or *use* of a work in order for it to be available for true interpretation rather than mere edification. "The writer's work must be open to displacement, otherwise it will remain an object of consumption rather than an object of knowledge."[26] In *Go Down, Moses* Faulkner forces the reader into making a judgment on Ike's actions or lack thereof. Significantly, discussing Ike's refusal some years after the publication of the novel, Faulkner clearly defines the latent and unavoidable political dimension of his writing.

Well, there are some people in any time and age that cannot face and cope with the problems. There seem to be three stages: The first says, This is rotten, I'll have no part of it, I will take death first. The second says, This is rotten, I don't like it, I can't do anything about it, but at least I will not participate in it myself, I will go into a cave or climb a pillar to sit on. The third says, This stinks and I'm going to do something about it. McCaslin is the second. He says, This is bad, and I will withdraw from it. What we need are people who will say, This is bad and I'm going to do something about it, I'm going to change it.[27]

The three-stage structure of this definition of human action and in-action is too complex and neatly expressed to have been a spur of the moment thought. In fact, Walter Taylor writes, Faulkner has given us examples of all three in Quentin Compson, Ike McCaslin, and Charles Mallison, chronologically presented over the span of writing his Yoknapatawpha novels.[28] What is most interesting, however, is the addition of an exhortation to political action following his description of Ike McCaslin's role in this three-staged system. Faulkner makes the very move away from the literary context to the world of real human actions that we must all make in our reading of his novels. The question of what to do about injustice, that is, "real" social injustice that is represented in the novel, is embedded in the presentation of that injustice, and the distance between fiction and political action is severely diminished.

CHAPTER 3

Great Works, Late Works:
The Representation of the Present

THE REFUSAL to read novels like *As I Lay Dying* and *Go Down,*
Moses for their obvious sociological and political implications
leads many critics to divide Faulkner's career into two unequal parts:
there is the "great" period from *The Sound and the Fury* to *Absalom,*
Absalom! (sometimes extended to include *Go Down, Moses* and *The*
Hamlet) which subsumes the apprentice stage of *Flags in the Dust* and
the earlier aestheticist novels; and there is the "late" period that begins
with *Intruder in the Dust* (sometimes with *Go Down, Moses*) and runs
through the last novel, *The Reivers*. The change from great to late, it is
claimed, defines Faulkner's loss of artistic power and the emergence of
his reactionary political consciousness. The implication, again, is that
art and politics are mutually exclusive. Singal is representative.

> As many have observed, these post–World War II novels are filled with
> explicit political statements of the kind Faulkner had avoided in the past.
> . . . Even Faulkner's style in these later works reflects his turn away from
> the depths of consciousness to surface matters—a "regression to lucidity,"
> R. W. B. Lewis has called it.[1]

For Singal, value-laden terms like "depth" and "surface" signify an
artistic distinction, describe a decline that needs no discussion. "Surface matters," the representation of social interaction involved in discursive practice, are treated as inherently unimportant because they
profess a more or less undisguised point of view. Singal accepts the

20

traditional formalist idea that art submerges or neutralizes the author's personality. On the other hand, Walter Taylor's alignment of Quentin, Ike, and Chick with Faulkner's three-stage structure of social/political action suggests a way of bridging the gap between the great/late divisions; for Taylor gives us the hint of a development in Faulkner's vision of the South and in his critical representation of it, a development that contained different responses and produced different narrative strategies—even different styles—in different novels.

Myra Jehlen, whose intelligent reading of Faulkner is the most complete of those few political interpretations now in print, also divides Faulkner's career into the traditional two parts; her argument, however, raises some interesting variations on the great/late theme. For Jehlen *Absalom, Absalom!* is the pivotal work that ends Faulkner's great period.

> Stylistically, *Absalom, Absalom!* spirals into confusing, sometimes self-parodying complexities. But this is also Faulkner's best work, the high point of his career which finally realized that potential we have traced unfolding in preceding stories but, paradoxically, was to be itself a sort of dead end. The most important of the writings following *Absalom, Absalom!* are the three Snopes novels and these show a marked shift in perspective toward a more conventional sociology and a more traditional style.

> Following the apotheosis which *Absalom, Absalom!* constitutes of his attempts to recapture the past, Faulkner took the logical next step and moved his fictional theater to the present.[2]

Many of Jehlen's most useful insights into Faulkner's representation of class structure in the South concern those novels written either prior to or long after the one she here designates as the best. Her discussion of class relations and prejudice in *Sartoris* establishes for us the tension, often raised in seemingly insignificant moments in the text, between the descendants of the old plantation owners like young Bayard Sartoris, for whom Faulkner evidences great sympathy, and poor whites like V. K. Suratt, whose depiction is more comic and alienating.[3] In addition, Jehlen convincingly demonstrates the depth of Faulkner's class prejudice against the Snopes characters, particularly in his agrarian bias against their urban commercialism. The Snopeses are largely "allegorical ciphers" in contrast to rounded and psychologically complex characters like Bayard.[4]

In Jehlen's treatment of *Sartoris* and the Snopes trilogy, class prejudice is central to the narratives, but in her development of this thesis in *Absalom, Absalom!* her discussion seems to miss the point. The focus of her interpretation is, naturally enough, Thomas Sutpen who embodies the basic class conflict of the old South between gentleman planter and redneck farmer. "On one level Sutpen as lord and peasant both can embody the entire white South corrupted and ultimately destroyed by the plantation system."[5] But there is curiously little discussion of Miss Rosa and her family alliance with Sutpen which introduces the middle class of small business people into the social equation, or of the Compsons as New South gentleman professionals, or even of Wash Jones, the redneck whose class outrage brings about the final destruction of Sutpen's design for an Old South cavalier dynasty. She treats Sutpen not as a projection of the thirties, of that southern project to rewrite the history of the South in order to sustain or recreate a myth, but rather as if he were an accurate representation of an antebellum aristocrat. This approach ignores the novel's narrative strategy, the retelling and recreating of a legend as an expression of present needs. Jehlen's treatment of this most complex narrative seems hasty, and her melodramatic conclusion, linking Faulkner and Quentin, lacks the subtlety of her readings of other novels.

> [Quentin] cries out, "I dont. I dont! I dont hate [the South]! I dont hate it!" Neither does Faulkner: but how to love it? At this moment, the culmination of his most creative period, he can neither go forward, which would mean to abjure at least the aristocratic tradition in Southern history, nor retract the terrible indictment the novel has constituted. After this Faulkner drew back, retreated, never again to expose himself to the terrors that had driven Quentin Compson to suicide.[6]

Her charge that Faulkner could not go forward here echoes the charge of Sartre that Faulkner fails to suggest a way beyond the conditions of his world as he saw them and represented them for his readers. Yet Jehlen praises the novel for sketching "a radically critical picture of the antebellum South,"[7] and notes that Faulkner does not retract this "terrible indictment."

In *Absalom, Absalom!* Faulkner's indictment is a "radically critical" demythologizing of the aristocratic cavalier myth; but rather than mark a cowardly moment of retreat, it prepares the way for the development of a different narrative strategy in his representation of the South.

That shift is visible in both *The Unvanquished* (which Jehlen misreads badly) and *Go Down, Moses* (which she dismisses as an inferior re-hash of the issues more artistically confronted in *Absalom, Absalom!*). It is not these novels, however, that Jehlen has in mind when she discusses the decline of Faulkner's writing after *Absalom, Absalom!*; it is *Intruder in the Dust* and the Snopes novels in particular which Jehlen sees as retreats and which convince her that *Absalom, Absalom!* was a dead end for its author, a terrifying experience that caused him to abandon his central thematics of southern history and lapse into reactionary politics. Such an explanation is not altogether acceptable. The reactionary tendencies were in Faulkner from the beginning, and the late novels are not such clear-cut cases of conservative thinking as Jehlen suggests. She is often prone to rather simplistic analyses of these late novels, as if declaring them to be artistically inferior deprives them of the right to serious interpretive attention. For example, she reads the voice of Gavin Stevens in *Intruder in the Dust* as an expression of Faulkner's racism[8] and claims that with Mink Snope's killing of his kinsman Flem, "*The Mansion* just disintegrates. Flem's defeat, which has been the central motive for the entire trilogy, is now accomplished without any consequences whatsoever. It means nothing."[9]

It is without question that Faulkner was unable to escape from his racist heritage despite his often demythologizing critical perspective on his society, and it is equally the case, as Jehlen asserts, that Faulkner simply did not like, and possibly feared, the Snopeses, a clear class prejudice. It is, nevertheless, inconsistent to credit him at one moment with an acutely sensitive response to his culture and its myths and prejudices and then condemn him at another for a lack of such critical sensibility, as if somehow in the meantime he forgot. Jehlen's reading of the final volume in the Snopes trilogy is a case in point. She argues that "the Snopes saga represents not a conservative resolution of the [class] conflict I have been tracing [between aristocratic planter and redneck farmer] but its last crisis,"[10] yet this interpretation does not inevitably lead to her conclusion that *The Mansion* is a meaningless finish to the story of Flem's defeat and of the Snopeses' rise and fall. Jehlen's problem here is, ironically, a formalist one: the unwillingness to read individual novels against one another.[11] In some crucial ways Flem Snopes repeats the tragic mistakes of Thomas Sutpen. Sutpen sought the power of socio-economic position, and his means of attaining that power were ruthlessness of action and the accumulating of wealth. His model of success was the Tidewater aristocratic planter, an image composed largely from the material trappings of plantation life, a simplified and purified version created in literature and movies. Sutpen is a representation of a representation and not a figure of actuality; he exists for us never as a character but only as a sign of that very simplification of the past that is symptomatic of the modern South's obsessive mythologizing. With Flem, however, the mythologizing has been pared away to reveal the raw motives that lie beneath the myths: desire for power and social position (prestige).

Jehlen is correct in identifying the internal conflicts of southern culture as destructive of that culture; these conflicts, as Faulkner expresses them, are centrally entangled in class relations which also involve issues of race and gender. What she does not grasp completely is that Faulkner was never concerned with the actuality of the antebellum South but always concerned with the living mythology of the southern past which found its expression in the everyday affairs of Southerners of the first half of the twentieth century. His critique of that mythology in *Absalom, Absalom!* is a critique of the present, and there is, therefore, no real shift of perspective in those novels written after *Absalom, Absalom!* The Snopes trilogy continues to trace the lingering effects of those myths of the past in the moral actions of those in the present; Flem Snopes repeats Thomas Sutpen—with a difference. In an important respect the Snopes stories critique the "historical" novels. When we reduce the distance between Snopes and Sutpen, then the Old South agrarian, aristocratic culture appears as little more than an early version of modern southern commercialism, the myth of entrepreneurial individualism and self-reliance gone wrong; Sutpen is nothing more than a businessman ruthlessly obsessed with the trappings of success: prestige, wealth, and power. The all-important questions of biological relations in Sutpen's dynastic "design" are rewritten, debiologized, unsexed in the story of Flem Snopes. The old mythology of power based on the primacy of the father has been stripped down in the Snopes trilogy, modernized into an impersonal power politics that dehumanizes and destroys society, and this without sentimental nostalgia for a golden past. Flem's death even repeats Sutpen's, for both die violently by the hands of profoundly disillusioned and repressed men. It would be hard to argue, even with all the romantic trappings of the Sutpen story, that Faulkner presented the mythology of the past as any more moral or desirable than the unscrupulous actions of Flem Snopes. There is in this a damaging critique of southern regionalism, for in the diminishing of the mythology of the aristocratic planter and the merging of Snopes commercialism and Sutpen aristocratic prestige into a common desire for power, the South seems less distinct from the dreaded North of commerce and industry than some southern apologists wished to claim. Faulkner was no such apologist.

CHAPTER 4

Roads and the Disintegrating Family

THE CULTURAL crisis which dominated the years between the two world wars reawakened in the South an interest in the past and spurred an extensive rewriting of southern history. The key to this revision was the still burdensome memory of defeat in the Civil War. Faulkner expresses the issues clearly.

> "It's all *now* you see. Yesterday wont be over until tomorrow and tomorrow began ten thousand years ago. For every Southern boy fourteen years old, not once but whenever he wants it, there is the instant when it's still not yet two oclock on that July afternoon in 1863, the brigades are in position behind the rail fence, the guns are laid and ready in the woods and the furled flags are already loosened to break out and Pickett himself with his long oiled ringlets and his hat in one hand probably and his sword in the other looking up the hill waiting for Longstreet to give the word and it's all in the balance, it hasn't happened yet . . . yet it's going to begin, we all know that, we have come too far with too much at stake." [1]

This was an obsessive theme for Faulkner as well as for many other southern writers and thinkers. The defeat was a barrier to regaining any regional pride; Gettysburg became a pervasive theme during Reconstruction, and it was revived in the twenties and thirties under the pressure of severe economic depression and the resultant changes in familiar social relations.

One important result was that despite the efforts of economic and political leaders, who shortly after the Civil War attempted to bring about an industrialization of the South, the southern mind-set con-

26

tinued to be dominated by Old South agrarian images and ideals long after the reality of an agrarian South had passed. By the 1920s cotton, the symbolic crop of the Old South, was no longer economically central; the agrarian South in general was in serious decline, the land exhausted, the timber harvested without adequate conservation. Traditional agrarian concepts of family and social order, therefore, conflicted with the economic realities of everyday life, and this conflict formed the ground for much of Faulkner's writing. Southern historian Thomas D. Clark notes that "eroded hillsides, depleted land, and wasted resources go far to document the Faulkner material,"[2] and that documentation played off against the enduring facticity of the Civil War leads to a partial unraveling of the southern mythology of the past, of the obsessive fascination with southern history that Faulkner represented for his readers in repetitious detail.

During the twenties and thirties, being a farmer, as Faulkner playfully characterized himself, was less feasible than being a millhand or miner or shopkeeper. Faulkner's agrarianism reflects the fact that Mississippi, the region of perhaps the most intense Old South mythologizing, lagged behind its neighboring Deep South states in industrial development; as late as 1960, 63 percent of rural Mississippians were farmers, and only one other southern state, South Carolina, was above 50 percent in this statistic.[3] Industrial options were not highly visible. But even so, farming in Faulkner's homeland was not what it once was. Modernization was apparent as agriculture became mechanized. Perhaps most symbolic of all, plow mules, a favorite Faulknerian motif, were rapidly being replaced in the fields by tractors. Moreover, in the South as nationally, farms grew in size while the number of family farms decreased, and insecure farm tenure led to extensive migration with the attendant results of poor education for migrant children and poor upkeep of sharecropped property. World War I had also uprooted significant portions of the population and helped initiate what was to become a major shift from rural to urban culture. Of most importance, however, are the alterations in attitudes which accompany such changes in circumstances. W. J. Cash, writing out of that period of change, offers a suggestive description of the effects of this unsettling of the traditional ways.

> The hunter who had formerly foraged for the larder while his women hoed the corn found himself with less and less to do. Lacking lands and markets which would repay any extensive effort as a farmer, lacking any

incentive which would even serve to make him aid the women at tasks which habit had fixed as effeminate, it was the most natural thing in the world for him to sink deeper and deeper into idleness and shiftlessness.[4]

There are two Faulknerian themes in Cash's theorizing. First is the romantic nostalgia for a lost "hunter" society, the frontier mythology that is one central theme in *Go Down, Moses*. As an old man Ike McCaslin dreams of this wilderness past where cavalier gentlemen tested their manhood in games of survival.

> "Eat," he said. "Eat it all up. I dont want a piece of town meat in camp after breakfast tomorrow. Then you boys will hunt. You'll have to. When I first started hunting in this bottom sixty years ago . . . Major de Spain wouldn't allow but two pieces of foreign grub in his camp. . . . It was to save until along toward the end of camp when everybody was so sick of bear meat and coon and venison that we couldn't even look at it."

> He seemed to see . . . the faces of the old men he had known and loved and for a little while outlived, moving again among the shades of tall unaxed trees and sightless brakes where the wild strong immortal game ran forever before the tireless belling immortal hounds, falling and rising phoenix-like to the soundless guns.[5]

In many ways Ike comes to represent that mythology of "better men" and more noble ways, a melancholy and politically reactionary resistance to change.

Second, Cash's characterization of the destructive effects of rapid social change on the individual spirit in the present recognizably fits Anse Bundren in *As I Lay Dying*. Despite the biting humor of Faulkner's treatment of the shiftless and hypocritical Anse, we should not dismiss too quickly the attitudes he expresses in his few chapters.

> It's a hard country on man; it's hard. . . . Nowhere in this sinful world can a honest, hardworking man profit. It takes them that runs the stores in the towns, doing no sweating, living off of them that sweats. It aint the hardworking man, the farmer. Sometimes I wonder why we keep at it.
>
> (*ALD*, p. 104)

Anse, of course, does not keep at it; what he voices here is merely a commonplace of the poor white farmer who is filled with resentment toward an increasingly urbanized world of apparent affluence and ease. This resentment, however, is only a symptom of far more complex fears. Anse's eccentrically comic thoughts on roads better express the feeling of personal and social disorientation general among southerners.

> Durn that road. . . .
> A-laying there, right up to my door, where every bad luck that comes and goes is bound to find it. . . . the Lord put roads for travelling: why he laid them down flat on the earth. When He aims for something to be always a-moving, He makes it longways, like a road or a horse or a wagon, but when he aims for something to stay put, He makes it up-and-down ways, like a tree or a man. . . . Because if He'd a aimed for a man to be always a-moving and going somewheres else, wouldn't He a put him longways on his belly, like a snake? It stands to reason He would.
> (*ALD*, pp. 34–35)

The Old Testament imagery adds doctrinaire moral force to Anse's commentary on the uprootedness of southern farmers in the twenties and thirties; migrating from place to place is *unnatural,* a violation of the prelapsarian divine will which created man erect above the lower creeping animals. The proper human way is to "stay put," to have a *place* to which one is rooted like a tree.

One culprit, another emanation of the industrial, urban North, was the automobile. In the 1920s there was an explosion of cars all across the country, their number increasing fourfold in the decade.[6] In rural America the conflict between the automobile and the horse or mule reflected a conflict of life-styles; the battle between the new and the old even works its way into the symbolic structure of Faulkner's first Yoknapatawpha novel, *Flags in the Dust.* A car, much scorned by the older generations, is instrumental in continuing the male Sartoris heritage of early and violent deaths. Road construction seriously lagged behind the booming manufacture of cars, yet this served only to increase the political and social interest in road building. During the Depression roads were a central goal of New Deal reforms in the South. Better roads, of course, made for easier travel, expanded horizons; those who had never ventured far from their ancestral homes were now encouraged to do so. The sense of place, rooted in the hereditary landholdings of the planter-farmer, was permanently undermined.

Anse is, of course, no cavalier with aristocratic pretensions, but his conception of "place" with its corollary of resisting change echoes Sutpen's desire to found an enduring dynasty on the land known, patriarchally, as "Sutpen's Hundred." The agrarian life assumes repetition, the cycle of seasons, crops, or generations all pivoting on a fixed point. Migrant farming or the insecurities of farm tenancy strike at the very heart of the southern agrarian mythology, and during the Depression years much farming was done by tenants who moved on the average of once every three years.[7] The effects of this unsettlement are remarkably narrated in a series of oral histories collected in the mid-thirties under the auspices of the Federal Writers' Project and originally published by the University of North Carolina as *These Are Our Lives.* Many of these "life stories" dwell on crop failures and children dying, yet the most consistently reported aspect of migrant life is the unsettled existence that is eloquently expressed in an interview with black sharecroppers.

> "Every day it's de same tale: 'I hain't found no place yet.' I hates to move; nobody knows how I hates to move!"
> "Yonder's somebody movin' now," Ola exclaims, looking out the window. All eyes turn toward the road. Over the deep ruts in the sand, wagon wheels grind slowly eastward; two wagons loaded with shabby furnishings wind around the curve out of sight.
> "Dat's de way we'll be soon—tore up and a-movin'. I wish I could have me one acre o' land dat I could call mine. I'd be willin' to eat dry bread de rest o' my life if I had a place I could settle down on and nobody could tell me I had to move no more. I hates movin'."[8]

Many sharecroppers harbored the dream of someday owning their own place, but ownership is more of an escape from the insecurity of tenancy than an end in its own right. One white tenant who would be most happy to rent tells us that his landlord

> "won't give me a five year lease and so I can't afford to make many improvements. If I was sure I could stay on, I would make over the house, fix up the terrace and clear some more land. The trouble is that just as sure as a tenant makes a farm more productive, the owner boosts his rent."[9]

Much of the narration in this collection is concerned with the raising of children. Any formal education is difficult; schools are inadequate for whites as well as blacks, and moving makes attendance that much harder. One small farm owner, who kept his moves to a minimum but nevertheless had to make several, says,

> "I tried to do the best for my children as they was growing up. They got all the schooling they was in the neighborhood. But most of them got no better schooling than I got."[10]

For the most part the desire for education is limited by a narrow assessment of possible goals.

> "I think too many boys and girls are going to college. They go just because they think it is the best thing to do. Every pupil ought to know what he wants to do before he leaves high school. Unless he is from a wealthy home he should begin preparation at once for his vocation."

> "I was talking with Professor Woods the other day. He teaches math in our high school. He has a little farm too, mostly a poultry farm. He gets about four hundred eggs a day during the winter. I have a lot of confidence in him. He tells me that there is no use for me to spend several hundred dollars sending Rufe to college unless he is sure he wants to do something that calls for college training."[11]

There are the familiar stories of young children pressed into work in order to bring in the crops, of the necessity of taking odd jobs to supplement the farm income. Tales of the children who move away to jobs in the cities are presented with a mixture of pride in those who can make a better life than that in which they were raised and nostalgia for a time when that move would not have been necessary.

> "The farms can't keep up the big families like they used to. Not near so many folks can live on the farms and work the land and make a living as a generation ago. The young folks have got nothing to look for ahead on a farm now as I did when I was a young man."[12]

Whatever the advantage of moving off the land, the old ways and old values died slowly. Anse Bundren's lament against modernism arises specifically from the fact that roads make leaving the farm easier: "Making me pay for Cash having to get them carpenter notions when if it hadn't been no road come there, he wouldn't a got them" (*ALD*, p. 35). Yet although many farms were still unmechanized and thus needed large families to work them, the decreasingly productive land could no longer support large numbers of children. Unfortunately, the result was not a slowing in the birthrate; large families continued to be the norm among poor southern tenant farmers, just as Anse expects Addie to bear him several sons. The Bundrens, like so many small farmers in the South at the end of the twenties, seem poised unknowingly on the brink of a treacherous transition which may well make it impossible to continue to claim, as Anse does, that he always managed to feed his family.

The most reprehensible reason for Anse's dislike of roads, of course, is that they provide too easy access to his remote farm for Dr. Peabody who has come to treat the dying Addie. Peabody will have to be paid. But Anse's mean-spirited motive should not cloud our understanding of the economic pressures which forced poor farmers to hesitate even in matters of life and death. One of the most powerful narratives from *These Are Our Lives* comes from a poor white sharecropper's wife, fictitiously named Irma.

> "When the second baby was four years old, he started gettin' pale and thin. We put him to bed one day because he looked so sick we thought he was going to die. We didn't call a doctor for a long while. You see, we didn't have any money then, and we'd heard that the doctor up in town wouldn't come unless you had the money ready." [13]

They do finally send for the doctor, but the child dies of meningitis.

Irma's story is filled with tragic events: the death of another infant, her own abused childhood at the hands of her father, the struggles of sharecropping and raising her other two children, and her husband's running off for three months with a sixteen-year-old neighbor girl, Amelia Carson, who bears him a child. But her life story moves toward what she depicts as a happy ending. The woman's point of view provides an instructive contrast to the many male narrators in *These Are Our Lives*, much as Addie's chapter counterpoints Anse and the other males in *As I Lay Dying*. In both Addie's and Irma's monologues the focus is on family and personal relations, including money, and not specifically on farming; these concerns, moreover, are abstracted into themes of love and fidelity and happiness or the absence thereof. Irma's and Addie's stories share much detail and thematic interest, but it is not content that is most important in either; it is, rather, their similarity as narratives, as ways of organizing, telling, and knowing. We realize that Irma's story is transcribed for us; it follows an outline set down by the interviewer in eliciting specific kinds of information, yet we learn at the very beginning that she is most anxious to talk about her life and that she has already formulated its generic classification.

> "No, I don't mind tellin' you about me and Morrison and the young'uns. . . . I'm mighty glad to have somebody to talk to. I use to tell Morrison our lives would make a good true story—like you read in the magazines and hear on the radio—Ma Perkins and the others." [14]

Irma's story, therefore, is made public willingly, almost confessionally; it follows the pattern of thirties soap operas where the key character roles are those of fathers, husbands, and sons as seen from the perspective of wives and mothers. We do not know if Addie's father abused her; we do know that her life before marrying Anse was not happy and she accepted Anse's proposal in part to get away from that world. So too, Irma married Morrison, having known him for only a few days, as a means of escape from her unhappiness at home. As husbands, both Morrison and Anse are woefully inadequate, although Irma sees (or hopes for) a reformed Morrison while, at the last moment of her life, Addie has ceased to care about any possible (or impossible) change in Anse.

The crucial factor here is that the two stories share an obsessive drive toward a conclusion: Irma's to a happy ending with the return of Morrison.

> " 'I been a damn fool, Irma. That crazy woman didn't want nothin' but my money. You ain't mad at me, are you, Irma?'
>
> "I said: 'I ain't got no right to be mad now, Morrison. You had your fling and done come home. We need you awful bad. We got to get out and hoe in the tobacco tomorrow. You better get some sleep.' " [15]

It is irrelevant whether or not this is an exact transcription of the conversation that took place on Morrison's return; it is clearly for Irma the climax of her soap opera, the denouement of her life story. It is the way she wants it. The tragic tone of her story is overthrown not by a sentimental forgiving of Morrison but by a declaration that his return "home" reestablishes proper relations, answers a fundamental need by enabling Irma to label Morrison's philandering a trivial "fling." All of this opens the way to the narration of a happy conclusion. They have purchased a house to be the destination of their final move, and, she tells us, "today there's no better man than Morrison." [16] There is even a bit of praise (it is hard to say if it is genuine or gratuitous) for Franklin Roosevelt and the New Deal. Such an ending would seem forced, of course, if not for a slight hesitation, a momentary perception of imperfection in the dreamed-for house.

> "They's only one thing bad about it though. It's right next door to where Amelia Carson lives—with her children. It's goin' to be hard to face her after what happened between her and Morrison. It'll take a lot of courage,

I guess—more'n I've got. I don't think she'll attempt again, though. He's learned his lesson." [17]

Addie's story is consistently bitter, its conclusion her death. But Addie also attempts to will order for her family.

> My father said that the reason for living was getting ready to stay dead. I knew at last what he meant and that he could not have known what he meant himself, because a man cannot know anything about cleaning up the house afterward. And so I have cleaned my house.
>
> (*ALD*, p. 168)

In Faulkner we are tempted to read "house" in the classical sense of "family," for Addie's goal is to settle all accounts in her home and leave it balanced and enduring as a testament to her spirit and being. She has marked all her children (with a whip until they bled) and revenged herself on Anse, in part by symbolically killing him (he becomes "not Anse"), and partly by forcing him to bury her with her people in Jefferson rather than on the farm. Like Irma's conclusion, Addie's is supposed to inscribe an end to the narrative of her family, but where Irma allows doubt about Morrison's steadfastness to spoil her vision of a settled and permanent home life, Addie simply misjudges her power. She mistakenly sends the family out on the dreaded road of change and disintegration.

Faulkner's novel tells a story of a journey from the farm to the city which transforms the Bundren family in fundamental ways. Until the final pages the subject of the novel is the seemingly irreplaceable loss of a mother and wife whose rapidly decaying body portends the almost as rapid disintegration of the family itself. It is her spirit, or memory, that seems to be the only force in the novel for order, yet this force confronts a nearly impossible task in a narrative filled with tragic losses and suffering: the drowning of horses, Cash's broken leg, Dewey Dell's unwanted pregnancy, and Darl's commitment to the state asylum. The tension between family members becomes incipiently violent. What we discover is that the journey's immediate cause, Anse's promise to bury Addie in Jefferson, ambiguously draws the family together into an uneasy joint effort while at the same time it signifies Addie's refusal to accept her identity as a Bundren, thus revealing a crack in the family's organic unity. The journey ultimately moves everyone away from an ordered, if harsh, life, and the road is what Anse dreaded it would be: fundamentally destructive of family and personal security.

In addition, there is a devastating culmination to this symbolic journey, an unprepared-for turn in the novel's plot that masquerades as a comic ending but in fact achieves no Aristotelian finality; it is, moreover, a direct rejection of Addie's will to final order. Much of the novel centers on the children's reactions to the death of their mother, but in the last sentences of the book this biological, natural, and absolute relationship has been displaced by a purely legal, functional, and conventional one. Anse buries Addie and a few hours later appears before what remains of his family to introduce, matter-of-factly, a new "Mrs. Bundren" (*ALD*, p. 250). At a stroke, the family is debiologized, removed from the realm of nature to that of convention. This is a radical, postmodern idea emerging in Faulkner's writing. To some extent this ending expresses Faulkner's neurotic fear of women; the new Mrs. Bundren is the author's revenge against the domineering Addie.[18] But the conclusion is also brought on by the organic structure of the novel itself. Reinforced by the fragmenting narrative form which isolates each character in his or her individual chapters, the plot leads the Bundrens nearer and nearer to a catastrophic disintegration. Only the intervening author can propose a happy (at least comic) ending to this story; only an authoritative imposition of an author's monologic voice on the heteroglot voices of the characters can rescue not only the Bundren family but also the tour de force novel Faulkner was writing. This impulse toward a narration of endings grows, as Faulkner presents it, from the soil of his native South. As much as any particular theme, Faulkner's novels embody a southern compulsion to talk, to tell stories. Within this drive to order and control we can locate concerns with the past and with the family as they reflect the conditions of social instability in the present.

Eventually, therefore, we must read *As I Lay Dying* in the context of Faulkner's other Yoknapatawpha novels, as a model of narrative style that later novels historicize, socialize, for *As I Lay Dying* forms only one piece of the discursive practice Faulkner represents for us. Much of that context will be developed in Part 2, but there is one further aspect of the theme of family disintegration brought on by rapidly changing social conditions that must be noted here. It is not an issue central to *As I Lay Dying*; it is a theme central to Faulkner's career project of representing the modern South. In a culture so deeply infused with an ideology of racial discriminations, racial identity and family identity function as interchangeable concepts. Thomas Clark quotes Howard Odum on racist attitudes following World War I.

At the close of the war there was fear in the minds of some that the returning Negro soldiers might cause trouble between the races and that some steps should be taken to prevent it. This fear proved groundless.[19]

Faulkner picks up on this theme in *Flags in the Dust* with the returning black soldier Caspy.

"I dont take nothin' offen no white man no mo', lootenant ner captain ner M.P. War showed de white folks dey cant git along widout de colored man. . . . And now de colored race gwine reap de benefits of de war, and dat soon."[20]

Faulkner also here daringly ventures on one of the male Southerner's most obsessive fears, the sexual threat of blacks.[21]

"Yes, suh. And de women too. I got my white in France, and I'm gwine git it here, too."

(*FD*, p. 67)

As if to illustrate Odum's assurance that these fears were groundless, Faulkner neutralizes the effects of Caspy's presence in the novel with the character of Simon, his father, whose devotion to the Old South mythology is itself obsessive. Caspy, perhaps too threatening, is never developed as a character.

Yet the war and the Depression did contribute to a movement in the South that was eventually to cause intense racial unrest. Singal describes the circumstances and accurately pinpoints one of Faulkner's most extended examinations of the issue in the character of Joe Christmas from *Light in August*.

In addition to the more formal challenges mounted by organizations like the NAACP and the Interracial Commission, the caste system was slowly being undermined by certain spontaneous changes taking place almost unnoticed at the local level. Younger blacks, in particular, restless with the prescribed codes of behavior, were beginning to see through the white mask and assert themselves. The depression added further momentum to these stirrings by uprooting hundreds of thousands of poor farm folk, converting them into an army of migrants tramping the roads in desperate search of jobs. Towns that had been relatively stable suddenly experienced a sizable influx of strangers whose origins were wholly unknown. Where once it had been highly unlikely for a resident to have "black blood" without the town knowing of it, the system of community genealogy was now doomed. As one character in *Light in August* remarks of Joe Christmas, "These country bastards are liable to be anything."[22]

The result is that the aristocratic planter's notions of racial purity are now dispersed throughout the white population. There had been an uneasy alliance all along between white planter and poor white against the black slave, reflecting perhaps the theory of John Calhoun that white superiority to blacks mediates a rigid class distinction; that is, poor whites participate in a fellowship with wealthy whites, one almost exclusively male, that functions as an exception to operational social codes limiting contact between aristocrats and peasants. This seems to be the basis for the relationship between Sutpen and Wash Jones in *Absalom, Absalom!* World War I and the Depression intensified the fear on the part of the poor southern whites that as a result of the loss of their identity as racial superiors to blacks, they were about to suffer the same cataclysmic fall that the aristocratic planter class underwent after the Civil War. In this way the fall of the Old South is interpreted as a narrative foreshadowing of the fall of contemporary southern culture. The extraordinary threat that Charles Bon poses to Henry Sutpen, therefore, merges miscegenation and incest themes to suggest a catastrophic undermining of social order. *Absalom, Absalom!* despite its focus on the past is a novel written for the present, representing present fears and venturing far beyond safety into the motivations and contradictions of southern mythmaking.

The narrative impulse of the modern Southerner reveals something more than an aesthetic concern with order and endings. The narrative of southern culture depicts family as a principle of order and stability, and this thematics cuts across class boundaries. The narrative of aristocratic genealogy and the narrative of oedipal family structure reflect similar desires. *As I Lay Dying* also unveils for us the fatal flaw in the narration of family order: tied to the classical journey motif, the Bundrens' story rests on a thinly disguised principle of disintegration and disorder. Though roads may signify precise destinations, in the modern, agrarian South they also represent the disruption of control, of certainty, of the past as a measure of permanence.

Faulkner's representation of the southern mind helplessly entangled in a continuing narration of its past becomes a powerful argument for a radical break with that past, for a forgetting that erases all previous narration. Yet it is the inability to forget, prompted by modern social instability, that dominates Faulkner's writing. Thus, his most ambitious representation of the South—*Absalom, Absalom!*—narrates precisely the southern mythmaking mind-set that Frank Vandiver eloquently states to have been the great tragedy of the Old South: "The myth holds that the South was so great when it fought with piteous ardor for a twisted past and for principles aged and vestigial, that there was no future left for it. Its future lay buried with its gray dead." [23] Faulkner clearly resisted extremes in his responses to this mind-set. He rejected nostalgia for the past as well as apocalyptic fatalism. After the sweeping southern family novels he even turned to confront directly contemporary social problems of race and gender in novels like *Intruder in the Dust* and *The Wild Palms*. Neither is a wholly successful effort to propose solutions or alternatives, yet neither disguises the issues. It is important to recognize, as most critics have not, that Faulkner's abandonment of the past in most of his late novels is motivated by a need to turn away from the trap of southern mythmaking, to escape from what he had represented as the destructive limitations imposed by a lingering southern mythology. Faulkner was pessimistic and fearful about change; from a man who saw so clearly and represented what he saw so faithfully we might have wanted more in the way of a visionary future. But that very hesitancy, a fearfulness that too rapid change risks destruction of all social order and value, is the condition of southern thought that produced Faulkner and that he never abandoned as his principal subject.

CHAPTER 5

Violence: Writing as Revision and Perversion

A DISTINGUISHED SOUTHERN historian, George B. Tindall, puzzles over the complexity of southern mythology and over the lack of unity among historians and sociologist in interpreting the vast mythmaking industry (in both the South and the North) which has created various and not always compatible visions of the southern experience. Yet despite the multiplicity of myths of the South, many Southerners, and more non-Southerners, believe that there is a "southern mind" and a southern character or cast of characters in a narrative that Frank Vandiver sees as obsessively focused on the Confederacy and the cataclysmic results of the Civil War. Southern mythmaking is concerned with establishing this narrative, and Tindall argues that southern historians ought to take such mythmaking seriously, although they rarely do.

> Certainly any effort to delineate the unique character of a people must take into account its mythology. "Poets," James G. Randall suggested, "have done better in expressing this oneness of the South than historians in explaining it." Can it be that the historians have been looking in the wrong places, that they have failed to seek the key to the enigma where the poets have readily found it—in the mythology that has had so much to do with shaping character, unifying society, developing a sense of community, of common ideals and shared goals, making the region conscious of its distinctiveness?[1]

Among those poets who have outstripped the historians, Faulkner is unquestionably the most accomplished at representing the South in its mythological self-projections. But his is a late representation; Faulkner entered a literary scene already well advanced in mythmaking. Perhaps most notorious was D. W. Griffith's transformation of Thomas Dixon's racist novel *The Clansman* into the film *Birth of a Nation* in 1915. Not much less widely known were the stories of Thomas Nelson Page. Dixon, Griffith, and Page were all Southerners whose sentimental attitude toward the Confederacy helped solidify the image of the Plantation South. Page in particular wrote nostalgic yarns that bemoaned the loss of the antebellum world, frequently putting laments in the mouths of ex-slaves. "Marse Chan" is typical wherein "his black narrator yearns for the homey comforts and fixed relationships of 'de good ol' days befo' de war.' 'Dem was good ol' times, Marster, de bes' Sam ever see.'"[2] The poets of the Vanderbilt Agrarian school, on the other hand, celebrated a very different antebellum world. Led by the historian Frank L. Owsley, the Agrarians espoused a reconstructed Jeffersonian ideal of the Old South based on the image of an individualistic yeoman farmer who at least could be said to have outnumbered the plantation aristocrats. It is this world also that Ellen Glasgow *(The Deliverance* [1904], *The Wheel of Life* [1905], and *Barren Ground* [1925]) wrote about with a healthy dose of southern populism added for good measure. Yet another perspective was offered by T. S. Stribling, who received a Pulitzer Prize in 1932 for the first volume of his Alabama Trilogy *(The Forge, The Store,* and *The Unfinished Cathedral),* and who wrote novels *(Teeftallow* [1926] and *Bright Metal* [1928]) that satirized southern hillbilly ignorance, violence, and fundamentalism.

These are but a few of the writers who helped create some of the myths of the southern experience. This is not an exhaustive list, but it does illustrate the wide divergences in attitudes about the South that existed in the literary world as Faulkner approached the writing of his first Yoknapatawpha novels. All of these aspects of the southern experience, and many more, and many perspectives on these, are embodied in the Faulknerian vision of the South, a richness of representation that all too often escapes Faulkner criticism. Faulkner critics have frequently interpreted the mythic content of Faulkner's work in a narrow manner, focusing on the "Lost Cause" of the Confederacy. Vandiver's depiction of this theme as obsessive among Southerners does find support in many of Faulkner's novels; it provides a unifying element for several narratives, and fundamental Lost Cause themes emerge from the repetition of character types and plot structures. But this single issue evolves throughout Faulkner's career to reveal a multitude of different perspectives and attitudes, and we must be concerned with these differences as means of understanding the southern world that Faulkner wishes to present.

Much of the postwar mythmaking in the South can be traced to the early Reconstruction period from 1870 to 1900 when a new text of beyond-the-Old-South was being composed. In 1886 Atlanta journalist Henry Grady proclaimed the future of a "New South" rising, phoenix-like, out of the ashes of the defeat. The primary strategy was industrialization which marked not only a departure from the old agrarian culture but also a reinterpretation of the Confederacy. The emphasis of the New South was on modernized economic principles and business management; the hope was to attract financial support from the North while maintaining home ownership. It was necessary, therefore, to abjure the slave economy of the past, but the distance of the new from the old South was not as great as these promoters claimed. Singal calls this a "New South version of the Cavalier myth,"[3] and Vandiver describes the effects of this attitude on southern society.

> While post–Civil War southerners were pushing as fast as they could into the New South, were grasping Yankee dollars with enthusiasm, they purified their motives in the well of Lost Causism. Politicians found it a bottomless source of bombast and ballots, preachers found it a balm and solace to somewhat reluctant middle-class morals, writers found it a noble and salable theme. What the South had been could be the touchstone for the future, could be the fundament of a section going into the industrial age with part of its heart and holding firm to the past with the other.
>
> Lost Causism came to fulfill a role similar to that of the pro-slavery argument in antebellum times. It offered justification for resistance to the leveling tendencies continued by harsh Reconstruction measures. It cloaked the lawless Klansman and lent license to the segregating Christian. It was, finally, the cornerstone of the New South.[4]

The new industrialism simply exploited the devastated economy of the South after the Civil War, and at the same time it accomplished the reactionary aims of southern racists and elitists in preserving in a new economic form the old social relations that the Confederacy had come to stand for. According to Melton McLawrin, the strategy was clear and relatively open.

> Southern industrialists employed any tactic to insure that labor would remain a commodity that could be purchased on a surplus market and controlled once purchased. Among the devices used were the company

village, scrip wages, company stores, child labor, the 'family wage' concept, and convict labor. The company village was an extension of the slave quarters system.[5]

The control of labor also deepened the racial antagonism between working-class whites and blacks, for the "threat of employing the South's black agrarian" laborers, who had been displaced in significant numbers from the farms and plantations, was constantly held before the eyes of whites who might have been ready to protest low pay and poor working conditions or, even more unthinkable, join a union.[6]

New South industrialism, therefore, brought with it new problems of class and race relations, for one of the South's major selling points to northern industrialists was the availability of cheap labor. A representative instance may be found in the southernizing of the American textile industry. A company like J. P. Stevens, which was founded in 1813 in New England, became a major player in the industrialization game and in the realm of labor relations. J. P. Stevens, militantly anti-union, was central to one of the South's most violent union episodes in Marion, North Carolina, in 1929. Workers walked out of the local plant to protest the extension by an additional twenty minutes of the twelve-hour workday. Police fired on the protesters; six were killed and twenty-five injured. The police officers were later tried and found not guilty while several strikers got six months at hard labor. Nor was this an isolated incident. In the late twenties and early thirties there were violent strikes among the coal miners in Kentucky, and other textile worker strikes in North Carolina, Tennessee, and Virginia.[7]

Faulkner was never very centrally concerned with labor disputes in his Yoknapatawpha novels, perhaps because, as noted above, Mississippi lagged behind its sister states in industrialization. Nevertheless, the conditions in which farm workers lived were quite similar to the conditions of those textile workers who were thrust into a violent struggle for a living wage in the mills. Tenant farming, according to Tindall, steadily increased during and after Reconstruction. By 1880 tenants operated 36.2 percent of farms in the South. By 1920 this was 49.6 percent, and in 1930, Tindall states, 58.5 percent. Plantation life was replaced by credit systems; farm commissaries supplied needs in exchange for crop shares, often to the extent of exceeding those shares. This latter practice is a familiar theme in the life stories narrated in *These Are Our Lives.*

> "Mr. Makepeace don't furnish us so much money a week like some landlords. He's got a store, and we go there and get what we need. He

don't complain about our account, but books what we buy. We've done had our settlement with him this year; our account was $375, which included our food and fertilizer and the labor for pickin' peas. We liked $220 payin' out. So we've got to start out the new year with that debt starin' at us."[8]

Tindall further discusses the burden of interest rates that assured the laborer's indebtedness; in the nineteen twenties and thirties, as Faulkner developed his southern chronicle, interest jumped from an average of 16.1 percent to 25.3 percent.[9] For those blacks who remained to work as tenants, as well as for poor white farmers, the possibilities were severely restricted.

In *Go Down, Moses* Ike McCaslin's repudiation of his ownership of the McCaslin farmlands dramatically centers on his reading, alone in the farm commissary, the old ledgers which tellingly merge the economic and social history of the McCaslin farm and family. Faulkner's description of this setting and what it stands for reiterates Tindall's claims. The commissary, Faulkner says, is "not the heart perhaps but the solar-plexus" of the farm:

the square, galleried, wooden building squatting like a portent above the fields whose laborers it still held in thrall '65 or no placarded over with advertisements for snuff and cures for chills and salves and potions manufactured and sold by white men to bleach the pigment and straighten the hair of negroes that they might resemble the very race which for two hundred years had held them in bondage and from which for another hundred years not even a bloody civil war would have set them completely free

himself and his cousin amid the old smells . . . and the desk and the shelf above it on which rested the ledgers in which McCaslin recorded the slow outward trickle of food and supplies and equipment which returned each fall as cotton made and ginned and sold (two threads frail as truth and impalpable as equators yet cable-strong to bind for life them who made the cotton to the land their sweat fell on). . . .

(*GDM*, pp. 255–56)

The mythmakers of the New South, therefore, did not repudiate so much as rewrite the story of the antebellum South. This involved more than clever rhetoric. The New South ideologues managed to articulate an ambiguous version of the Old South which described how a noble social vision had been fatally distorted by a mysterious madness. Singal calls this "the familiar plea of not guilty by reason of insanity" used by New South intellectuals "to condemn and defend their society simultaneously."

The tactic—pre-Freudian in conception—permitted them to "explain" slavery or lynching by arguing that circumstances had somehow conspired to paralyze the South's reasoning faculty, a situation presumably remediable through social and industrial progress, while at the same time enabling them to hurl charges like "frantic delirium" at the slaveholders. For older southerners such a strategy represented a psychological necessity: it allowed them to maintain their adherence to the Lost Cause while expressing their barely hidden hostility toward the antebellum regime for bringing the South to defeat.[10]

A critical result of this argument, however, is the embedding of the irrational within the rational, the savage within the civilized and cultured, creating thereby a figure of the cavalier gentleman who can barely repress the violence of his passion and ambition. It is a stereotype that Faulkner utilizes in the bizarre scene where Thomas Sutpen engages his slaves in a ritualistic fight.

> It seems that on certain occasions, perhaps at the end of the evening, the spectacle, as a grand finale or perhaps as a matter of sheer deadly forethought toward the retention of supremacy, domination, he would enter the ring with one of the negroes himself. Yes. That's what Ellen saw: her husband and the father of her children standing there naked and panting and bloody to the waist and the negro just fallen evidently, lying at his feet and bloody too. . . .
>
> (*AA*, p. 29)

This repressed violence at the heart of civilization is part of what Ellen Glasgow called the "gothic" dimension of Faulkner's writing, and it provided eastern intellectual reviewers like Clifton Fadiman with a wealth of material for mocking attacks on the writer's excesses of style and subject matter.[11] Fadiman's is perhaps the most infamous review of *Absalom, Absalom!* but Bernard De Voto, no less critical than Fadiman, makes a more serious effort to grasp Faulkner's representative southern themes. De Voto, whose perspective reflects the ascendancy of "realist" fiction among the eastern intellectual establishment (Fadiman preferred Jack London to Faulkner), attributes the difficulties of Faulkner's style and the bizarre content of his novels to the author's retreat into "witchcraft" as an inadequate substitute for clear and rational explanations of characters' motivations. "Witchcraft," De Voto argues, "like all magic, is a spurious substitute for fundamental knowledge."[12] Although this argument about obscured motivations seems foolish to us today, De Voto is correct in noting the fascination Faulkner evidences for the irrational and the violent.

Mr. Faulkner is exploring the primitive violence of the unconscious mind. Nothing else can explain the continuity of rape, mutilation, castration, incest, patricide, lynching, and necrophilia in his novels, the blind drive of terror, the obsessional preoccupation with corpses and decay and generation and especially with the threat to generation.[13]

De Voto gives us here both an accurate catalogue of Faulknerian motifs and a set of essential fears that underlay the New South ideology. What Singal calls the "insanity defense" introduces a crucial weakness into the mythologizing of antebellum society that trades one sort of guilt for another. As a result the stereotypical Southerner became the soft-spoken, cultured gentleman by day who rioted at cross-burning ceremonies, or lynchings, at night. Such a stereotype seeks to justify the use of violence to control the threat of a greater violence seen within southern society itself. The insanity that infected the Old South and led to its defeat in the Civil War was subject to two forms of repression in the New South: projection onto the blacks who were seen as potentially antisocial forces descending from primitive African slaves, and repression of working-class whites who were necessary to the establishing of a New South version of the cavalier gentleman, now an industrialist rather than a plantation master.

In *Flags in the Dust* Faulkner treats this ambiguous New South myth mostly as a comic theme. In the character of Virginia Du Pre he dramatizes for us the shifting attitudes necessary to the maintaining of an ambivalent perspective on the past. She, herself a Sartoris, is the repository for the tales of Sartoris heroes in the Civil War.

It was she who told them of the manner of Bayard Sartoris' death prior to the second battle of Manassas. She had told the story many times since (at eighty she still told it, on occasions usually inopportune) and as she grew older the tale itself grew richer and richer, taking on a mellow splendor like wine; until what had been a hair-brained prank of two heedless and reckless boys wild with their own youth, was become a gallant and finely tragical focal-point to which the history of the race had been raised from out the old miasmic swamps of spiritual sloth by two angels valiantly and glamorously fallen and strayed, altering the course of human events and purging the souls of men.

(*FD*, pp. 13–14)

Ironic to be sure, this passage with its authorial insertion of the truth behind Miss Jenny's highly embellished tale, nevertheless illustrates the tangled perspectives that were a part of the Lost Cause mythology. A reckless prank, riding into the enemy camp to retrieve anchovies, serves to build a tale of tragic proportions, a narrative articulated in the language of the Old Testament and imaged as postlapsarian. The prank is valiant and angelic but it also tells of a fall from grace, of a kind of madness and self-destruction that underlies all reckless heroism. Even without an authorial intrusion we find that Miss Jenny's attitude toward the Sartoris legend is never simply worshipful; it is consistently ironic and sometimes bitter. She has repeatedly witnessed the suicidal recklessness of Sartoris men in her long life, a lingering insanity and self-destructive violence that extend far beyond the Civil War into the modern age of automobiles and airplanes, and she (along with Faulkner) associates this self-destruction with the lost cause of the Confederacy.

Miss Jenny's counterpart in *Absalom, Absalom!* is Rosa Coldfield, but in this later novel Faulkner does not approach the issue of violence and madness in a comic manner. The insanity plea is rewritten as the mysterious and irrational eruption of evil within the idyllic antebellum world. Rosa's depiction of Thomas Sutpen as a demon spirit who "out of quiet thunderclap . . . would abrupt. . . upon a peaceful scene . . ." (*AA*, p. 8) is, according to Quentin Compson, her explanation of "why God let us lose the War" (*AA*, p. 11); she thus perceives the historical calamity in mythical terms, transforming event into causality. The South was fated to fall from grace just as Sutpen's dynastic design, according to Rosa, was doomed from the start.

> *Because he was not articulated in this world. He was a walking shadow. He was the light-blinded bat-like image of his own torment cast by the fierce demoniac lantern up from beneath the earth's crust and hence in retrograde, reverse; from abysmal dark to eternal and abysmal dark completing his descending. . . .*
>
> (*AA*, p. 171)

It is Rosa, then, who best exemplifies De Voto's charge of willful mystification of motivations, but De Voto misses the fact that the remainder of the novel is a complex narrative of demystification. Rosa initiates a dialogue that will be rewritten because it is repressive and the repressed cannot be explained away. The strategy of this mystification is to divert attention from the fact that the central issue of the Civil War, the true insanity of the Old South, was slavery, that the evil at the heart of the antebellum society was racial violence. But Sutpen effectively disperses this issue for Rosa who sees him as an abstraction rather than as a representation. In this manner Rosa's mythmaking, as many critics have suggested, sets the tone for all of the narrators, but not in the sense that her exotic version of the past is the foil for other narrative repudiations and corrections. Her narration is the enabling force for succeeding narrative revisions. Mr. Compson, whose nostalgic vision of the Old South leads him to aestheticize Sutpen, transforms him from demon to tragic hero complete with tragic flaw: his "innocence" (*AA*, p. 220). In a way, Mr. Compson's version of Sutpen's life story completes Rosa's; together they express the fundamental themes of Lost Causism, narrating the tragic tale of a noble past gone inexplicably mad. No less mythic, of course, is Quentin's obsession with "incest" which rewrites the stories told by Rosa and his father in terms of a universal, not a regional, law of rational social decorum and order, the Freudian reworking of original sin. Quentin swerves the narrative focus from Sutpen to his children, a necessary shift that allows him to produce another powerful narrative of mystification. It remains for Shreve to enter into this deadly serious game of mythmaking and to push rewriting to its limits. Shreve breaks into Quentin's painful narration, asserting his right to "play a while now" (*AA*, p. 280), and the freeplay of his narration transcribes Quentin's incest theme into that of miscegenation. As a result the mediating function of the mythmaking is dislocated, brought down to earth or raised from the unconscious.[14] The compulsion to retell the story of the South, the story of Thomas Sutpen, is dissipated, and the novel is concluded.

Shreve's raising of the repressed, however, should not lead to a reductive reading of *Absalom, Absalom!* Faulkner allows Shreve's perspective on the South to go essentially unchallenged; the racial violence exemplified by Henry's killing of Bon is made visible through the clouded mythmaking of Quentin's Freudian obsession. Nonetheless, Shreve's version of the story does not cancel out the others; his is not a psychoanalytic exorcism but a narrative rewriting which is never free of the intertextual traces of the other narrations. The issues of Sutpen's story, as Faulkner presents them (while refusing to resolve them), are multiple not single; they include fratricide, class violence, genealogical destiny, power, wealth, incest, and miscegenation. In fact, it is not racism as such that motivates Sutpen; it is his emergence into class consciousness:

> he himself seeing his own father and sisters and brothers as the owner, the rich man (not the nigger) must have been seeing them all the time —as cattle, creatures heavy and without grace, brutely evacuated into a world without hope or purpose for them, who would in turn spawn with

brutish and vicious prolixity, populate, double treble and compound, fill space and earth with a race whose future would be a succession of cut-down and patched and made-over garments bought on exorbitant credit because they were white people, from stores where niggers were given the garments free. . . . as he came out of the woods . . . and looked at . . . his sister pumping rhythmic up and down above a washtub in the yard, her back toward him, shapeless in a calico dress and a pair of the old man's shoes unlaced and flapping about her bare ankles and broad in the beam as a cow, the very labor she was doing brutish and stupidly out of all proportion to its reward: the very primary essence of labor, toil, reduced to its crude absolute which only a beast could and would endure. . . .

(*AA*, pp. 235 and 236)

Two years after the publication of *Absalom, Absalom!* Faulkner approached this issue of class violence again through the figure of Ab Snopes in "Barn Burning." The raw and unexplained anger expressed in Ab's destructive acts against his landlords springs simply from class hatred. His actions are irrational and frightening because he is a purer, more unself-conscious version of Wash Jones. We are not given a specific "class insult" which motivates Ab as we are with Wash and with Sutpen himself. Here Faulkner is concerned simply with violence in his southern society; there is no apparent link with the Civil War or slavery. Ab's anger seems endemic. To some extent Ab's violence links the class anger and humiliation of a Sutpen with a more extreme representation of southern violence: the character of Popeye from *Sanctuary*. Suffering from hereditary syphilis and impotence, and threatened with insanity, Popeye is pure, perverse irrationality. But he would have no connection with southern society if Faulkner had not made Temple Drake his willing victim and established Horace Benbow, the stereotypical representation of an effete southern gentleman, as the agonized observer-interpreter of Temple's fall from grace. The bitterness of Faulkner's misogyny in *Sanctuary* sometimes distracts our attention away from the effort to represent the South as burdened with guilt and founded on an irrational drive toward self-destruction. The theme is, nevertheless, still derived from Lost Causism and its insanity plea. Popeye is merely the agent for Temple's self-destruction; he is thus an evil that the South discovers ready at hand, at the heart of the mythical southern character, a figure in a southern morality play. He can be seen, as Eric Sundquist argues, to symbolize the fear of black sexuality that underlies the racism of southern whites.[15] But Popeye belongs to no race and no class. He is a function of social relations, a perverse principle of violence available for any occasion, representing as easily the pent-up violence of whites as the racial hatred of blacks.

The tracing of themes reflecting the cavalier myth of the Confederacy, through the trauma of defeat and Reconstruction, to the rewriting of the Old South mythology in the Lost Causism of the New South ideologues is Faulkner's subject matter. There is, however, a further revision of this history of mythmaking that Faulkner articulates. By the 1930s the failure of New South industrialism to regenerate the region while preserving its unique, southern character had become painfully clear. No doubt this failure had become irreversible much earlier, but the point was driven home by a dramatically increased dependence on outside, or federal, economic support. The Depression became a second defeat echoing the primal fall of the Civil War, and it was closely followed by a second reconstruction in the form of the New Deal. The myth of the Confederacy, of course, did not disappear; it was perhaps even more violently asserted, but the second failure marks a final break between myth and social reality. The New South rewriting of the Confederacy myth no longer contained a viable plan of social and economic reform; it now functioned solely to bolster the idea of a peculiarly "southern" state of mind. As such it remained a potent force which, as Vandiver argues, retarded real social and economic progress, and as such it became the focus of an endless play of critique and defense. The critical dimension of this discourse dominates Faulkner's writing, although his representation of southern mythmaking exposes us to both sides of the controversy.

According to Clark the Depression merely deepened an already severe economic and social crisis. By "1930 the South had fallen behind the nation in every positive statistical category."[16] Industrialization in textiles and timber was at a standstill; mill closings and resultant unemployment were rampant. Economic conditions in Mississippi were particularly bad, reaching a crisis in 1933 in unemployment and scarcity of capital for new economic ventures. Clark summarizes these conditions in a comment on the government pamphlet published in 1934 entitled *The South, The Nation's Number One Economic Problem*, a study, he says, which "left no doubt that people, land, agricultural systems, human character, and credit methods had failed."[17] Interestingly, Clark suggests that conditions were so universally bad that they could not be ignored. The decline of the South was visible for all to see and was captured on film by photographers who helped disseminate its image throughout the region as well as the rest of the nation. The second failure, therefore, had an aesthetic dimension, wearing away at any lingering complacency. Clark also finds that one of the most successful of all the federal projects, rural electrification, symbolically represents the growing awareness among Southerners of the conditions which the old mythmaking designedly sought to cover up. The TVA signaled not only a move into "modernity" but also, Clark claims, the "first burst of bright light revealed the shabby surroundings to many rural southerners in a manner that was impossible for them to see without electricity."[18] One result was to deepen the sense of guilt and shame that accompanied the second failure, but at the same time it seemed to spur on an enlightenment period of critical stocktaking. As never before, the South set out to examine itself from within.

Of course, this Depression era enlightenment does not mark the first of such critical studies in the South; to some extent this spirit had belonged to the New South intellectuals who set out to resurrect the region on more modern principles—except where the issue of race relations was concerned. These were the "genteel progressives," according to King, who "were born generally between 1855 and 1875" and thereby were free of the taint of the madness of the Lost Cause. They represented a middle class "ethic of work and rationality."[19] Serious critical work on the issue of race was often detached from this New South boosterism; it came from scholars like Andrew Sledd at Emory writing on the Jim Crow laws as early as 1902 or in Howard Odum's sociological study of race in 1911.[20] Yet by the 1930s there existed a whole other set of relationships between young intellectuals and the southern past. The Civil War and certainly the Confederacy for these men and women belonged not only to a time they had not experienced but to a past for the most part beyond the memory of their living relatives. This generation, which comprised the great-grandchildren of those who actively participated in the Civil War, "was born around the turn of the century and lived through the cultural crisis of World War I." They "came to feel increasingly estranged from the tradition" which "loomed distressingly distant and overpoweringly strong, insupportable yet inescapable."[21] King's discussion of the relation of this perspective to a tendency to render the real world "fantastic" (Hannah Arendt's term) is vitally important, for it explicates the urge toward Lost Cause mythmaking that intensifies itself to the point of advocating violence as a response to the underlying awareness that the world depicted in the myth has separated itself from social and economic reality.

He is speaking here of Faulkner's generation and, among others, notes Faulkner's fascination with the mythmaking drive and his connection of that southern obsession to a tendency toward violently defensive positions. Faulkner's repeated use of a four-generation schema to represent his southern families, his sense of a generational decline away from an original heroism accompanied by the ambiguous longing for and rejection of those last heroic times, illustrate Faulkner's own experience: he was himself the great-grandson of a legendary Civil War hero. As a result of the crisis of the Depression, however, the crucial element of a revitalized critical attitude was added to this complex set of cultural-historical motivations. Faulkner's four-generation schema, which will occupy us centrally in succeeding chapters, also provides him with a protective distance and the possible freedom for a truly critical evaluation of self and society. It is this attitude that allows Faulkner to sympathize with yet reject, as author and Southerner, a character like Gail Hightower. Or more pointedly, it explains Faulkner's attitude toward his fellow Southerner, and nostalgic Old South traditionalist, Will Percy who, Faulkner said, was "like a little boy closing his eyes against the dark of modernity."[22] Faulkner resisted modernity himself but in the critical spirit of the enlightened South after the second defeat of the Depression.

During the 1920s and 1930s, therefore, southern resistance to modernity was accompanied by a shift from Old South nostalgia to critical examination of a culture in crisis. The South could not refuse modernization in this period of deepening economic depression, but it did look upon intrusions, like those of the New Deal, as unavoidable cultural disasters. The active boosterism of the New South movement was transformed into a mood of passive acceptance, almost melancholy in tone. Something like this attitude among southern intellectuals is reflected in Faulkner's short story "The Tall Men" which tells of a poor but self-sufficient family of white farmers confronting the regulations and restrictive procedures of New Deal reform projects. A draft board investigator, who is an outsider in the community, is accompanied by a local marshal on an official visit to the remote farm of the McCallums with warrents to be served to two McCallum sons who failed to register for the draft. They arrive to find Buddy McCallum with his leg badly injured about to undergo amputation surgery without benefit of anesthetic. The melodramatic situation here is used to drive home the moral lesson that the McCallums, who resist any form of government economic aid, espouse a more heroic, individualistic code of behavior than that produced by the modern world of crop subsidies and price supports. The lesson is made more emphatic since the story shows only male McCallums and, in somewhat guarded language, contrasts their stoic heroism with those weak and effeminate people who are willing to accept government handouts.

> "Only even when they didn't raise cotton, every year the county agent's young fellow would come out to measure the pasture crops they planted so he could pay them for that, even if they never had no not-cotton to be paid for. Except he never measured no crop on this place. 'You're welcome to look at what we are doing,' Buddy says. 'But don't draw it down on your map.'
>
> " 'But you can get money for this,' the young fellow says. 'The Government wants to pay you for planting all this.'
>
> " 'We are aiming to get money for it,' Buddy says. 'When we can't, we will try something else. But not from the Government. Give that to them that want to take it. We can make out.' "

> "We have slipped our backbone; we have about decided a man don't need a backbone any more; to have one is old-fashioned. But the groove where the backbone used to be is still there, and the backbone has been kept alive, too, and someday we're going to slip back onto it. I don't know just when nor just how much of a wrench it will take to teach us, but someday."
>
> (CS, pp. 57 and 59)

All of this is spoken by the marshal and is set against the dark humor of the very reluctant investigator helping the marshal bury the bloody stump of Buddy's leg in the McCallum family graveyard. It is a prophecy but not a nostalgic one of return to the good old days. The focus here is an attack on the New Deal and on the modern, urban world that is imagistically associated with these reform programs. Yet despite this attack on the modern, the world of the McCallums is clearly an anachronism; it is not presented as a viable alternative to modernization. The story's tone is somber, reflecting in part the stoic attitude of Buddy McCallum, an attitude that occasionally slips from the heroic to passive acceptance. The McCallums' resistance to the intrusion of the modern is partial and not very successful. They refused price guarantees for their cotton but were thereby forced to shift their efforts to raising cattle; their simple world has been revised by the violent intrusion of the modern in several ways, and there is no reason to believe that such revision will not continue. Faulkner's portrayal of the McCallums in this Depression era story is itself a revision of their earlier appearance in *Flags in the Dust*. The earlier version handles their eccentricities gently and humorously; their rough home provides a retreat for young Bayard Sartoris in his futile effort to escape his past, the burden of an ancestry that can be traced to a legendary great-grandfather, Colonel John Sartoris. In *Flags in the Dust* the McCallums offer an alternative to that doomed pseudo-aristocratic heritage that is so much a part of young Bayard's self-destructive temperament. In "The Tall Men," however, the doom is that of the McCallums, this time a fate traceable not to the Lost Cause of the Confederacy but to the crushing power of the modern world, to the finality of the second defeat.

> He heard the truck start up and back and turn and go down the road, the sound of it dying away, ceasing, leaving the still, hot night—the Mississippi Indian summer, which had already outlasted half of November—filled with the loud last shrilling of the summer's cicadas, as though they, too, were aware of the imminent season of cold weather and of death.
>
> (*CS*, p. 54)

Faulkner's revision of the McCallums has a very significant parallel in the rewriting of the Sartoris myth in *The Unvanquished*. The most crucial action of that novel occurs in the final chapter, "The Odor of Verbena," which was written specifically for this collection of earlier-published stories. The most significant shift is in the character of John Sartoris; in *The Unvanquished* he is actually brought into the narrative in a manner that severely diminishes his legendary stature as depicted in *Flags in the Dust*. Even for his son, Bayard, to see him demystifies him, and the juxtaposition of the legend and the childish games of heroic action played by Bayard in the first stories of the novel reinforces this demystification. In *The Unvanquished* John Sartoris is simply cruel and ruthless; he blindly cultivates his own legend in the name of the Confederate myth. His wife, Drusilla, interprets his action for Bayard and for us in a pointed contrast between Sartoris and Sutpen. For her, Sartoris is a symbol of the South struggling to throw off Reconstruction and assert itself as a new South nevertheless true to its old ideals, whereas Sutpen acts only out of self-interest.

"Nobody could have more of a dream than that."
"Yes. But his dream is just Sutpen. John's is not. He is thinking of this

whole country which he is trying to raise up by its bootstraps, so that all
the people in it, not just his kind nor his old regiment, but all the people,
black and white, the women and children back in the hills who don't even
own shoes—Don't you see?"

"But how can they get any good from what he wants to do for them if
they are—after he has—"

"Killed some of them? I suppose you include those two carpet baggers
he had to kill to hold that first election, don't you?"

"They were men. Human beings." [23]

The exchange between Drusilla and Bayard undercuts the legend
of John Sartoris by insistently breaking off from Drusilla's efforts to
aggrandize John's actions. Bayard's disbelief here is further reinforced
by the fact that it was Sartoris and not Sutpen who "organized the night
riders to keep the carpet baggers from organizing the Negroes into an
insurrection" (*UV*, p. 256). It was Sartoris who was deposed as leader
of his regiment to be replaced by the coldly rational Thomas Sutpen,
and it was Sartoris and not Sutpen who used a not altogether honorable
weapon, a derringer, to dispose of his enemies. That Sutpen, for all of
his ruthlessness and coldness, comes out the better in this comparison
with Sartoris finalizes the latter's fall from legendary stature.

"The Odor of Verbena" contains another crucial revision of the Sartoris figure. John Sartoris here is not so much the Civil War hero sharing
the glory of a reckless career with his brother Bayard but a businessman, an entrepreneur, and a politician. His "dream," therefore, as Drusilla presents it, reflects the dream of the New South ideologues with
their Lost Cause mythology. His business partner, Ben Redmond, kills
him because Sartoris forced Redmond out of a partnership in a railroad.
The central theme of revenge in this story rests against a backdrop of
unsavory business deals and ruthless killing and is not a manifestation
of the cavalier code of honor. The community expects Bayard to challenge Redmond to a duel. He does not; his challenge, if it is a challenge,
distorts the idea of honorable revenge by depicting it in straightforward
terms and emphasizing the violence of the action. Bayard's confrontation with Redmond ironically repeats his father's final, and suicidal,
act of facing Redmond unarmed when he knew Redmond planned to
shoot him, but the outcome of Bayard's act is vastly different. Redmond deliberately misses Bayard, firing two shots at point-blank range.
Bayard's courage, as John Irwin notes, "unmans Redmond," and he
disappears from the community never to be seen again. [24] To make sure

that the reader does not miss the distinction between these two courageous yet suicidal acts Faulkner inserts a commentator on the action,
George Wyatt, a Civil War comrade of the brothers John and Bayard.

> "You ain't done anything to be ashamed of. I wouldn't have done it
> that way, myself. I'd a shot at him once, anyway. But that's your way or
> you wouldn't have done it.
> "Maybe your right, maybe there has been enough killing in your
> family."
>
> (*UV*, p. 289)

For Wyatt, who sees himself as of another world and time, there is the
clear perception of an end to that "way" and perhaps the intimation of
a new way, a rewritten code that would eschew the violence of the old.

As in all rewriting, the old lingers in its transformation. Bayard per-
formed an act of revenge earlier in the novel, and for that act he was
declared to be "John Sartoris' boy" (*UV*, p. 213). Even that act, however, did not strictly conform to the old code; the revenge was for
Granny Millard, not his blood kin. It was a courageous and somewhat
brutal act that was also an extension of his childhood war games. Rosa
Millard, unlike John Sartoris, was indeed a humanistic figure, raising
money by tricking northern officers and redistributing it to the needy
in her community. As with many of Faulkner's older women, she is an
androgynous character who very ably fills the roles of the men who are
engaged in the more masculine heroics of the Civil War. Her murder requires some form of justice, but it is only as a mature man that Bayard
realizes that his killing of Grumby repeated his father's violent life, and
it is that past that Bayard rejects when he faces Redmond unarmed.
Myra Jehlen startlingly misreads *The Unvanquished* on this point.

> Bayard has neither qualified nor modified the John Sartoris myth; all he
> has done is to translate the fairy tale into adult terms. The uncharacteris-
> tically clear, moderate tone in which Faulkner wrote *The Unvanquished*
> has just this function vis-a-vis the myth it extols. Failing (or refusing) in
> this work to distinguish between myth and history, he does away rhetori-
> cally with the distinction itself and achieves a general credibility through
> a language which seems sufficiently reasonable (or perhaps only bland
> enough) to be factual.[25]

Unquestionably the stylistic shift of this novel is crucial to our understanding of it, but a plain style here does not confuse myth and history.

History, by which Jehlen means "facts," is never at issue; anything resembling a fact is quite rare in the narrative, subject to being qualified as what merely seemed to be or what Bayard heard to be the case. Joanne Creighton rightly notes that the change of point of view from earlier stories is crucially related to the plain style.[26] In "The Odor of Verbena" we are asked to look at John Sartoris from the perspective of a mature Bayard who perceives with clarity not only the facts but more important the differences between the child's credulity and the adult's skepticism. The result is a deeply critical tone, a disbelief that unmasks the myth and sets up the narrative for revision.

The tactic of revising is Faulkner's strategy for critically representing southern mythmaking. Revision of the narrative text and revision of the discursive practices of his society are the same, and this revisionary strategy places the author inside his text/society, implicates him in the critique he expresses. In one sense we recognize that no author can actually place himself outside of his world in order to write about it, in the same way that he cannot be outside of the language of his world and still express himself in that language. But in his Yoknapatawpha novels Faulkner self-consciously accepts this limitation and transforms it into a strength, adding a dimension of reflexivity to his representation of the South. From such a perspective revision appears as a perversion. It is not so much a critique from a privileged position—which is what Jehlen seems to want from Faulkner—as a willful distortion which masks itself sometimes in playfulness and sometimes in vulgarity. Perversion is a twisting or turning away from the norm, or perhaps just away from the familiar. Faulkner's perspective on the South, therefore, is debasing and corrupting, but that corruption appears to emerge from the very nature of southern mythmaking itself, as a perversion that abrupts," like Sutpen, from within.

In *The Unvanquished* the principle of perversion is figured for us in Drusilla. Drusilla's is an exemplary case for Faulkner, involving that crossing of the boundaries of gender difference that signifies a twisting of the norm. Faulkner found those boundaries difficult to bridge, a limitation that plagued his efforts to give us an authentic feminine voice in his women characters. The "otherness" of gender difference removed women, just as the otherness of racial difference removed blacks, from the easy intimacy that he felt with his white male characters. His women characters emerge in his narratives as exotic, sexless figures like Rosa Coldfield or as mystically silent, voiceless symbols of desire like Caddy Compson. This radical gender difference is a central element of his southern heritage, a difference that penetrates all registers of meaning: psychological, biological, social, literary, and historical. The rigidity of this sexual barrier, of course, enhances the impact of his perverse violation of it in Drusilla Sartoris. She is a shadowy double of John Sartoris in dress, action, and ideals. Even in Bayard's thoughts of her waiting for his return in the expectation of his revenge against Redmond, her sexuality fluctuates and she plays two roles simultaneously.

> We rode on, toward the house where he would by lying in the parlor now, in his regimentals (sabre too) and where Drusilla would be waiting for me beneath all the festive glitter of the chandeliers, in the yellow ball gown and the sprig of verbena in her hair, holding the two loaded pistols (I could see that too, who had had no presentiment; I could see her, in the formal brilliant room arranged formally for obsequy, not tall, not slender as a woman is but as a youth, a boy, is, motionless, in yellow, the face calm, almost bemused, the head simple and severe, the balancing sprig of verbena above each ear, the two arms bent at the elbows, the two hands shoulder high, the two identical duelling pistols lying upon, not clutched in, one to each: the Greek amphora priestess of a succinct and formal violence.
>
> (*UV*, p. 252)

She is both Sartoris' double, his other self, and his wife, the other than himself, an unstable condition in the psychology of both traditional social behavior and traditional literary technique. Her mother says that she has "deliberately tried to unsex herself" (*UV*, p. 217), a mistaken view of what is actually the doubling of her sexuality, but the mother's judgment comes from the context of Old South mythology. Bayard reads to us the letter which contains her conception of what is "proper."

> *But when I think of my husband who laid down his life to protect a heritage of courageous men and spotless women looking down from heaven upon a daughter who had deliberately cast away that for which he died. . . .* That's how it sounded . . . there had been reserved for Drusilla the highest destiny of a Southern woman—to be the bride-widow of a lost cause—and now Drusilla had not only thrown that away, she had not only become a lost woman and a shame to her father's memory but she was now living in a word that Aunt Louisa would not even repeat but that Granny knew what it was. . . . Drusilla had been gone for six months, . . . and then one night she walked into the cabin . . . in the garments not alone of a man but of a common private soldier and told them how she had been a member of Father's troop for six months. . . .
>
> (*UV*, pp. 219–20)

Drusilla's perverted departure from the antebellum myth, however, is not her only significance for Bayard in the narrative. If it were, she would simply represent a corruption springing from within the myth itself, leaving Bayard critically outside. Faulkner's narrators have no such privileged position because the author has none. He implicates Bayard by having Drusilla seduce him, draw him into a brief incestuous kiss that she clearly hopes will lead to a violent confrontation between father and son since she urges him to tell his father immediately. But Drusilla is not just Bayard's stepmother; she is also his father's double. This is no simple oedipal seduction, for it is homosexual as well as heterosexual. As a result, the violent confrontation does not come when Bayard confesses to his father.

> "I have now accomplished the active portion of my aims in which you could not have helped me; I acted as the land and the time demanded and you were too young for that, I wished to shield you. But now the land and the time too are changing; what will follow will be a matter of consolidation, of pettifogging and doubtless chicanery in which I would be a babe in arms but in which you, trained in the law, can hold your own—our own. Yes. I have accomplished my aim, and now I shall do a little moral housecleaning. I am tired of killing men, no matter what the necessity nor the end. Tomorrow, when I go to town to meet Ben Redmond, I shall be unarmed."
>
> (*UV*, p. 266)

The father's wrath is transformed into a seduction of another kind, a formal passing on of power, a willful relinquishing that acknowledges history and social change but takes no notice whatever of Drusilla. Ultimately she too disappears from the novel, like Redmond, because the changing world rejects her. John Sartoris, however, would not disappear were it within his power to prevent it. In the act of relinquishing he seeks to guarantee his continuation in the world he made. His final speech to his son echoes the grand design of Sutpen, and reflects the same blindness, the same egocentric vision of the South. What the father gives to Bayard is the burden of carrying on the father's name, and with that the codes of behavior, values, and meanings of the myth of the Confederacy. All accomplishment, all glory returns to the father as origin of this noble design. It is truly a seductive burden, no less so than Drusilla's forbidden kiss, but it is one that Bayard nonetheless perverts in his refusal to seek revenge against Redmond.

Faulkner revises the Old South myths most effectively by perverting them. His response to his world is nonetheless a critique for being embedded within the culture he sought to demystify. He is not, of course, everywhere a master of his own strategy, overindulging in the playfulness of perversion at times while at others intellectualizing his technique. The former fault makes problematical the character of Joanna Burden in *Light in August*, whose motivations appear muddled or inconsistent. Clearly Faulkner overintellectualizes with the character of Gavin Stevens in *Intruder in the Dust*, where the strategy of evolving a critical perspective from within the culture means arguing that problems of race relations in the South can be solved only if the South is freed from outside interference, a reactionary "state's rights" dogma. Very often, however, Faulkner is true to his mark, his "gothic" temperament raising to consciousness the very issues that southern mythmaking repressed.

In this sense *Sanctuary* is an exemplary novel expressing the difficulty and danger of cultural critique in the Faulknerian mode. Temple Drake's story is filtered through the experiences of Horace Benbow; Temple's corruption, the perverse debasement of the Old South ideal of the "spotless woman," reaches out to corrupt the ideal that Horace tries to erect for his daughter, Little Belle, the same ideal he tried to erect for his sister Narcissa in *Flags in the Dust*. Singal insightfully identifies Horace as a prime vehicle of Faulkner's bitterest attack on the South.

> His anxiety is compounded as he frantically searches for Temple, building to a fever pitch when he finally locates her in Memphis, listens to her story, and realizes she is "recounting the experience with actual pride, a sort of naive and impersonal vanity." As Cleanth Brooks points out, the interview makes clear to him not only that a sweet young girl can come into contact with evil, but also that she might actually invite and enjoy it, thus shattering the bedrock belief in unassailable innocence on which Horace had constructed his entire world view. Once again his photograph of Little Belle is transformed by his imagination from "sweet chiaroscuro" to "voluptuous promise," but this time the fantasy descends into a nightmare vision of Little Belle substituted for Temple atop the corn shucks. . . . Sick to the very core of his being, Horace barely reaches the bathroom in time.[27]

There seems no question that Faulkner's fitful yet troubling misogyny led him to associate perversion with the feminine, just as he associated writing with femininity and the perverse with writing. Temple as well as Joanna pushes over the boundaries of the revisionary perverse, and Faulkner seems too often in *Sanctuary* to strive merely for the shocking effect. If as Singal suggests, however, it is Horace and not Temple who represents the South, represents it not as Temple would as an irrational, even insane, self-destructive evil but in its more modern incarnation as self-deluding in its mythmaking, then the critical awakening of Horace could be brought about only by a woman whose perversity violated every traditional code of feminine purity and innocence that he held dear. What must also be remembered is that this dream of innocence for Horace had its first manifestation in *Flags in the Dust* as an incestuous fantasy involving his sister. There Narcissa was embodied in Horace's small "almost perfect vase" that he calls by her name, describes in Keats's terms as a "still unravished bride," and keeps by his bed (*FD*, p. 190). In *Sanctuary* that vase has become Little Belle's picture, and although she is not in fact his daughter, his vision of her echoes that incestuous desire for perfect innocence that Narcissa once represented for him.

In his famous introduction to *The Sound and the Fury* Faulkner described Caddy Compson as the sister he never had and the daughter he lost. She is a beautiful yet "doomed" little girl whose fate it is to be swept into "dishonor and shame."[28] He does not explain why her fate must be dishonor, but in the novel the desire for perfect innocence expressed in Quentin's interior monologue seems part of that doom if for no other reason than that Caddy represents for him an impossible ideal. Caddy, of course, functions only as an object of consciousness in the narratives of others; she is never allowed to speak for herself, and consequently she is for the reader a figment of the other characters' imaginations. Temple Drake is very much a presence in the novel and is allowed to speak for herself. But we may nevertheless read Temple through the imagination of Horace, and the consequence, as with Caddy and Quentin, is the destruction of the Old South ideal.

The impact of the feminine perverse in all these cases is directly proportional to the extremity of the delusion of purity; the more intense is the ideal, the more devastating is its collapse. It is as if in his revisionary strategy Faulkner strains toward a representation of the South that is cataclysmic. He allows us to glimpse this cataclysm in Rosa Coldfield's demonology of the fall of the Confederacy, to experience it in the tortured and suicidal obsession with the Lost Cause in the mind of Quentin Compson, and to see it in terms of a modern second defeat in the existential nausea of Horace Benbow. This endless and often self-defeating revisionary process Faulkner says he learned in composing *The Sound and the Fury*. The writing of the Benjy section in particular taught him "both how to write and how to read," and the production of the other revisionary sections led him to an even more important lesson which he summarizes in the story about another vase so like that beloved by Horace: "There is a story somewhere about an old Roman who kept at his bedside a Tyrrhenian vase which he loved and the rim of which he wore slowly away with kissing it."[29] Faulkner's representation of the South is just this sort of loving, incestuously perverted wearing away. In striving to depict his society's cultural crisis, Faulkner could do no more than lovingly revise the very myths that lay at the base of that crisis. It is that revisionary task that generates his most moving stories and produces his most extraordinary narrative forms. His is an aesthetics of revision, of how to write and how to read, that enabled him to move toward an impossible goal: the full and honest confrontation of his culture and himself.

CHAPTER 6

"Art and Southern Life": Revision, Repression, Perversion

THE REVISIONARY strategy which marked Faulkner's engagement with southern mythmaking generated a conflict in his mind concerning the aesthetic goals of his Yoknapatawpha novels. The conflict is a traditionally romantic one between art and life, and Faulkner never resolved it. This lack of resolution, moreover, is central to the curious relationship between Faulkner and the Vanderbilt Agrarians. The Agrarians were Faulkner's contemporaries in an emerging regionalist consciousness, but many of the Agrarians ultimately abandoned their southernism in favor of a rigidly antiregionalist, antirepresentationalist formalism. These prominent Agrarians founded the New Criticism, and the New Critics, ironically for all of their antiregionalist aesthetics, were centrally responsible for the early readings of Faulkner's southern novels which established his literary reputation. The link between the Agrarians, the New Critics, and Faulkner is complex, based in part on their shared southern heritage and in part on the New Critics' consistent misreading of the Yoknapatawpha novels. To separate Faulkner from his southernist contemporaries and his formalist interpreters, however, demands a close critical reading of them all.

In 1925 Faulkner wrote and then abandoned a story called "Elmer" about an artist who failed in his commitment to his art. There is much of Faulkner in this story about the doubts and fears of a young writer deeply influenced by the aesthetic theories of symbolism and fin-de-siècle aestheticism. "Elmer," somewhat reminiscent of Browning's "Andrea del Sarto," defines art as opposed to life, a theoretical dichotomy that Faulkner was never able to give up even though his narrative practice was deeply representational, intimately involved with his life as a Southerner. By the writing of *Mosquitoes* in 1926, Faulkner had begun to distance himself critically from the demands of artsakism, but the interminable conversations of that narrative are nonetheless filled with aestheticist dogma. A more radical change took place in 1927 when Faulkner began writing a narrative called "Father Abraham," his first long Yoknapatawpha story which he set aside that same year to write *Flags in the Dust* and did not revive for over a decade when it reappeared, much changed, as the first Snopes novel, *The Hamlet.* The period from 1925 to 1927, therefore, spans a critical disjuncture between "Elmer" and *Mosquitoes* on the one hand and "Father Abraham" and *Flags in the Dust* on the other; that disjuncture hinges on a career decision that moved Faulkner away from aestheticism to representationalism, away from art toward life.

The artsakist ideal nevertheless remained to haunt Faulkner, both in his own evaluation of his achievements and, again in modified form, through the New Critical tradition that championed his artistry in the 1950s and 1960s. Faulkner's self-evaluation is most evident in his comments in *The Sound and the Fury*, a novel he felt to be an artistic failure, although redeemed by the purity of his aesthetic designs. In the crucial introduction, which was written five years after the novel's original publication, Faulkner described the joy and agony of composition. His lack of commercial success to that point in his career left him, he claimed, without ulterior motive; he was free to undertake a project for the pure joy of it: "I said to myself, Now I can write. Now I can just write."[1] The result was Benjy's narrative and the creation of the enigmatic figure of Caddy Compson. Benjy's section of *The Sound and the Fury* is a purely lyrical exercise freed from the limitations of time and space because it is the expression of a naive consciousness. This was, by his own account, the last of Faulkner's purely artistic moments of composition, for the corrupting influences of publication forced him out of the world of pure art and by stages more and more toward revision and representationalism, toward the narration of consciousness ever more tainted by time and place, by the world.

> The story is all there, in the first section as Benjy told it. I did not try deliberately to make it obscure; when I realized that the story might be printed, I took three more sections, all longer than Benjy's to try to

clarify it. But when I wrote Benjy's section, I was not writing it to be printed. If I were to do it over now I would do it differently, because the writing of it as it now stands taught me both how to write and how to read, and even more: It taught me what I had already read, because on completing it I discovered, in a series of repercussions like summer thunder, the Flauberts and Conrads and Turgenievs which as much as ten years before I had consumed whole and without assimilating at all, as a moth or a goat might.[2]

The dichotomy of art and life expressed here is a cliché of symbolist aestheticism; the focus is on the corrupting nature of print, that is, the opposition between language as social exchange and language as expressive creativity. In addition to this rather overblown romantic theory of composition, moreover, the opening paragraphs of the introduction establish a specific geographical context for this conflict; Faulkner begins with the claim that "art is no part of southern life."[3] The corruption of print is tied both to the demands of writing for an audience, of being understood, and to the revisionary technique that through repetition and difference moves Benjy's lyrical expression toward a narrative representing Faulkner's South. The successive sections expand Benjy's romantic ode to Caddy beyond the merely personal to a public world of social action, practice. The first movement away from pure art is in Quentin's oedipal lament at his inability to escape from time and place, an escape granted to Benjy. The second movement seems more radical: to Jason's very unlyrical diatribe against Compson genealogy, an expression which constitutes a powerful affirmation of time and place. Finally we move to a third-person narration, the shift in point of view emphasizing the focus on a slice of southern life, a new perspective on social-historical context which is remarkably unconcerned with Caddy or lyrical expressiveness. From this point on in his career Faulkner's writing intimately engaged southern social history, at first by imitating the discursive practices of southern mythmaking and finally by critiquing those practices. The protagonist of this myth of the Old South was, of course, the cavalier gentleman, a trope already introduced in *Flags in the Dust* and destined to remain central to Faulkner's writing through *Go Down, Moses.*

At the same time that Faulkner made his move from aestheticism to southernism, the Vanderbilt "Fugitives" made a similar move from the avant-garde, symbolist internationalism associated with *Fugitive* magazine (1922–25) to the militant southern regionalism of "Agrarianism."

In 1925 Donald Davidson began work on his celebration of Tennessee pioneers in *The Tall Men*. A symposium designed as a revaluation of southern culture was proposed in 1927 and was warmly endorsed by John Crowe Ransom, later the founding father of the New Criticism. This symposium eventuated in the publication of an Agrarian manifesto, *I'll Take My Stand*, in 1930. In 1928 Allen Tate, another future New Critic, began work on his most famous poem, "Ode to the Confederate Dead." The flurry of critical and literary activity that marks the transition from the *Fugitive* to *I'll Take My Stand*, Daniel Joseph Singal claims, "came about so fast that even the future Agrarians themselves were taken by surprise."[4]

The immediate causes of this new passionate southernism are difficult to locate. No doubt the infamous Scopes trial in 1925, with the unfavorable notoriety it gained for the South in the Northeast, acted as a spur to defensive regionalism. The ridiculing attacks of northern intellectuals like H. L. Mencken demanded a response that would disprove the suggestion that the South was an intellectual and moral wasteland.[5] Perhaps, as with Faulkner's contemporaneous emergent southernism, no simple cause can be found; what is certain is that the Agrarians undertook to revise the Old South myth of the cavalier by attacking the stereotype of the aristocratic southern planter and substituting an image of the Southerner more in line with populist historicism, an image provided by Frank Owsley's study of the southern "yeoman farmer."[6] But for the Agrarians the yeoman image was thoroughly permeated with cavalierism; as Singal argues, the Agrarians "declared flatly that the ideal embodied in the Cavalier was indispensable for social happiness and artistic creativity."[7]

The paths of the Agrarians and Faulkner did not intersect until after the Agrarian transmutation into the New Criticism in the 1940s and 1950s. There is no reason to quarrel with Cleanth Brooks's claim that no evidence exists for any direct influence of the Agrarians on Faulkner in the early (1920s) stages of Faulkner's southernism. Faulkner and the Agrarians did, however, share a number of attitudes that link them at the level of regionalist consciousness. Both deeply distrusted industrialism and espoused a nostalgia for what had come to be mythologized as the antebellum chivalric code of honor. In both, therefore, there is an aristocratic bias. For Faulkner this is tempered by an ongoing critique of cavalierism insofar as it was associated with the legendary exploits of his great-grandfather, although the code of honor is never absolutely rejected in his novels. There is, by contrast, no true critique of cavalierism among the Agrarians, not even in their final mutation as New Critics. An elitist aesthetics and social theory are founded on a vague ideal of leisure and Jeffersonian classism. The Agrarian revision of Old South cavalierism rewrites the defunct New South ideology of the Lost Cause, rejecting at the same time the New South celebration of industrialization as a mode of reconstructing the region to its former, antebellum glory.

From these roots it is possible to trace an evolution in thought from Fugitive symbolism to Agrarianism, and through Agrarianism and an Arnoldian high culture conservatism to the New Criticism. Moreover, a central tenet of New Critical formalism—the exclusion from literary interpretation of any concerns with social history, influence, biography, intentionality, and representationalism—serves, conveniently, to repress the Agrarian origins of New Critical aesthetics. Faulkner's own public disavowels of representation and sociology, along with his aestheticist ideal of pure art, appealed to the New Critical sensibilities and seemed to make him available for appropriation. Faulkner was, consequently, institutionalized as a powerful case proving that a southern writer could produce pure art. The conflict within Faulkner's work between art and southernism, aesthetics and representation, theory and practice was ignored.

Agrarian conservatism, which Richard King characterizes as "the closest thing to an authentic conservative vision which America has seen,"[8] is embedded in New Critical formalist aesthetics. The Agrarian-to-New Critic genealogy reveals itself in an essay by Cleanth Brooks entitled "Faulkner and the Fugitive Agrarians." Brooks devotes considerable space to a defense of the Agrarians; in particular, he responds to Daniel Aaron's charge that the Agrarians were reactionary regionalists who never developed, as did Faulkner, a critical attitude toward the Old South. Brooks argues that with the exception of Donald Davidson and Andrew Lytle the Agrarians never overpraised the Old South. He suggests that the Agrarian focus on the yeoman Southerner excluded any nostalgic cavalierism, and he goes on to argue that Faulkner, too, had a similar respect for the small farmer of the South.

> His characters like the McCallums or V. K. Ratliff possess backbone and determination and also moral force. We make a grave mistake if we take as representative of this class of yeoman farmer the despicable Anse Bundren or the ridiculous I. O. Snopes.[9]

But in his haste to disassociate the Agrarians, and Faulkner, from reactionary cavalierism Brooks characteristically uses Davidson as the

Agrarian scapegoat and ignores what is crucial in Faulkner's writing: the tension between cavalierism and all of its oppositions in the thematics of class, gender, and race. Oddly, the New Criticism becomes at this point uncritical, slipping into a simplistic account of Faulkner's "representative" class types. It is not at all clear what the McCallums, Ratliff, Anse Bundren, and I. O. Snopes have in common, but they are not all yeoman farmers of the same stripe. They are, perhaps, all *versions* of a class type, variations on a single theme, but as such they reveal not Faulkner's class allegiance so much as his revisionary technique.

Even critics who are not, like Brooks, doctrinaire New Critics miss this dimension of Faulkner's revisionary narrative practice. An exemplary case is the way certain readers interpret Faulkner's reworking of the cavalier John Sartoris in *The Unvanquished*. Both Singal and Joseph Blotner fail to recognize the critical difference in Faulkner's two major treatments of the Sartoris legend. Singal argues that in *The Unvaquished* "Faulkner . . . was trying to have it both ways, to assail the myth and keep it too." In that sense he concludes that "Faulkner would never repudiate the Sartorises" and their cavalier heritage.[10] Repudiation, however, is no real option for Faulkner; revision is. Having it both ways is less an escape than a critical engagement. Blotner also fails to see the depth of Faulkner's revisionary strategy, describing the Sartoris of *The Unvanquished* as just a "more violent self-centered ruffian than he had appeared" to be in *Flags in the Dust*.[11] But Blotner's dismissal of difference here seems psychoanalytically naive. The distance between the early and late version of John Sartoris, a figure drawn so clearly from the image of Faulkner's legendary great-grandfather, encompasses a shift in the author's stance toward both the cavalierism of the Old South myth and toward his sense of his own Falkner heritage. The difference is crucial.

The revisionary strategy that exposes John Sartoris performs a similar operation on the character of Thomas Sutpen. Here the New Critical exclusion of political and historical interpretation is more significant than with Sartoris' cavalierism. Brooks, in *William Faulkner: The Yoknapatawpha Country*, declares that Sutpen is so unique a figure that he cannot be said to represent the Old South aristocratic planter in any way. He returns to this same issue, prompted by critical response to his earlier claim, in *William Faulkner: Toward Yoknapatawpha and Beyond*. In an appendix entitled "Thomas Sutpen: A Representative Southern Planter?" Brooks reworks his earlier argument in a further effort to short-circuit nonformalist readings of *Absalom, Absalom!* To accomplish this task he departs from formalist procedures long enough

to enlist the aid of two distinguished historians of the South, Eugene
Genovese and C. Vann Woodward. His discomfort at the implications
of this approach force him into a disclaimer: "What any historian may
have to tell us will not, of course, be decisive for the meaning of *Absalom, Absalom!* or for the interpretation of the characters of that novel
—including Thomas Sutpen." [12] Given this, why the tortuous argument
that follows? This is a desperate move.

The answer lies in Brooks's reading of Genovese's thesis that the Old
South was distinct in its cultural attitudes; it was not dominated by the
ideology of capitalism gone slightly awry but was founded on a slave
economy which expressed itself in a precapitalistic or anticapitalistic
paternalism. Brooks quotes the following passage from Genovese who
is taking direct aim at the work of W. J. Cash.

> The question remains: What social vision informed these men's dreams?
> What kind of life did they seek for their children? Parvenus are parvenus,
> but bourgeois parvenus are not necessarily slaveholding parvenus once
> one gets beneath appearances. Cash has so far begged the question.
>
> After alleging that the Virginians who went west generally failed miserably, Cash makes a small admission, which like most of his small admissions compromises his argument: "Some of them . . . did nevertheless
> succeed. There were few parts of the South, indeed, in which it was not
> possible to find two or three—occasionally a small colony—of them."
> Influence, not numbers is here in question, and Virginia influence need
> not have meant a recapitulation of the Virginia experience. The questions
> come to these: Did the rising planters of the Southwest during the 1830's
> have before them, as an ideal future for themselves and their children, Virginia or Massachusetts? the Cavalier or the financier? Were they, in their
> economy and social relations, going down a bourgeois or an aristocratice
> road? [13]

For Genovese, of course, the ideal in the mind of the antebellum Southerner was that of the cavalier, which would appear to bring Sutpen
firmly into the realm of representative type. But for Brooks that is mere
appearance. First, Brooks claims, Genovese describes paternalism as
based on the concept of the extended family, and Sutpen has no sense
of family at all. "Frankly," Brooks argues, "it is difficult to imagine
Sutpen's ever carrying the boy Henry on his back or jogging him on his
knee." [14] This argument, surely, is irrelevant to Genovese's claim and a
dangerous bit of fanciful, extratextual speculation for a New Critic.

Whatever its merits, this argument is hardly as important as the second argument which infuses Woodward into Genovese to produce yet another image of the Old South cavalier based on the idea of aristocratic leisure, a quality not evidenced, says Brooks, by Sutpen.

> The South, to the despair of a people who have wished it well but insisted that it hustle more, has always reserved a large place for leisure. Woodward, to be sure, is properly cautious in drawing hard and fast conclusions, and he concedes that a concern for leisure may appear to another's more jaundiced eye as simply "laziness."[15]

Sutpen's character, Brooks believes, owes more to what Woodward defines as the New England Protestant ethic.

> Woodward quotes from Ernst Troeltsch's *Protestantism and Progress*: "For this spirit displays an untiring activity . . . it makes work and gain an end in themselves . . . it brings the whole life and action within the sphere of *an absolutely rationalized and systematic calculation*. . . . The last phrase applies to Sutpen in precise detail.[16]

Brooks weaves a pattern for the southern planter out of threads from Woodward and Genovese in order to establish that Sutpen is atypical of Old South cavalierism. Conversely, as a New Critical advocate of the Agrarian dogma of yeomanry, he is perfectly willing to argue that the McCallums and Ratliff are typical of the yeoman class. Representation is a convenient device.

In the essay on Sutpen's typicality Brooks's main purpose is to use Woodward and Genovese to separate southern paternalism and Yankee capitalism. This accomplished, Sutpen can be banished as unsouthern, as, ironically, "northern" in the simplistic (and perhaps centrally Agrarian) dichotomy of North and South. But Brooks's merging of Woodward and Genovese may tell us more than he wishes to say. Sutpen's exaggerated rationalism and single-minded drivenness may not be so atypical of the Old South as Brooks's reactionary cavalierism would have it. The Weberian spirit Sutpen represents may be read as undermining Genovese's separation of capitalism and paternalism, a controversial point that Brooks does not take up because it likewise undermines his attempt to deny Sutpen any representational function with regard to Old South cavalierism.

Carolyn Porter does engage Brooks and Genovese on precisely this issue in a finely tuned analysis of *Absalom, Absalom!* Porter questions Genovese's conclusions without rejecting his analysis, thereby reopening the door to an interpretation of Sutpen as representative of the mingled paternalistic and capitalistic ideologies of the southern planter.

It is the aspiring men of the antebellum South with whom we are chiefly concerned here, and Genovese is certainly correct in seeing them as thoroughly committed to the plantation myth and the paternalism ascribed to it. In accounting for this, however, it is not necessary to see the myth as validating a distinct slave economy in the South; it is just as plausible, if not more so, to see the myth as validating the use of slave labor by the plantation capitalist. . . . The paternalistic ideology of the Southern planter could and did serve . . . to confirm the dominant slaveowning class's right to dominate. . . . What destroyed this neat congruence of self-interest and idealism was not the intrusion of the cash nexus from without, but the exposure of the cash nexus within the plantation as a unit of production. . . . The plantation myth, in effect, proved vulnerable for the same reasons it had once been so powerful; it had provided a means for fusing within one social vision what in the end could not be fused because they were fundamentally contradictory—family and marketplace values.[17]

Porter accomplishes here a considerable narrowing of the gap between Genovese's Massachusetts and Virginia. More important, she demolishes Brooks's argument that Sutpen is not representative of the southern planter myth. She even suggests an extension of her argument that emphasizes Faulkner's revisionary strategy and his ultimate refusal to protect the cavalier myth from critical analysis.

The short stories in *The Unvanquished* were put together during roughly the same period as *Absalom, Absalom!* and of its hero. To compare the two heroes [Sartoris and Sutpen—as Faulkner does in the *The Unvanquished*] is to realize that Faulkner was playing for much higher stakes in *Absalom, Absalom!* . . . , producing a novel which appreciably undermines the nostalgia emanating from the pages of *The Unvanquished*. It almost seems as if *The Unvanquished* helped him to write *Absalom, Absalom!* by syphoning off his own romantic attachment to the cavalier legends.[18]

Porter's judgment of *The Unvanquished* is harsher than mine, for I find that retreat from nostalgia in *The Unvanquished* itself, however more forcefully it is accomplished in *Absalom, Absalom!* Nevertheless Porter provides a crucial support for my contention that Faulkner gradually abandoned his commitment to pure art with its defensive (repressive) denial of representation. Sutpen, therefore, must be seen as a type, but he does not represent a monolithic social order. He stands for the complex of contradictory images, attitudes, and practices that comprise the mythology, and the mythmaking, of both the old and the new South.

He unveils ideology through the thematics of race, class, and gender—particularly race, that southern family affair so central to the obsessive, repetitive narration of the South's great cultural trauma: the loss of "The War." Faulkner's narration of this narrative obsession constitutes the power of novels like *The Unvanquished* and *Absalom, Absalom!* for his revisionary technique critically confronts, not always without nostalgia or even regret, and surely always with uncertainty, his own legendary ancestor and the representative southern cavalier in the figures of John Sartoris and Thomas Sutpen. This writing is at the heart of the author's psychological and social identity, a location where art and life intersect.

We have already met the art-versus-life dichotomy of Faulkner criticism in the debate between Louis Rubin and Richard King. Nevertheless, Rubin's perspective reflects a widespread contemporary theory of language and literature, and such a theory deserves further discussion here. Rubin claims:

> The novelist's responsibility to truth is through and in art; and the morality, racial or otherwise, of a work of fiction must lie not in a prescription for action but in its exploration, in language, of the human experiences it recreates.[19]

Two forms of language stand opposed in Rubin's definition; the "prescription for action" is excluded from the artistic "exploration" of recreated "human experiences." The aestheticizing of language can be traced back from the New Critics through I. A. Richards to Coleridge; it is a naive conception at best, claiming for artistic uses of language an innocence that grants it immunity from all forms of critical practice other than formalist appreciation. Rubin's argument, however, establishes more than a linguistic division; he also posits a peculiar aesthetic "truth" which apparently we are to understand as having no issue in real, lived experience. Its value seems questionable. Rubin here sets up a basis for critical judgment: novels of true artistic quality (and language) resist the language of prescription. The measure of Faulkner's greatness as a writer rests on those novels which successfully defend against the intrusion of social and political issues like race relations in the South.

Walter Sullivan goes even farther, reading the lapse into prescription as evidence of the downfall of all modern literature. Joyce is a particular enemy, but Faulkner's late Snopes novels are equally guilty of these impurities. Sullivan quotes Peter Swiggart's judgment that *The Town* and *The Mansion* lack the depth of Faulkner's earlier ("great") works. "The result," Swiggart claims, "is a writing impasse that the author tries to escape principally through rhetorical means."[20] Swiggart's evaluation not being sufficient, Sullivan supplements it: "Or, one might add," Faulkner "tries to escape through a new commitment to the social and political clichés of our time."[21] The source of the problem, according to Sullivan, is the growth of secularism and gnosticism: "Modern man is continually tempted to think that he can modify the terms of human existence. . . . He is mistaken because he is not trafficking in essential truth as was Christ, but in secondary realities."[22] This gnostic pride, he claims, has resulted in a decline of more than just southern literature: "For the first time in history . . . a democratic society has forced art into the subservient and distorted function of pursuing political and social ends."[23]

Sullivan, although a minor Faulkner critic at best, is the last of the Vanderbilt line spawned by the Agrarians, and his argument crystallizes the Agrarian and New Critical dogma that isolates art from life, the artistic (essential or Christian) truth from the secular world of politics. He shares this set of attitudes with another scholar of southern literature, Robert Jacobs. Jacobs' Faulkner meets the moral and religious criteria advocated by Sullivan: "*Absalom, Absalom!* is a tale that affirms the existence of a moral order above and beyond man by the very completeness of destruction."[24] There is an important link here between moral order and completeness which contains both a doctrinaire morality and an aesthetic ideal of formal closure. The result is a particularly forced and blind reading of Faulkner's novels, for anything that suggests incompleteness or open-endedness must be explained away. The real enemy for Jacobs is the individual who refuses to be bound by tradition or by social codes regardless of traditional social injustice. To disagree, resist, question, or criticize, to refuse to accept one's assigned role is an act of overweening pride, a form of antisocial behavior and a denial of moral order. Such rebellion Jacobs mistakenly terms "solipsism": "Faulkner's tragic theme is solipsism, the isolation of the individual behind the walls of Self, but he shows clearly the way to breach those walls. It is the old way."[25]

The particular orthodoxy which constitutes the "old way" for Jacobs is irrelevant to our discussion. What is important is the juxtaposition of solipsism and the idea of "endurance," a term tellingly borrowed from Faulkner: "Man's freedom is an inner and moral one. It is his responsibility to endure and attempt to expiate the evils which he inherits from the past."[26] Endurance is primary, and the evils from the past hardly could include social injustice (racism) given Jacobs' castigation of sociological critics who read the story of Joe Christmas as one about a "victim" of racist violence. We understand better what he means when we realize that it is Byron Bunch, Sam Fathers, and Dilsey who compose a list of Faulkner characters exhibiting the "inner" moral strength and "freedom" of endurance: "[They] have the humanity to feel love and compassion and the courage to endure and to sacrifice for something or someone beyond self."[27] Whatever "freedom" these characters have must surely be "inner" because evidence of it otherwise is limited. Jacobs has read uncritically the implicit classism, racism, and sexism in Faulkner, transforming these weaknesses into a universal moral principle. One need not question the social and political implications of Faulkner's novels, Jacobs suggests, since the acceptance of repression is a mark of moral strength. It is a moral strength possible only for the repressed. Given this perspective, Faulkner's great novels have few loose ends; fate, suffering, acceptance all seem ordained and imply a static society as well as a closed aesthetic form.

The New Criticism, with its provision of a sacred space and time in the midst of chaotic reality, wrings artistic success out of social and political failure, redeems that failure in the realm of the imagination, in a dream of an ideal world. Art writ large, as "Culture," is a fragile shore against the ruins of modernism; the New Criticism defines the world and the self that comes to dwell within it and thus provides a metaphysical justification for a kind of aesthetic status quo. Art remains free of the taint of life until life has been purified in the fires of creative productivity. Art is thereby removed from life and, as a consequence not always acknowledged, removed from critical analysis. Art traffics with art alone; the images of art are drawn from art itself, one of the most famous being that articulated by Brooks as the "well-wrought urn." It is not by chance, of course, that the urn also serves Faulkner as an image for pure art; in *Flags in the Dust*, his first novel beyond the early period of his fascination with aestheticism and symbolism, he depicts, in Keatsian terms and not without a touch of irony, Horace Benbow's hobby of "making glassware."

[Horace] produced one almost perfect vase of clear amber, larger, more richly and chastely serene [than his other efforts] and which he kept always on his night table and called by his sister's name in the intervals of apostrophising both of them impartially in his moments of rhapsody over the realization of the meaning of peace and the unblemished attainment of it, as Thou still unravished bride of quietude.

(*FD*, pp. 190–91)

An alignment of Brooks's New Critical image and Faulkner's Keatsian reference is tempting, and it is tangled with other resonances in the New Critical appropriation of Faulkner that established his reputation as an artist and still provide the basis for critical analysis of his work. One of the best of those influenced by formalism in reading Faulkner is Olga Vickery, who also centers her discussion of Faulkner's narrative structure on the image of the urn. The problem is that Faulkner's narratives do not seem to be well wrought. She offers what she calls the "grand pattern" of his fiction as something of an excuse for his lack of narrative closure; the Yoknapatawpha novels, she suggests, must be read not singly but rather as a grand design consisting of several novels. It is a promising idea, but one that her formalist bias cannot sustain. She also assumes an art-versus-life dichotomy, appealing to Aristotelian formalism for a distinction between the historian who is "relentlessly factual" and the artist who eschews social and historical facticity. To support her position she quotes a passage from Faulkner's *Intruder in the Dust* (one which echoes an argument put forward by Ike McCaslin in *Go Down, Moses*). Her reading of this passage also supports the claims of Agrarian defenders like Rubin, Sullivan, and Jacobs. In art, she hears Faulkner say, the interest is not in "facts but long since beyond dry statistics into something far more moving because it was truth; which moved the heart and had nothing whatever to do with what mere provable information said."[28]

But Vickery takes this passage out of context. Her aim is to associate art with a truth beyond lived experience. Furthermore, she jumps from this old dichotomy to one of the most persistent pieces of critical misreading ever proposed about Faulkner: the characterization of him as a "failed poet:"[29] "Faulkner, the self-styled 'failed poet,' makes prose fiction approximate poetry which he equates with the lyric and defines as 'some moving, passionate moment of the human condition distilled to its absolute essence.'"[30] As a result, she bemoans the lack of formal integrity in Faulkner's narratives, ultimately agreeing with Malcolm Cowley (with whom at first she seemed to disagree) that Faulkner's novels suffer from "structural weakness." Like Cowley she invokes Poe in her definition of Faulkner as a better short story writer than novelist since his longer prose works are little more than a "series of pieces." Ranging widely for her analogies, she characterizes these stories as lyrical moments, as "figures" in a Jamesian carpet woven from the fabric of Yoknapatawpha.

> In viewing the carpet one therefore moves inevitably from an awareness of vibrantly living characters to the perception of an intricately related series of lyrical stases. Individually these recall Keats's Grecian Urn capturing the essence of the moment, while collectively they constitute a modern prose equivalent to the Renaissance lyric cycle.[31]

Vickery's terminology, the image of the Renaissance sonnet cycle, the storehouse of exemplary theories drawn from Aristotle, Keats, Poe, James, and implicitly Brooks prevent her from seeing that the Yoknapatawpha novels are a single narrative, one that is open, continuous, and revisionary. And this blindness also turns her attention away from the representational, that is, profoundly social and political, implications of Faulkner's open-ended narrative. Her critical terminology and cast of formalist authorities bind her within a lyric prejudice that makes it impossible for her to discuss narrative at all. Thus Faulkner's truth of the heart is mistakenly, if inevitably, associated with art rather than with the vision of social injustice (racism) that forms the cultural and historical context of the passage from *Intruder in the Dust* that she quotes.

If we read carefully, Faulkner's urn imagery always falls short of perfection, indicating his skepticism about the aesthetic ideals he had borrowed from artsakism and symbolism. The Keatsian vase of *Flags in the Dust* is "almost perfect," but that qualification opens the closed vessel to psychological and social calamity, to incestuous desiring that no amount of metaphorizing can transform into aesthetic innocence. The urn ideal has in Faulkner its analogue in the Old South ideal; both are forms of mythmaking. Moreover, the ideal of pure art, like the Old South myth, is seductive, but Faulkner could not affirm the ideal enough to escape from life, from the present, from narration of his world. The revisionary technique is, therefore, no celebration of art by art; it is a gesture toward a reality, an insistent voice among other voices; it is an expression and a quotation, an engagement of form and reference, art and life.

Reading Faulkner raises critical awareness of the complex relationship between author and text. To write is profoundly autobiographical, and

Faulkner incorporates his life as a southern writer into his narratives with uncommon zeal. Formalism represses the struggle that Faulkner's writing articulates because it represses the narrative genre itself, attempting to resolve tensions that are, left unresolved, the essence of narrative. Formalism insists on a unified voice, but true narrative is a polyvocal representation of what Mikhail Bakhtin called "heteroglot" discursive practices.[32] Narrative arises from listening and discerning, a source made explicit in Faulkner's novels of storytelling, or story-listening. The novelist's infusion of social discourses into his fictional discourse represents a critical engagement with society, both a distance from and implication in the reality that always grounds narration. Biography, from this perspective, is not merely a chronological account of the author's life but a critical interpretation; the fundamental issues in the relation of author and text are the "career" decisions everywhere present in the text which derive from the author's critical response to his life. Biographical criticism, therefore, blends psychoanalysis, biography, and formalism, a far from comfortable association of critical modes. This concluding segment of the first part of our reading of Faulkner anticipates a discussion of career, and beyond that a discussion of central issues regarding narrative form, narrative voice, and the problematical thematics of Faulkner's most enduring novels: racism, classism, and sexism. The preliminary question of Faulkner's attitude toward writing is the topic here.

The slow emergence of biographical and psychoanalytical interpretations of Faulkner's novels in the 1970s signaled a final break in the formalist stranglehold on reading Faulkner. Yet the departure from formalism is incomplete; aesthetic and biographical approaches make contact only through cautious, inconclusive, and frequently self-defeating marriages. Such is the case with David Minter, a most astute critic and biographer, who nonetheless struggles heroically to bridge the theoretical gaps that a true critical biography must overpass. Minter's involvement with Faulkner is of long standing. His first book concluded with a reading of *Absalom, Absalom!* wherein his formalist biases are clear in his use of Sutpen's "design" as a representative principle of structure in American prose. For Minter the "design" is less purely lyrical than the well-wrought urn and more representational, opening onto southern discursive mythmaking and the southern problematics of social order and traditional social values, but his reading of the "design" presents it as an ideal. Unfortunately, in Faulkner's novels, as in his urns, the design is flawed.

The aesthetic dimension of Sutpen's design derives, for Minter, from the oppositional relationship between Sutpen and his interpreters, from the discursive play of voices that forms the narrative. Implicit here are representations of Sutpen as Old South cavalier, as a man of action obsessed with a dream expressed in his life design. Yet these issues are muted by Minter's formalist perspective.

> It is, in brief, through Faulkner's effort to bring order to the lost lives of his men of design and interpretation, through his effort to give pattern and meaning to the action and thought of Yoknapatawpha, that the story of Sutpen and his interpreters is transformed into Art and thereby redeemed . . . from time itself.[33]

Southern history here disappears into "Art," elevated by its capital. Interestingly, not all of Sutpen's interpreters are "men." Minter inadvertently raises a critical issue, for the transformation of life into art in Faulkner is tangled in the problem of gender identity. To write is to exhibit a conflict of feminine and masculine characteristics for Faulkner. The masculine characteristics are artistic control, authority, and prestige (wealth and fame); the feminine, as we shall see, are a perversion of masculine authority. Formalism's metaphor for that sense of control is the extraordinary imaginative power of transformation. Thus it is not surprising that both "transformation" and "redemption" are prominent in New Critical jargon; the distinction between sacred art and profane life stifles (represses) representation, which, as feminine, challenges (masculine) authority. Minter's critical posture vis-à-vis the dichotomy of art and life is typically defensive. He derives his image of Faulkner's redemptive art from W. H. Auden; *Absalom, Absalom!* "is 'mere' poetry, a created and human song 'of human unsuccess' sung 'in a rapture of distress.'"[34] His eloquence persuades because his deep sympathy with Faulkner's struggle to succeed as an author is movingly articulated. Yet the image of Faulkner as a failed poet and the false humility of Auden's "mere" poetry distort our reading of the novels. Faulkner redeems very little of his troubled world; he represents it.

Minter's sympathy for Faulkner enabled him some years after this initial reading of *Absalom, Absalom!* to produce a very ambitious biography. The mechanics of biographical inquiry necessitated a departure from formalism, but there was no radical break. The pivotal point of his analysis and exposition is the relationship between *The Sound and the Fury* and *Absalom, Absalom!*; it was the former, Minter argues, that "focused Faulkner's attention on the problematic relations between novelist and his novels."[35] The latter contextualized these problematic relations within the narrative as a relationship between "teller and tale," very much in the manner of Jamesian "dramatization."[36] The problem here for Minter as biographer is to explain the interaction of author and text (expressed in the interaction between teller and tale) in terms of the relationship between life and art. The crucial critical discourse that forges this link for Minter, as it was for Judith Wittenberg in a biography that appeared the year before Minter's, is psychoanalysis. Wittenberg labels Faulkner's writing the "transfiguration of biography," using another religious term related to "transformation." Both Minter and Wittenberg draw on the merging of psychoanalysis and formalism found in John Irwin's *Doubling and Incest: Repetition and Revenge.* Irwin appropriates biography for psychoanalysis; he overemphasizes the character of Quentin Compson, as so many formalists have done, to produce not so much a reading of Faulkner as a definition of art as oedipal conflict, as a "suicidal, incestuous struggle between the writer and the other self of his book."[37] For Irwin writing is lyrical; all voices merge egoistically to express the self (or desire for the unitary self), so that all writing becomes a simplified form of the interior monologue. Irwin rewrites New Critical aesthetic unity as authoritarian law or the struggle for authority. Minter and Wittenberg rescue biographical detail from Irwin's misappropriation, but neither challenges the formalism implicit in his oedipalism.

Minter's move from biography to art is gradual. He describes the power of *Absalom, Absalom!* in its "inclusiveness," listing an array of contexts for the novel.

> It touches not only the geography and history but also the prehistory of Yoknapatawpha, and it makes contact with each of its social elements— including dispossessed Indians, enslaved blacks, and a variety of whites, from Wash Jones and the Coldfields to the Compsons. Through its action it reaches back into the early nineteenth century, when Yoknapatawpha was "still frontier." Through its French architect it reaches back to Europe. Through Thomas Sutpen's family it reaches back both to the splendor of Tidewater Virginia and to the simplicity of a primitive Appalachian community. Through Sutpen's slaves it reaches back to the West Indies and Africa. It provides, therefore, a sense not only of the people and history of Yoknapatawpha, but of its sources.[38]

The promise of this reference to "sources" might be to take us beyond the fictional Yoknapatawpha to the South of Faulkner's own experiences. The next move of the critical biographer is to explain this link between art and life. Minter's formalist instincts, however, lead him most immediately to associate *Absalom, Absalom!* with other Faulkner novels and then to construct a literary genealogy which includes the Bible, Greek drama, Cervantes, Shakespeare, Melville, and Conrad. The assessment is certainly correct, the honor deserved, but the result is to retreat from all sources that are not strictly literary. "The larger source of the power of *Absalom, Absalom!*" Minter argues, "is formal."[39] The relation between Sutpen's design and its interpretations in the text emerges again to plant Minter's reading of the novel firmly within the parameters of formalism. His image of art here is borrowed from Wallace Stevens, a favorite source of aesthetic principles for Minter: "*Absalom, Absalom!* becomes both a narration of great action and an exploration of human minds and imaginations engaged in acts of discovering what will suffice."[40] The sufficiency of art in Stevens' "Of Modern Poetry" affirms the unbridgeable gap between the lyric imagination and life, and what will suffice here not only echoes Minter's earlier aesthetics of redemption but also anticipates his final words on Faulkner the artist: "What Christ was to sin and death—their only possible antidote—art is to man's [Faulkner's] sense of failure, imperfection, and impending death. Art becomes, in these terms, man's subtlest strategy."[41] The repeated return of formalism to the sacred is designed to divide art and life and defend against critical interpretation by consecrating art as a holy mystery.

The appropriation of sacred terms for the defense of art in the discourse of the New Criticism can be traced again to the Arnoldian roots of Agrarianism. The short distance between the aestheticizing of the sacred and the formalizing of psychoanalytic theory makes possible Minter's employment of the strategies of psychoanalysis in his explanation of the merging of Faulkner's life and work. The early novels and particularly stories like "Carcassonne" (1925) and "Nympholepsy" (1925) provide a focus for Minter's dichotomy of purity (art) and decay (life) that has mingled sexual, religious, and aesthetic implications. Sexual difference, or sexual identity, emerges as central to Faulkner's conception of being an author. Irwin first locates in Faulkner's introduction to *The Sound and the Fury* the critical principle that Minter later develops; writing is an oedipal struggle. Irwin focuses on Faulkner's story of the "old Roman" and "the vase he kept by his bedside" whose rim he "wore . . . slowly away with kissing it":

[Faulkner] understood that a writer's relation to his material and to the work of art is always a loss, a separation, a cutting off, a self-castration that transforms the masculine artist into the feminine-masculine vase of the work. He knew . . . that the writer ends up identifying himself not with what remains but with what is lost [Faulkner's sister, daughter, Caddy, novel], the detached object that is the work. It is precisely by a loss, by a cutting off or separation that the artist's self and his other self, the work, mutually constitute one another—loss is the very condition of their existence.[42]

Irwin's image for the author/text relationship constantly shifts its reference. It is conventionally oedipal: "The masculine self as related to the feminine-masculine work of art immediately suggests the man-woman-man interaction of the Oedipal triangle."[43] It is also "auto-erotic . . . , the self making love to the self, a kind of creative onanism," or it is the image of "the self . . . continually spent and wasted in an act of progressive self-destruction."[44] What remains stable in Irwin's theorizing is the perspective on writing as masculine; Irwin's particular variation on the famous Keatsian urn ideal merely emphasizes what has been often repressed: the dimension of performance anxiety, the deeply egoistical and romantic fear of lost potency, of not being able to do it again. Minter's dichotomy of pure art and decaying life has its source in Irwin's psychoanalytic meditations, and for both of them art's transcendence of life represents the miracle of a sacred triumph over time, history, and human experience, the achievement of immortality, an escape, figured in Quentin Compson, from life, from sexuality. Irwin:

And this process of literary self-dismemberment is the author's response to the threat of death; it is a using up, a consuming of the self in the act of writing in order to escape from that annihilation of the self that is the inevitable outcome of physical generation, to escape by means of an ablative process of artistic creation in which the self is worn away to leave only a disembodied voice on the page to survive the writer's death, a voice that represents the interruption of the phallic generative power of the creative imagination.[45]

The unitary voice which represents "the phallic generative power of the creative imagination" is so stridently egocentric and sexist that it outreaches even Faulkner's infamous misogyny. Irwin's uncritical use of Oedipus here—yet another metaphor for aesthetic purity and lyric form—serves to rarefy and isolate art, to cramp representation. "Self-dismemberment" evokes the "failed poet," and here, too, that failure is transformed into triumph. The radical displacement of life by art is purchased at the expense of driving biography into psychoanalytical truisms, self-evident propositions. Sexism aside, the only response to such a reading of Faulkner is that the interpretation is dismally reductive.

Minter is less tempted by masculine oedipalism than Irwin and is much more aware of the broader agony of Faulkner's struggle to accept his career as a writer. The failed poet remains the reference point; the introduction to *The Sound and the Fury* again provides the source of information.

> Like imperfect success . . . indirect knowledge and indirect expression imply partial completion and carry several connotations. Both Faulkner's need to approach Caddy only by indirection and his need to describe his novel as a series of imperfect acts only partially completed ally it with the complex. His descriptions of *The Sound and the Fury* are in part a tribute to epistemological problems and in part an acknowledgement that beauty is difficult. . . . But the indirection and incompletion that his descriptions stress are also useful strategies for approaching forbidden scenes, uttering forbidden words, committing dangerous acts.[46]

The strategies of indirection are indeed useful to Faulkner, not merely for exploring the savage psyche, but for confronting the images of the self handed down from his ancestors and codified in the southern myth of the cavalier. Ultimately Minter cannot follow this lead; Irwin's perspective intrudes: "Imaginatively [Faulkner] is able to open closed doors, approach forbidden figures, and commit dangerous acts as well as make life a prolonged and inspired defiance of death by turning it into art."[47]

Nor can Irwin, distracted by his image of phallic power, perceive how near he comes to escaping from his aesthetic trap:

> What Faulkner describes here [introduction to *The Sound and the Fury*] is the author's sense of loss of the original virgin space ("that ecstasy, that eager and joyous faith and anticipation of surprise which the as yet unmarred sheets beneath my hand held inviolate and unfailing") and his mature acceptance of repetition ("The unreluctance to begin, the cold satisfaction in work well and arduously done, is there and will continue to be there as long as I can do it well").[48]

What Irwin calls Faulkner's "mature acceptance of repetition" Faulkner calls his learning to read and write, the beginning of the most productive period of his career bounded by the universally acknowledged "great" works *The Sound and the Fury* and *Go Down, Moses*. What originates with the writing of *The Sound and the Fury* is a departure from his early aestheticism, an initiation into an understanding of narrative, the representation of discursive practices in the multiple voices of his stories, the crucial recognition of the problem that he phrased as an uncertainty whether he "had invented the world" of his narratives "or it had invented" him.[49] Most important of all, however, *The Sound and the Fury* fails because it misrepresents the conditions under which the Compson, and Faulknerian, obsession with Caddy emerges. *The Sound and the Fury* only grudgingly gives way to the master theme of Faulkner's most moving narrations: the South. It distorts and digresses from the powerful thematics of race, class, and gender which become central to Faulkner's career for the next two decades.

Faulkner was a self-conscious writer, and his frequent statements on writing tellingly reveal a deep uncertainty about his sexual identity that is involved in his career decision to write. For Faulkner the masculine was all too often linked to the image of a man of action whose affairs of the world seemed to exclude the isolated, antisocial, and contemplative experiences of the creative artist. Again, the choice rests on a basic dichotomy of art and life: "those who can, do, those who cannot and suffer enough because they can't, write about it" (*UV*, p. 262). But when Faulkner searches for images to depict the act of writing, life overwhelms art.

> So I put people in [*Flags in the Dust*], since what can be more personal than reproduction, in its true way, the aesthetic and mammalian. In its own sense, really, since the aesthetic is still the female principle, the desire to feel over the bones spreading and parting with something alive begotten of the ego and conceived by the protesting unleashing of flesh.[50]

The birth/writing metaphor here is not the conventional one that inspired Irwin's autoerotic aesthetics. Irwin simply appropriates the "female principle" for his own purposes, but Faulkner's version is less violent and more daring, asserting the "desire to feel" the pain of labor, to be like a woman rather than displace her. Irwin must rummage through his Freudian lexicon for some male equivalent for the pain of childbirth; the best he can find is the fear of castration. For Irwin, giving birth, whether metaphorical or biological, merely suggests a primal loss of self. Faulkner emphasizes the mingled desire and pain that more sensitively represent the complex emotions of fear and joy, courage and dread that accompany childbirth.

Crucially, Faulkner's metaphor situates its images on the body, in the real. Irwin only repeats the conventional metaphor of birth/creativity, leaving it hopelessly symbolic. Irwin debiologizes whereas Faulkner insists on the return of biology. The distinction is important. In *Mosquitoes* Faulkner comments on the metaphor itself.

[Art is] more than that. It's getting into life, getting into it and wrapping it around you, becoming a part of it. Women can do it without art—old biology takes care of that. But men, men. . . . A woman conceives: does she care afterward whose seed it was? Not she. And bears, and all the rest of her life—her young, troubling years, that is—is filled. Of course, the father can look at it occasionally. But in art, a man can create without any assistance at all: what he does is his. A perversion, I grant you, but a perversion that builds Chartres and invents *Lear* is a pretty good thing.[51]

The masculine bias of the birth/writing metaphor is made clear in this passage, although the masculine imagery gets tangled with that of motherhood. The conventional masculine issues of composition are the preservation of a threatened ego, the establishing of paternal authority and the legitimacy of descent, and the unchallengeable ownership of the products of one's labors. Yet the central point for Faulkner is not birth but the relation of art to life. In the first two sentences he reverses the infamous aestheticist doctrine articulated by Oscar Wilde, once so strong an influence on the young artsakist Faulkner. It is not life that imitates art; rather here something more akin to a traditional mimetic theory displaces artsakism. The remainder of the passage critically reprises the birth/writing metaphor; *critically* reprises it by labeling this masculine convention, the appropriation of the feminine, a "perversion."

This passage, moreover, echoes an earlier one in *Mosquitoes* which eventuated in a discussion of modern poetry.

"Hermaphroditus," he read. "That's what it's about. It's a kind of dark perversion. . . ." I mean, all modern verse is a kind of perversion. Like the day for healthy poetry is over and done with, that modern people were not born to write poetry any more. Other things, I grant. But not poetry."

(*MO*, p. 252)

Here we read Faulkner's apology for abandoning poetry to write narratives (those "other things"); the critically popular theme of Faulkner as a failed poet turns out to have generic and not personal validity. Modernism deflates poetry, deflates the romantic metaphoric ideal of a perfect union of differences by reducing it to hermaphroditic monstrosities. In the Yoknapatawpha novels this idea finds its expression in a series of approaches to the subject of incest. Initially, the creation of unity out of oppositions is depicted in a way that supports Minter, as a forbidden but ideal pleasure; in a typically romantic metaphor for art it takes the form of brother/sister incest. This theme has a romantic and ideal development in Quentin Compson's fatal obsession tied to the desire to escape from time, from life. But the theme is significantly rewritten in *Go Down, Moses*, moved away from the aesthetic ideal toward violence and exploitation in the incest (which is also miscegenation) of father and daughter. Here romantic ideality is historicized and socialized; the escape from life into art is prevented by both the thematics of race and gender and a narrative dispersal (fragmentation in formalist terms), rather than preserved by lyric monologue. Faulkner discovered that the issues of racial and gender difference have no place in the romantic world of forbidden, idealized unions and aesthetic appropriations of life.

Faulkner does not, however, eschew the perverse; the modern writer, he argues, self-consciously cultivates it. Faulkner discovers a subversive power in writing, an enlightenment he celebrates in the introduction to *The Sound and the Fury* and associates with that "female principle" he earlier had called the aesthetics of perversion. It refers to the irreparable crack in the Faulknerian urn, the repressed fault in the romantic, New Critical ideal. This subversive power has one of its best expressions in *Absalom, Absalom!* in Mr. Compson's repeated lament that "something is missing" in the Sutpen story which defers understanding and truth (*AA*, p. 101). What is missing, of course, is the conventional phallic symbol of completeness and authority that would allow Quentin's father to put an end to narration, to cut off his son's narrative voice (to say nothing of Rosa Coldfield's voice) before Quentin can usurp the game. Freudian discursivity finds its way into Mr. Compson's narration rather too obviously. And this psychoanalytical discourse merges easily with the "literary" language which informs much of Mr. Compson's celebration of the heroic cavalier past. The latter is Aristotelian (that is, formal), defining a tragic inevitability for the story of the Sutpens (the South). *Oedipus Rex*, we should recall, was Aristotle's model of tragic closure; formalism is implicit in Freudianism.

Mr. Compson's authoritarian drive, however, is disrupted, perverted and dispersed, by other discourses that are audible in his narration and that subvert the unity of his voice. He speaks many languages. The first is that of legal practice, particularly that of marriage contracts. Mr. Compson's tale of Sutpen hinges on the play of marriages acknowledged and unacknowledged. The key is Charles Bon's black mistress in New Orleans, a motive, he argues, for Henry's refusal to allow Bon to marry his sister, Judith (*AA*, p. 104). But this key, unfortunately, unlocks no revealing (forbidden) doors; something is still missing, and Mr. Compson is compelled to reconstruct (rewrite, revise) his portraits of Henry, Bon, and Judith. He seeks incriminating evidence, and in his desperation another discourse enters, one decidedly Faulknerian in its decadent aestheticism and obvious reference to Wilde. The young Faulkner particularly admired Wilde's passionate play of seduction, *Salome*,[52] and Mr. Compson's description of a feminized Charles Bon might well have been in imitation of a Beardsley-like sketch of Wilde:

> —this man whom Henry first saw riding perhaps through the grove at the University on one of the two horses which he kept there or perhaps crossing the campus on foot in the slightly Frenchified cloak and hat that he wore, or perhaps (I like to think this) presented formally to the man reclining in a flowered, almost feminized gown, in a sunny window in his chambers—this man handsome and elegant and even catlike and too old to be where he was, too old not in years but in experience, with some tangible effluvium of knowledge, surfeit: of actions done and satiations plumbed and pleasures exhausted and even forgotten.
>
> (*AA*, p. 95)

The feminized portrait, with its satirical portrait of the satiated Byronic hero, serves as critical background for Mr. Compson's narrative of perverted oedipal relations. The plot of his tragedy now follows a chain of seductions (from Henry's by Bon to Judith's by Henry in the name of Bon) and not the course of heroic actions of men (*AA*, pp. 96 and 97).

Even a character so monologically authoritarian, so oedipal as Mr. Compson cannot write a perfect story; what is missing, the crack in the urn, is not castration, loss of potency, creativity, but, for Faulkner, the space where creativity, as revision and not mere repetition, is possible. Also missing is the opening onto what is real and what is historical. The solitary, romantic Quentin of *The Sound and the Fury* is displaced into *Absalom, Absalom!* where his voice is penetrated by a "commonwealth" (*AA*, p. 12). Quentin's narration is derived from the narratives told by Rosa and his father and is dialogically juxtaposed with the narrative of Shreve. In the process *Absalom, Absalom!* historicizes and socializes *The Sound and the Fury*, a revisionary act glimpsed in the novel's intertextual disruptions. Shreve's substitution of a thematics of race for Quentin's more romantic fantasy of brother/sister incest marks the crucial transition from a narrative of self-expression to a narrative representation of a discursive practice. The "something missing" of *Absalom, Absalom!* is not a lack but a space for revision, for other voices and other versions. It is in this space that Faulkner's theory of writing as feminine perversity is located. Clearly Faulkner does not here reject the masculine stereotyping of the female as a deviant form of the male, but he does, perhaps unknowingly, rewrite the stereotype of the feminine as lack, making of the feminine a principle of creativity, of productivity and reproductivity, even if it remains for him a perversion.

We must understand, therefore, that the feminine perverse served Faulkner in very complex ways. Thematically he insistently depicts the fall of southern culture as a rupture within the South itself and not as a defeat by outside forces. His struggle is to narrate this internal contradiction through the play of contradictory voices, the clash of contradictory discursive practices. The representation of the South, of southern mythmaking, undergoes revision in the name of arriving not at the true version but at a form of deviant behavior, a perversion of the ideals that southern mythmaking sought to perpetuate. The perverse unleashes voices that Faulkner may not have wanted to hear, but he leaves those voices a space for articulation, if an often firmly circumscribed one. These voices emerge in the formal structuring of his narratives as incompatible with the dominant, the familiar, the authoritative, the repressive, the legitimate, white masculine voices of the myth of the Old South. They are black voices, and female voices, and juvenile voices, necessarily "other" since they express Faulkner's own perversion of the Old South, his personal perversion of his Falkner heritage. These voices do not merely endure or symbolize. Here, then, are Minter's forbidden subjects, in Faulkner's hermaphroditic modernism, whose roots lay in the modern South's depression and its antebellum delusions. The subject of his novels is a cultural crisis embedded in a crisis of aesthetics, thematized as a family crisis, expressing a crisis of personal identity.

PART II

Reading the Texts

CHAPTER 7

Genealogy and Writing

FAULKNER'S INTEREST in genealogy was personal and aesthetic. In both instances he concerned himself not with simple chronicle but with a foreshortened structure of descent. The crucial schema was limited to four generations within which the typical pattern displayed a confrontation between the first and fourth generations. The First Ancestor is a great-grandfather, a legendary figure whose authority in family history rests on his role as founder, as originating force. This powerful father of fathers, a mythic character, gives his name to his descendants, determines family identity, confers on his heirs a sense of legitimacy and belonging. His counterpart, which we may call the Descendant, at three removes from the First Ancestor, confronts not a real being but a ghost. The First Ancestor is known only through stories, legends, myths, handed down from generation to generation. The Descendant inherits those stories as well as the function of retelling them. It is an ambiguous power involving a test of wills, the one a legend's bequest, the other a present desiring.

William Clark Falkner, the Old Colonel, was William Cuthbert Faulkner's First Ancestor.[1] Colonel Falkner was a man of heroic proportions, a soldier in two wars, a planter, lawyer, politician, railroad builder, and, not incidentally, a novelist. He was also self-destructively daring, romantic, independent, violent, reckless, and controversial. He was born on July 6, 1825, to a poor family that had migrated from South Carolina to Tennessee and later moved to Missouri. Sometime between 1839 and 1842 (the stories vary) the boy left home and traveled alone, mostly on foot, to Mississippi, then very much a part of the great American frontier. His uncle, John Wesley Thompson, a schoolteacher and lawyer, of Ripley in Tippah County, took the boy into his home and educated him. When he was about twenty, Falkner wrote a pamphlet based on the true confessions of an ax murderer whom he had helped rescue from a lynching party. On the day of the man's execution, he sold 2,500 copies to onlookers and made a tidy profit. His rise to fame and fortune had begun.

He read law with his uncle, married, and stabbed a man in an argument. Found innocent of murder by reason of self-defense, Falkner stepped from the courthouse only to be attacked by the brother of the man he had killed, and in the ensuing struggle he shot and killed another man. He was again acquitted, but other encounters and several duels followed. He gave his first son, John Wesley Thompson Falkner, whose mother died soon after his birth, to his uncle Thompson to raise. He then married a woman who, as the story goes, had been a little girl who gave him water on his first arrival in Mississippi. At the outbreak of the Civil War he raised a regiment of cavalry; called "The Knight of the Black Plume," he was a brave, daring, and hot-tempered soldier praised for his heroics in leading a regiment to glory at Manassas. His men, however, eventually turned against him for his harshness and ruthlessness, for his severity and recklessness, and selected a new commander.[2] He promptly rode back home to Ripley and raised another regiment.

He emerged from the Civil War, after a mysterious absence when he was apparently running blockades around Memphis, with enough money to build a railroad in partnership with Richard J. Thurmond. It was a small line, but this was clearly a bold venture under the circumstances of the times. He eventually owned a 1,200-acre plantation, a mill, and other property, and entered into politics, winning election to the legislature. He built a new, pretentious, and grotesquely designed house, and, mostly as a pastime, he wrote verse, drama, and novels. One novel was *The White Rose of Memphis*, a melodramatic work which was based on his own life. It was a popular success and was followed by *The Little Brick Church* in 1882. Both of these novels depict a curious incestuous brother-sister relationship. By this time he had decided to drop the "u" from the spelling of his surname—an alteration that remained in effect in the family until his great-grandson, William Cuthbert Faulkner, restored it.

In the late 1880s he collected enough money to buy out his railroad partner. Thurmond, who felt he had been swindled, shot down the Old Colonel in the streets of Ripley in 1889. Prior to his death, Falkner had commissioned an enormous, eight-foot-high marble statue of himself, and this monument was erected over his grave in Ripley with the single word FALKNER carved on all four sides of the fourteen-foot-high pediment. There is little that is exceptional about the statue except its size and that behind the figure of the Colonel, seemingly merging into his coat, is a stack of books.

The Old Colonel's life was courageous, glamorous, romantic, but most interesting is that it is hedged about with what Judith Wittenberg calls "dark substrata of violence and moral ambiguity."[3] If his personality and drive attracted success, they also surrounded him with controversy. One version of his leaving home depicts a poor boy of seventeen courageously setting out after his father's death to find in the virgin frontier of Mississippi the means to support his mother and brothers and sisters. But a better-known story has him leaving home at age fourteen after a quarrel with his brother in which he bloodied his brother's head with a hoe. His father whipped him so severely that he ran away. Another version omits the beating and says that, thinking he had killed his brother, he fled immediately.[4] Violence, the suggestion of fratricide, echoes of the story of Cain and Abel are all a part of the Old Colonel's legend.

There is a coldness reflected in his relations with members of his own family. He gave his infant son to his uncle to raise, and that son would always refer to his father as "Colonel Falkner," an indication of respect but also of distance.[5] Perhaps the most telling story concerns his son William Henry Falkner, the first son of his second marriage. According to family legend, Henry was given to gambling and reckless living; he once accidentally toppled a fellow student at the University of Virginia to his death from the roof of a building. More important, however, is one story told of Henry's death. Henry had begun an affair with the wife of a crippled jeweler in Ripley, and when the long-suffering husband had had enough, he shot his wife's seducer. Then he called on the Old Colonel, telling him, "Colonel, I hate to tell you this, but I had to kill Henry." The Colonel reportedly received the news silently, and when he finally spoke he told the man, "That's all right. I'm afraid I would have had to do it myself anyway."[6] Henry's sister would always insist that her brother had been a complete gentleman who died of a ruptured appendix, but the more sensational story was the most widely believed. Henry was buried in the family plot with but a single name, HENRY, engraved on his plain marble vault.[7]

In order to build his railroad, the Old Colonel leased convicts as laborers, and he used what is an all-too-familiar system of coercion to induce various towns along the line to contribute to its construction so that it would not pass them by and ruin them economically. He ran for the legislature, in part so that he could secure a rate increase bill beneficial to his railroad. Standing only five foot seven, Falkner was nonetheless an overbearing man, and, according to his great grandson, it was his arrogance that led to his death. William Faulkner believed that "the old man probably drove [Thurmond] to desperation—insulted him, spread stories about him, laughed at him," and he noted that the Old Colonel was deliberately unarmed the day he was shot, even though he was known always to carry a pistol.[8] Falkner knew of Thurmond's intentions and had drawn up a will; for this reason his death appeared almost suicidal, even to his great-grandson.

Although much of the sotry of the Old Colonel is subject to dispute, his legend takes its life from the more spectacular elements. It is a characteristic of all legendary First Ancestors. Such narratives which honor the family progenitor nevertheless also cluster around him tales of sins against the family. The Old Colonel is associated with an attempted fratricide, a willingness to kill his own son, two murders, the suggestion of suicide, and, in his novels, the repeated theme of incest. Edmund Leach argues that the examples of First Ancestors in many myths of human origin and kinship—of genesis—carry similar patterns of symbolic suggestion, contradictions between an orderly lineage and a darker side.

> Every human society has rules of incest and exogamy. Though the rules vary they always have the implication that for any particular male individual all women are divided by at least one binary distinction, there are women of *our kind* with whom sex relations would be incestuous and there are women of the *other kind* with whom sex relations are allowed. But here again we are immediately led into a paradox. How was it in the beginning? If our first parents were persons of two kinds, what was that other kind? But if they were both of our kind, then their relations must have been incestuous and we are all born in sin. The myths of the world offer many different solutions to this childish intellectual puzzle, but the

prominence which it receives shows that it entails the most profound moral issues.[9]

The Lévi-Straussian schema here is not at issue; what Leach provides for our reading of Faulkner is a source for a narrative structure. Old Testament myths serve as instructive examples of the paradox Leach sees as crucial to the concept of the First Ancestor. In Genesis Adam and Eve are said to be of "one flesh" (Gen. 2.24), but when they eat of the forbidden fruit and become aware of their nakedness and sexual difference, there is the implication of incest. Eve, as the "mother of all living" (Gen. 3.20), is associated with the great oppositions of Life and Death, because of the tangled relationships of incest (or its prohibition) and procreation. Cain and Abel repeat the antithesis between monosexual unity in the other world (Paradise) and bisexual duality in the fallen world. Abel's offering of the living world, the product of the union of two (the "firstlings of his flock" [Gen. 4.4]), is more pleasing to God than Cain's first fruit of the ground, for plants are described as monosexual in Genesis 1.11, as that "whose seed is in itself." Moreover, Cain's fratricide compares to Adam's incest, and God's questioning and cursing of Cain has the same form and sequence as his questioning and cursing of Adam and Eve. Cain's sin, Leach argues, is "not only fratricide but also incestuous homosexuality." God tells Eve in Genesis 3.16 that her "desire shall be to thy husband, and he shall rule over thee." In Genesis 4.7 we are led to equate Abel with Eve when God repeats himself speaking to Cain: "And unto thee shall be his [Abel's] desire, and thou shalt rule over him." The linguistic patterns of similarity do not confuse fratricide with incest but link them, equate them as elements of the origin myth. Leach elaborates: "In order that immortal monosexual existence in Paradise may be exchanged for fertile heterosexual existence in reality, Cain, like Adam, must acquire a wife [Gen. 4.17]. To this end Adam must eliminate a sister [Eve as Adam's sister is exchanged, rewritten as his wife]: Cain a brother [the homosexual pairing of Cain and Abel is eliminated to clear the way for Cain's heterosexual productivity]. The symmetry is complete."[10] The crucial factor here is that incest seen as a logical paradox is never presented directly in any origin myth; it is always mediated by a third term that introduces a third category. This "middle ground," as Leach calls it, is the space occupied by the First Ancestor in genealogical narrative. It is an inherently ambiguous, even contradictory, position or function, "the focus of all taboo and ritual observance."[11]

This account of a radical breach of sexual morality makes the story of Sarah and Abraham seem almost virtuous, Sarah being Abraham's half-sister by the same father. Yet Leach suggests that "the barrenness of Sarah is an aspect of her incest. The supernatural intervention which ultimately insures that she shall bear a child is evidence that the incest is condoned." [12] Here again a deep concern is repeated in a disguised form. The problem is a contradiction embedded in beginnings.

The biblical sources of Leach's analysis were familiar stories to Faulkner who once proclaimed his fondness for the Old Testament because it was full of "scoundrels and blackguards doing the best they could just like people now." [13] It is not surprising, therefore, that Faulkner would pattern his genealogical narratives on those genesis myths which focus on the figure of the founder as a scoundrel or blackguard. There is abundant evidence from Faulkner's biographers that Colonel W. C. Falkner was among the strongest influences on William Faulkner's life. When Faulkner was born, the Old Colonel had long been enshrined as a "household deity." [14] It is of no consequence, of course, that he was not the actual first ancestor of the Falkners; he nonetheless "dominated the family's imagination. Telling stories about him was more than a pastime; presided over by the unvanquished aunts whom Faulkner later immortalized, it was a ritual in which everyone participated." In addition to the family members, the servants and the survivors of his Confederate regiments "told and retold the story of their founder." He was, in their minds and apparently his own, "a giant." The ritualistic retellings gave his life story "the flavor and dimensions of a saga, or even a myth." [15] Yet in this commemorative act there is a fascination with that dark substratum of violence and immorality that the retellings preserve and enhance. As Leach describes it, the ritual obsessively returns to the suggestion of the taboo. As for William Faulkner, when asked in childhood what he wanted to become, he answered, "a writer like my great-grandfather." [16] Faulkner's brother, Murry, wrote that Bill "more or less unconsciously patterned his life after the Old Colonel's." [17]

William Faulkner's attitude toward his great-grandfather nonetheless was contradictory. He desired to be like him, but when he came to write about such First Ancestors he stinted nothing in the revelation of that traditional dark substratum of evil and sin. The key, of course, is in the very fact of contradiction, which provides a psychosocial dimension to Faulkner's representation of the Old Colonel and the Old South. Writing presses that contradiction on Faulkner in his genealogical novels: a cultural past to be rejected with regret, a heroic model to be emulated with full awareness of all that it entails socially and morally. Writing about one's First Ancestor implicates the narrative itself in the ambiguity of commemoration and critique. Eric Sundquist puts the issue clearly.

> Whether that act takes the form of idealization or criticism, calm veneration or violent attack, what is at issue is the authority generated by dependence upon, or independence of, a genealogy; and it is precisely in the very personal terms of such a question that authorship may find its own power. . . . Experiments in authorial desire must risk the possibility that they too will either become repetitive commemorations in the name of an overthrown authority, or else find themselves at a loss before the very absence of that authority. . . . The two cannot be untangled.[18]

Genealogical writing becomes entangled in rejection and preservation, in the futile struggle to locate one's identity and, hence, one's authority over the telling of that story and over the figures represented in that story. For Faulkner this effort spans a career.

The "firstness" of the First Ancestor is exhibited in his catastrophic appearance. The origin of a family or of a culture depends upon a transgression of the binary opposition between nature and culture. Derrida notes that this passage has no explanation. It is "uncertain and precarious, but since nothing in the previous [natural] state contained the structural ingredient to produce the subsequent [cultural] one, the genealogy [of humankind, of a family] must describe a rupture or a reversal, a revolution or a catastrophe."[19] Culture, the family, the First Ancestor are associated with rules and order; the origin of such order is sudden rather than gradual, not unlike the sudden appearance of Thomas Sutpen in Yoknapatawpha County, who, Faulkner writes, "abrupts" on the scene (*AA*, p. 8).

Derrida, following Lévi-Strauss, links culture and writing through genealogy; culture, writing, and genealogy are all expressions of their own need to exist. Furthermore, by excluding nature and prohibiting its disorder and rulelessness, culture, writing, and genealogy assert their adherence to orderliness and law. Because the fundamental, foundational law of culture and family is the prohibition against incest, Derrida claims that "society, langauge, history, articulation . . . are born at the same time as the prohibition of incest."[20] According to Lévi-Strauss, the incest prohibition is "at once on the threshold of culture, in culture, and in one sense . . . [is] culture itself"; it is marked by an "inherent duality to which it owes its ambiguous and equivocal character."[21] This is the locus of the infamous Lévi-Straussian "scandal."

> Let us suppose then that everything universal in man relates to the natural order, and is characterized by spontaneity, and that everything subject to a norm is cultural and is both relative and particular. We are then confronted with a fact, or rather a group of facts, which, in thelight of previous definitions are not far removed from a *scandal:* we refer to that complex group of beliefs, customs, conditions and institutions described succinctly as the prohibition of incest, which presents, without the slightest ambiguity, and inseparably combines, the two characteristics in which we recognize the conflicting features of two mutually exclusive orders. *It constitutes a rule, but a rule which, alone among all social rules, possesses at the same time a universal character.* That the prohibition of incest constitutes a rule need scarcely be shown. It is sufficient to recall that the prohibition of marriage between close relatives may vary in its field of application according to what each group defines as a close relative, but sanctioned by no doubt variable penalties, ranging from immediate execution of the guilty parties to widespread reprobation, sometimes merely ridicule, this prohibition is nevertheless to be found in *all* social groups.[22]

The scandal at the origin of the foundation of culture and family infects genealogy and writing. Derrida comments that incest "is at once spoken and forbidden by all signs. Language is neither prohibition nor transgression, it couples them endlessly." Like genealogy, language reveals contradiction. "The birth of society is therefore not a passage, it is a point, a pure fictive and unstable, ungraspable limit";[23] this limit, moreover, is generative—the origin of "freeplay," of supplementation and exchange that always risks exposing itself as a scandal, a perversion, a subversion of cultural, genealogical order. Writing about genealogical order leads to the discovery of genealogy as writing itself, as a tracing of relations that undermines orderliness through the insistent power of rewriting, revision.

Genealogy is a narrative which, as Edward Said puts it, "represents the generative process—literally in its mimetic representation of men and women in time, metaphorically in that by itself it generates succession and multiplication of events after the manner of human procreation."[24] Writing and procreation are linked metaphorically; it is an old cliché that requires further examination below. For the moment we will take it at face value and read it back onto the First Ancestor who stands at the abrupt origin of genealogy, family, culture, and writing. This figure Faulkner appropriately depicts as "self-progenitive" and monstrous. Such figures "name" themselves, as the Old Colonel altered the spelling of his family name, usurping the place of his progenitor. But a First Ancestor has no definite progenitor. Said says that "in such a case the image of man conceals behind its facade multiple meanings and multiple determinations,"[25] and it is precisely this multiplicity that generates supplementarity, for multiplicity is a polite term for contradiction, the repressive mediating of which is the foundation of all orderly descent and law. The inevitable failure of any particular mediation, moreover, propels genealogical narrative forward into the endless play of retelling.

Genealogical writing rests on an incurable anxiety, a fact that Faulkner discovered in the composition of his family novels. It is the anxiety of all Descendants who are the preservers of the genealogical narrative, of the legends of the First Ancestor. For a modern writer like Faulkner the anxiety is Freudian and existential; it rests on the traditional southern/Faulknerian theme of the burden of the past and of the ambiguity of a family name. Yet that same anxiety at the heart of beginnings is also a source of power, the basis of rejection and revision. For Faulkner it is a power that comes to rest not in the legendary figures of Sartoris and Sutpen but in a character like Lucas Beauchamp who exposes the contradictions of his genealogy and culture. Lucas plays multiple roles, and he alone of Faulkner's Descendant figures seems to triumph over genealogy.

Faulkner's own genealogical anxiety sent him in search of similar triumph. The place of the Descendant at three removes from the First Ancestor, however, is by definition weak. Faulkner considered the intervening generations between himself and the Old Colonel to be a decline, marked by failure. Faulkner's grandfather, John Wesley Thompson Falkner, was a successful man, a banker, but his title, the Young Colonel, was merely inherited since he fought in no wars. He was, one grandson recalled, "the loneliest man I've ever known."[26] Faulkner's mother was a strong, dominant woman, but his father, Murry Falkner, was a pale figure when compared with the Old and Young Colonels. Dominated by his father, who sold from under him the railroad, his life's ambition and his first and "lasting love," Murry was an ineffectual man who rebelliously failed at most of the jobs his father obtained for him. He was "widely regarded as the failed descendant of a legendary grandfather and a successful father."[27]

William Faulkner's reaction to this family history is instructive, for whenever real fathers show such weakness there is a movement toward establishing a more suitable substitute. Michael Paul Rogin discusses this movement toward what he calls "imaginary fathers." If the child is an orphan or feels wronged and neglected, he may substitute a mythical or famous hero for his own father. The imagined father may, in the fantasy of the son, rescue him from maternal domination, especially in a traditionally male-oriented society. Imaginary fathers may exert a more powerful influence over sons than real fathers. "Absent from a child's experience, a missing father is bigger than life, and split into heroic and villainous parts."[28] The usual process of reduction of the father to normal size as the child matures does not occur, because the fantasy father is removed from the normal impact of reality. He is beyond the child's emulation, therefore, and his restrictive power over the child's aggressive wishes and desires is correspondingly greater than that of a real father. Rogin goes on to show that after the Revolution, Americans, who no longer had a king, turned not to their living fathers, whose authority in the leading families of America had been weakened by the Revolution itself and by the rise of capitalism, but to the founders, the Revolutionary fathers, idealized as a dying generation which had "secured rights for their children" through their bravery.[29] It is easy to see a parallel displacement onto the founding fathers of the Old South on the part of those sons of the South stranded in the modern crisis of a lingering defeat.

Although Faulkner's Sartoris family is most directly patterned on his own Falkner ancestry, it is the Compsons who best illustrate the functioning of the imaginary founding father. Quentin Compson, the Descendant figure, is removed from strictly genealogical anxiety in *The Sound and the Fury*, where he appears as little more than a neurotic young man; nevertheless, his tragic suicide, Faulkner said, was a "basic failure Quentin inherited through his father or beyond his father."[30] That "beyond" is spelled out in *Absalom, Absalom!* where the missing First Ancestor appears as Thomas Sutpen. Sutpen is no kin to Quentin, yet his stature is so magnified that he comes to represent a whole cultural past that Quentin sees as his personal fate. Rogin's model fits perfectly Quentin's participatory narration of the Sutpen story. It also links the creation of an imaginary father with narration itself, illuminating Faulkner's self-conscious struggle with his role as Descendant-writer. In one of his most suggestive remarks about the Old Colonel he discloses a host of motivations and attractions.

People at Ripley talk of him as if he were still alive, up in the hills some place, and might come in at any time. It's a strange thing; there are lots of people who knew him well, and yet no two of them remember him alike or describe him the same way. One will say he was like me and another will swear he was six feet tall. . . .[31]

The focus is on narrative variations and the sense of the legend as "still alive." The inevitable comparison between the Colonel and Faulkner emphasizes a crucial ambiguity that either equates the First Ancestor and the Descendant or positions the Descendant in childlike inferiority. Faulkner continues his description in another interesting way.

There's nothing left of the old place, the house is gone and the plantation boundaries, nothing left of his work but a statue. But he rode through that country like a living force. I like it better that way.[32]

The claim that nothing remains of the Old Colonel's work reveals more wish than reality even as it contradicts the previous statement about how people at Ripley still talk of him as if he were alive. Faulkner's preference is to think of him in the past tense. More interestingly, the passage opens with a reference to "boundaries," a sense of limits pushed back to open the narrative of the Old Colonel to a freeplay of revisions already legitimized by the Ripley folk who never agree on details. The lack of boundaries is a fundamental representational principle associated with the "fictive" and "ungraspable point" of intersection between nature and culture, the "limit" set by the First Ancestor, emphasizing especially his darker side.

That darker side also grounds another of Faulkner's comments on his relation, as a writer, to the Old Colonel: "I may have inherited the ink stain from him."[33] The inherited "stain" bespeaks talent but also something rather more ominous: a gift with a curse attached.[34] What is inherited, as both familial and cultural, is an ambiguity that discloses a contradiction. Genealogical writing cannot avoid that contradiction; to write is to engage it, to mediate it endlessly. Edward Said characterizes the anxiety involved:

The collapse of the one into the many, of the genealogical line into a plurality. . . , of systematic linear analysis into a tangled skein of problems —all these leave sustained effects in consciousness. For the writer a major effect is that the authority of what he says is undermined by the possibility that, unconsciously, he either does not or cannot say what he means.[35]

Each story, each version of the family has its complement in another story, never cancels out a previous narration but rather supplements it.

This, although he could not have known it at the time, was the meaning of his statement in *Mosquitoes* that a book is the writer's "dark twin," a "secret life," and "you can't reconcile them."[36]

Faulkner's ink stain generated a series of narrated families which he admitted to be "the same story over and over," a story of "myself and the world." He also depicted it as a struggle for completion, for a narrative ending, and for this he hit upon a rather contemporary model: "I'm trying to say it all in one sentence, between one Cap and one period."[37] There is something more here than an unintended joke on the infamous Faulknerian sentence. What we must read is a profound sense of restriction, self-imposed to be sure, but reflective of genealogical structure with its demands for strictly linear, chronological, order. Writing becomes a seeking after a period, a resistance to digression and disruption, an authoritarian closing out of other voices. But genealogical narrative ruptures its own boundaries, traces its own digressions in the very branchings of descent that destroy any sense of strict linearity. That lesson Faulkner learned by writing; it defines his career. It is as if genealogical writing refuses to lie when mediation functions as repression. Said's comment on genealogical writing describes this crisis in authorship. Not to be able to say what one means displaces meaning from the self to language, from the Descendant-writer to the genealogical narrative that he writes. Telling a story becomes tangled in hearing stories. Narrative mediations give themselves away.

Early on Faulkner had two working titles that he never used. One was "Abraham's Children" for a manuscript containing the germ of the Snopes material. It recalls the biblical First Ancestor and the tribes that issued from him, tribes of such number that a genealogical table threatens to disperse into chaos. The other was "The Dark House," a beginning for both *Light in August* and *Absalom, Absalom!* Here the Greek suggestiveness of the term "house" recalls the major Yoknapatawpha families of his greatest novels.[38] Faulkner seemed to sense from the beginning that in the darkness of the old, patrilineal lines lay the cultural contradiction which generated dispersal, disruption, and digression, and in these unused titles is much of the source of what he considered his life's labor, the creation of his "heart's country."[39] It was a demanding task that forced him to confront repeatedly the flaw at the base of his culture. All of his Descendant figures, those children of Abraham, inherit the ink stain of their dark houses; and, since he was a Descendant figure himself, it is not hard to understand why his most passionate sympathies lay with those children.

CHAPTER 8

"They ain't my Sartorises . . . I just inherited 'em"

FAULKNER'S EARLIEST treatment of his family's history is probably the unfinished sketch he wrote in the latter 1920s entitled "And Now What's to Do?" This two-page manuscript, composed shortly before *Flags in the Dust*, is remarkable in its obvious autobiographical dimensions.[1] This fragment links the actual and legendary facts of Faulkner's family history with his first major fictionalization of a genealogy. The central four-generational structure is prominent.

> His great-grandfather came into the country afoot from the Tennessee mountains, where he had killed a man, worked and saved and bought a little land, won a little more at cards and dice, and died at the point of a pistol while trying to legislate himself into a little more; his grandfather was a deaf, upright man in white linen, who wasted his inherited substance in politics. He had a law practice still, but he sat most of the day in the courthouse yard, a brooding thwarted old man too deaf to take part in conversation and whom the veriest child could beat at checkers. His father loved horses better than books or learning; he owned a livery stable, and here the boy grew up, impregnated with the violent ammoniac odor of horses. . . . By the time he was twelve he had acquired from the negro hostlers an uncanny skill with a pair of dice.[2]

There are some significant changes here in Faulkner's four-generation genealogy. The great-grandfather has "killed a man," not merely bloodied his brother's head with a hoe as Colonel W. C. Falkner was reputed to have done. There is also no evidence that the Old Colonel was a gambler.[3] But the motif of games is important in Faulkner's narratives, suggesting particularly a masculine world of ritualistic behavior.

101

In genealogical novels like *Flags in the Dust* and *Go Down, Moses* games of cards are closely intertwined with the structure of family history and with genealogical writing, almost as representations of social/familial rules of exchange involving slaves, women, money, and property. Skill at cards earns legendary respect and is associated with skill at business.

In this fragment of a story the boy develops an "uncanny skill with dice," a fact that links him, as Descendant, with his great-grandfather, the First Ancestor. Faulkner is overleaping generations in a mode quite typical of his family narratives; the reaching back to the remote past acts as a corrective for the Descendant's sense of belatedness, reflecting Faulkner's own sense of the decline of the Mississippi Falkners. The Old Colonel, if not a gambler, nonetheless had added to his holdings, his prestige and legend, by means of games of obviously high risks and high stakes. Intervening generations had "wasted inherited substance" revealing an impotence at masculine power games.

The sense of decline also is expressed through the boy's attitude toward his father's business. At age sixteen, he becomes aware that his friends' fathers are all members of "genteel professions," lawyers, doctors, or merchants. His feeling of inferiority, however, is "defiant": none of the other boys "could make a pair of dice behave as he could." "There was a giant in him, but the giant was musclebound."[4] We never learn the fate of the boy after he hops a train and leaves town, and we do not know if the giant ever emerged. Yet there is a hint of the form that such a releasing will take. The title, "And Now What's to Do?" foreshadows the famous statement made by Bayard Sartoris in *The Unvanquished*: "Those who can, do, those who cannot and suffer enough because they can't, write about it" (*UV*, p. 262).

Should the boy's fate be that of the writer, we have much evidence of what that suffering might be in the struggle that Faulkner underwent himself in the latter part of 1926 when he began *Flags in the Dust*. Two years after the completion of that novel he wrote an account of its genesis. He recalled that he had been "speculating idly upon time and death" when he began searching for a "touchstone," a "simple word or gesture,"

> but having been these two years previously under the curse of words, having known twice before the agony of ink, nothing served but that I try by main strength to recreate between the covers of a book the world I was already preparing to lose and regret, feeling with the morbidity of the young . . . that growing old was to be an experience peculiar to myself

alone out of all the teeming world and desiring, if not the capture of that world and the feeling of it as you'd preserve a kernel or a leaf to indicate the last forest, at least to keep the evocative skeleton of the dessicated [*sic*] leaf.[5]

According to Faulkner, he began writing without much purpose or interest until he "realized that to make it truly evocative it must be personal":

> So I put people in it, since what can be more personal than reproduction, in its true way, the aesthetic and mammalian. In its own sense, really, since the aesthetic is still the female principle, the desire to feel over the bones spreading and parting with something alive begotten of the ego and conceived by the protesting unleashing of flesh.[6]

The world of *Flags in the Dust* is peopled with evocative skeletons of his own past; its narration is a genealogy both in subject matter and in its expression of his sense of writing as reproduction, a kind of repetition that renews and revises.

According to Blotner, Faulkner originally began *Flags in the Dust* with a scene of old Bayard Sartoris in the attic of his home musing over the family genealogy.[7] The Toledo blade and Mechlin lace that Bayard examines date the Sartorises back to the time of the Plantagenets. Faulkner later revised this material, condensing it to delete the Sartorises who fought at Agincourt, shortening the genealogy to an essential four generations. Again the parallels between Sartorises and Falkners are clear, but what is most interesting about *Flags in the Dust* is a peculiar omission; the third generation is left out of the novel. We are told that John Sartoris, the father of the fourth-generation Descendant figures, the twins Johnny and young Bayard, dies of "yellow fever and an old Spanish bullet-wound."[8] Yet when asked why he skipped over this generation in the narrative, Faulkner replied that he had done it for dramatic reasons and that the twins' father had come along at a peaceful time when "nothing happened to Americans to speak of," when "there was nothing that brought the issue to him to be brave and strong or dramatic. . . . But he had to be there for the simple continuity of the family."[9]

In dismissing his father's fictional counterpart in the novel, Faulkner gained a certain kind of revenge. Murry Falkner had not understood his son or his son's writing; at times the father had been abusive psychologically. Whatever his conscious or unconscious feelings toward his father, however, this abrupt dismissal of the third generation functions as a novelistic strategy to foreshorten the genealogy and move his own generation into closer proximity with the founding figure. The invitation is to closer comparison of Descendant and First Ancestor. Moreover, Faulkner doubled both the First Ancestor and the Descendant figures thereby further stressing the association. Blotner notes that "it was as if Faulkner worked from his own longings and dreams of heroism and fatality in creating these two Sartorises whose exploits would come near to those of the men of their great-grandfather's generation." [10]

This doubling and foreshortening also intensifies the masculine dimension of the genealogy, emphasizes the patrilineal structure. The role of women in the Sartoris family is marginal, passive, just as the metaphor of writing/birth he used to describe the genesis of *Flags in the Dust* represents female reproductivity as passive. Only Jenny Sartoris Du Pre, who has no children of her own, plays an appreciable role in the Sartoris story—and that largely as the source of commemoration. Aunt Jenny is modeled on Faulkner's great-aunt Alabama Falkner, whom he pushes back a generation in the Sartoris narrative to the status of sister to the First Ancestor figures, John and Bayard. Aunt Jenny's role is enhanced in part by this primary association.

But other women do not receive even this reflected glory. There is no mention in *Flags in the Dust* of the first wives of the Old Colonel. Only later in *The Unvanquished* does Faulkner depict Rosa Millard, the mother of John's first wife, and his second wife, Drusilla Hawk. The wives of other descendants receive rather rough treatment at the hands of Sartoris men. According to Sally Wyatt, Lucy Sartoris, mother of the twin Descendant figures, lost her identity to the Sartoris myth, to "those folks, thinking there wasn't anybody quite as good as a Sartoris."

> Even Lucy Cranston, come of as good people as there are in the state, acting like it was divine providence that let her marry one Sartoris and be the mother of two more. Pride, false pride.
>
> (*FD*, p. 75)

And Caroline White Sartoris, young Bayard's first wife, apparently shared this attitude. Miss Jenny says:

> Soon as she found out about the baby, she named it. Named it nine months before it was born and told everybody about it. Used to talk about it like it was her grandfather or something. Always saying Bayard won't let me do this or that or the other.
>
> (*FD*, p. 56)

Jenny concludes that Caroline's dying in childbirth, after young Bayard left her in Jenny's care when he went off to war, was her revenge. It is revenge bought at a high price.

> "Poor woman," she said, "I reckon we do have to take our revenge wherever and whenever we can get it. Only she ought to have taken it out on Bayard."
>
> (FD, p. 57)

Other mothers are also missing from the novel. Narcissa and Horace Benbow's mother, Julia, "died genteelly when Narcissa was seven" (FD, p. 58), and both wives of Virginius MacCallum are deceased (FD, p. 310). Narcissa also seems aware of her fate, accepting the role of "self-sacrificial martyr and mother of more Sartorises."[11] Accepted or revenged, an early death awaits most of the women; and even the headstones of the Sartoris wives, whom the men "had dragged into their arrogant orbits," are overshadowed by the grand statue of John Sartoris in the cemetery. Their membership in the Sartoris family is merely by "alliance"; and "despite the pompous genealogical references" on their stones, they are reduced to insignificance beneath the masculine power of the First Ancestor. Their graves, Faulkner tells us, seemingly through Aunt Jenny's consciousness, are as "modest and effacing as the song of thrushes beneath the eyrie of an eagle" (FD, p. 427).

There are also few daughters in *Flags in the Dust* other than Narcissa and little Belle; the two daughters of Colonel John Sartoris, old Bayard's sisters, are mentioned only once (FD, p. 16). The suppression of sisters, whose primary function in the patrilineal family structure would be one of exchange in marriage alliances, further evidences the rigid narrowness of the Sartoris male-oriented genealogy. It is crucial to note here that the relationship of alliance suppressed in *Flags in the Dust* becomes central in later genealogical novels, a shift of focus that betokens a fundamental destabilization of the Old South, cavalier mythology that dominates the early Sartoris narrative. Thus in the revised Sartoris story in *The Unvanquished* women play a much more significant role, even to the point of displacing the traditional male figure of heroism. In this initial telling of the myth, however, women seem to exist only for the sake of continuity, to bear male children or to transmit the legend itself, both functions equated in the writing/birth metaphor. Ironically, this function of continuity is the same as that assigned by Faulkner to his father's generation in *Flags in the Dust*, that of filling out the four-generation genealogy.

What we see in this restricted genealogy of the Sartorises is an over-emphasis on blood relationships. Genealogy itself has been reduced to descent; all collateral relations are suppressed. Michel Foucault associates this overemphasis on blood kinship with a broader cultural revision of the idea of sexuality. In the late seventeenth and eighteenth centuries in Europe, a culture formerly ordered by kinship alliances is invaded by a new conception of sexuality focused primarily on reproduction as a function of economic and political power.[12] The collateral relationships between husband and wife are gradually weakened by a new emphasis on relations of production between parent and child, and in the patriarchal system of the American South the productive relation between fathers and sons receives particular emphasis. Old Man Falls best expresses this new overemphasis on blood kinship when he argues that "a feller kin take a wife and live with her a long time, but after all they aint no kin" (FD, p. 264). In this the American South, for all of its feudal trappings and agrarian mythology, reveals itself to be little more than a belated participant in the modern industrial tradition. The obsession with blood relationships is at the center of the Sartoris myth; even Miss Jenny says that young Bayard "ought to have a wife . . . let him get a son, then he can break his neck as soon and as often as he pleases" (FD, p. 92). This begetting just before death, a masculine metaphor linking orgasm and death, repeats a story told about young Bayard's father, thereby functioning as a further intensification of the legend of Sartoris male fatedness.

The novel also contains another important expression of this masculine genealogy. The eccentric MacCallum family provides young Bayard with a few days' decidedly masculine retreat from his Sartoris fate. Eighty-year-old Virginius MacCallum, "straight as an Indian" and towering "above his sons by a head," is as dominant a patriarch in the flesh as Colonel John Sartoris is in legend (FD, p. 361). And just as old Sartoris' hawklike features are reflected in the planes of young Bayard's face, so all of the MacCallum sons (there are no daughters!) are emblems of their father, "their dark saturnine faces all stamped clearly from the same die." Even the twins, Stuart and Rafe, bear "no closer resemblance between them than between any two of the others, as though the die were too certain and made too clean an imprint to be either hurried or altered, even by nature" (FD, p. 363). Faulkner's exaggerated description of the replication of the father's image rests on a classical distinction between nature and culture. The former defaces the images of coins, destroys the authority and value of the father whose power is traced through his inscription of primacy and ownership on the bodies (currency) of his children. Culture, on the other hand, is defined by a repetitive inscription of names and values, from the First Ancestor down through the genealogical chart. With all of the focus on coinage and the image of patriarchal authority, the MacCallums seem injected into the novel for the sole purpose of reinforcing the Sartoris patrilineality.

In this light, the youngest son, Buddy, young Bayard's contemporary, has a special function. The son of Virginius' second wife, he has inherited her reddish hair and hazel eyes in contrast with his brothers' dark coloring, but "the old man had stamped Buddy's face as clearly as any of the other boys', and despite its youth it too was like the others" (FD, pp. 380–81). In one other respect Buddy differs from his brothers, although not from his father. He is the tallest of the sons, standing "eye to eye with that father" (FD, p. 381), and thus as his equal. His father's response is to mock his son's height, calling him a "long, spindlin scoundrel"; but Buddy is clearly marked as the inheritor, and, therefore, as the displacer of the father, a fact that goes a long way to explain his father's subdued hostility. The other sons all look at Buddy "with the same identical thought; a thought which each believed peculiar to himself and which none ever divulged—that some day Buddy would marry and perpetuate the name" (FD, p. 381).

Buddy also bears his father's name, Virginius, but when he joined the army in World War I and the men called him "Virge" he fought them, "steadily and thoroughly and without anger" (FD, p. 381). While he is not developed fully as a character, Buddy clearly parallels young Bayard as the Descendant of a dominant family founder. Buddy's father, who fought at Stonewall Brigade bridge at sixteen, then "built himself a house and got married" (FD, p. 357), is a contemporary of Colonel John Sartoris and could easily be twenty-year-old Buddy's great-grandfather. The two generations of the MacCallum family span the same time frame as the four generations of the Sartorises (and the Falkners of Mississippi). Buddy's brothers (Jackson, the eldest, is fifty-five, Henry is fifty, the twins forty-four, and the others somewhere between forty and twenty) fill out the two missing generations. Buddy, as the equivalent of a fourth-generation Descendant figure, is brought into direct conflict with a First Ancestor who happens in fact to be his father.

Faulkner's obsessive tracing of the implications of reproductive relationships leads him into one further interpolation within the MacCallum/Sartoris overlay. This new variation seems perversely comic, but

its implication within the southern mythology of male blood relationships is quite clear. The MacCallums, of course, do not repeat
the Sartoris fatedness, a mythology obviously reserved for the cavalier
class. The foreshortened genealogy of the MacCallums does not em-
phasize decline or dramatize a simplistic oedipal confrontation between
father and son. Buddy accommodates himself well to the double bind
of replicating and repudiating his father, whereas the Sartorises are
not so successful in their confrontations with the destructive tensions
that accompany the restricted genealogy of blood descent. Yet if the
MacCallums themselves do not reproduce the Sartoris self-destruction,
Faulkner includes within the MacCallum segment a strangely relevant
episode concerning the mating of the MacCallums' hunting dog, significantly named "old General," with a fox called Ethel (renamed Ellen
in *Sartoris*).

In an experiment designed, as Jackson says, to "revolutionize the
hunting business" (*FD*, p. 372), the MacCallums seem to have trans-
gressed a fundamental taboo. The products of this cross-breeding are
described in terms that contrast explicitly with the MacCallums themselves and implicitly with the Sartorises. It was

> as strange a litter as Bayard had ever seen. No two of them looked alike,
> and none of them looked like any other living creature—neither fox nor
> hound, partaking of both, yet neither; and despite their soft infancy there
> was about them something monstrous and contradictory and obscene,
> here a fox's keen cruel muzzle between the melting, sad eyes of a hound
> and its mild ears. . . .
>
> (*FD*, p. 374)

Such genetic engineering, though comically treated, threatens more
serious consequences: the breakdown of binary differences and the dissolution of social order. The most striking aspect of the passage is that
these creatures defy language; they can only be described as "strange"
or as "partaking of both" sides of absolute opposites. They are "something" but nothing recognizable, "monstrous" and "obscene." They are
unresolved and unmediated contradictions that allow the monstrous
otherness of nature a brief but terrifying presence within culture. The
experiment, tellingly, is a "business" venture gone wrong, but the most
damning denial of legitimacy comes from the seat of paternal authority,
not merely Old Man MacCallum but old General himself.

> Rafe went to the door and called, and presently General entered, his claws
> hissing a little on the bare floor and his ticked coat beaded with rain, and

he stood and looked into the old man's face with grave inquiry. "Come hyer," Mr. MacCallum said, and the dog moved again, with slow dignity. At that moment he saw the puppies beneath Jackson's chair. He paused in mid stride and for a moment he stood looking at them with fascination and bafflement and a sort of grave horror; then he gave his master one hurt, reproachful look and turned and departed, his tail between his legs. Mr. MacCallum sat down and rumbled heavily within himself.

(FD, p. 375)

It is appropriate that Faulkner began writing his vast chronicle of Yoknapatawpha with the scene of old Bayard visiting the attic room where souvenirs of the legendary Sartoris past are preserved in an old trunk. The episode is occasioned by Old Man Falls's gift to old Bayard of John Sartoris' pipe; remembering that he has the pipe in his pocket, old Bayard makes a "sudden decision" and climbs the stairs to enter the dark attic room which smells of "dust and silence and ancient disused things" (FD, p. 93). Such are the places of remembering in Faulkner's novels, Rosa Coldfield's "office" and the dorm rooms of Quentin and Shreve in *Absalom, Absalom!* and the commissary where Ike reads the McCaslin family ledgers at midnight in *Go Down, Moses*. These rooms are closed to the present world, wholly given over to the past; they define the space of narration itself. In the souvenir relics they contain they express the overpowering desire within narrative for contact with authentic experience. These are the places and moments of writing as re-presentation. The objects exposed in old Bayard's attic function as what Susan Stuart calls "traces of authentic experience." The souvenirs represent events that are "reportable" but not "repeatable," "events whose materiality has escaped us" and which therefore can "exist only through the invention of narrative."[13] Faulkner here begins writing about a world he was "already preparing to lose and regret" by initiating a narrative that both preserves and transcends that world, by creating a narrative whose basis is the deep nostalgia of the modern South for its mythical past, a past recreated out of present recollection. Stuart insightfully captures the paradox:

first, the assumption that immediate lived experience is more "real," bearing within itself an authenticity which cannot be transferred to mediated experience, yet second, the assumption that the mediated experience known through language and the temporality of narrative can offer pattern and insight by virtue of its capacity for transcendence. It is the meeting of these two assumptions, in the conjunction of their *symptoms*, that the social disease of nostalgia arises. By the narrative process of nostalgic reconstruction the present is denied and the past takes on an authenticity of being, an authenticity which, ironically, it can achieve only through narrative.[14]

None of the objects enumerated in Bayard's ceremony of remembrance takes on any sacred meaningfulness; the importance of the "things" he reveals to us, aside from their signification of materiality, their "authenticity," is their metonymic richness. The verbal equivalent for these objects is the "list," or in narrative terms what Northrop Frye once called the "anatomy." The nature of nostalgic narrative is the displacement of metaphoric fetishism with the supplementarity of desiring. Bayard's attic room is cluttered with things that are like "patient ghosts holding lightly in dry and rigid embrace yet other ghosts—a fitting place for dead Sartorises to gather and speak among themselves of glamorous and disastrous days" (*FD*, p. 79). Bayard's opening of the old trunk which had remained closed since the death of his son John in 1901 is something less than an unleashing of Pandora's box; we are told, nevertheless, that "each opening was in a way ceremonial, commemorating the violent finis to some phase of his family's history" (*FD*, p. 80).

Among the items in the trunk the most important is the "huge, brass-bound Bible" that Bayard raises up and opens to read the names that trace the family's history backward to an ambiguous origin. The link between genealogy and nostalgic narration is measured by the space between the legible and the illegible, between two orders of significant yet meaningless blankness.

> Beginning near the bottom of the final blank page, a column of names and dates rose in stark, fading simplicity, growing fainter and fainter where time had lain upon them. At the top they were still legible, as they were at the foot of the preceding page. But halfway up this page they ceased, and from there on the sheet was blank save for the faint soft mottlings of time and an occasional brownish penstroke significant without meaning.
>
> (*FD*, pp. 81–82)

The "simplicity" of the Sartoris genealogy reflects its patrilineal rigidity. Faulkner's dark and closed spaces are mausoleums commemorating patrilineality. Lawrence Stone traces this locus of a sacred space within the household to the reorganization of the family in the late sixteenth century: "The parish tended to be replaced by the household as the main agent of piety, prayer, and moral indoctrination, in part because of the failure of the Anglican Church under Elizabeth to fulfill this urgent need, and in part because of the Puritan stress on the household for these purposes." [15] The family thus "served as a substitute for the parish" with a consequent strengthening of the "patriarchal aspects of the internal power relationships within the family." [16] Faulkner's attic mausoleum moves the Bible and sacred relics from the parish into the household. Either the Anglican or the Puritan heritage of the American South would have preserved the tradition. Stone argues:

> The household was the inheritor of much of the responsibilities of the parish and church, the family head was the inheritor of much of the authority and powers of the priest. The transubstantiated host, carefully preserved at the east end of the church, was replaced by the Holy Bible on a lectern in the hall or kept in a bible box. It was a book which also, significantly enough, often served at all levels of society to record the family genealogy. Thus the Word of God was removed from the parish church and transferred to the private home; the Holy Spirit was domesticated. [17]

This sacred domesticity accords with Foucault's account of sexuality within the family. At the beginning of the seventeenth century, according to Foucault, sexuality was becoming less public and more "confined."

> The conjugal family took custody of it and absorbed it into the serious function of reproduction. On the subject of sex silence became the rule. The legitimate and procreative couple laid down the law. The couple imposed itself as model, enforced the norm, safeguarded the truth and reserved the right to speak while retaining the principle of secrecy. . . . Nothing that was not ordered in terms of generation or transfigured by it could expect sanction or protection. [18]

Faulkner's treatment of old Bayard's ceremonial opening of the family Bible, therefore, unlocks a host of cultural traditions. The private family history, genealogy as generation, establishes a narration of patriarchal authority, legitimacy, and desire for authenticity. Bayard as father/priest writes in the sacred domestic text the names of those whose lives have been legitimized by their Sartoris fate.

> He stirred again and sighed quietly, and took out his fountain pen. At the bottom of the column he wrote:
> "John Sartoris, July 5, 1918"
> and beneath that:
> "Caroline White Sartoris and son, October 27, 1918."
>
> (FD, p. 83)

That entry in the genealogical narrative is supported by the addition of one more authentic souvenir to the collection; it is neither the last nor the most important, Colonel John Sartoris' pipe.

> When the ink was dry he closed the book and replaced it and took the pipe from his pocket and put it in the rosewood box with the duelling pistols and the derringer and replaced the other things and closed the chest and locked it again.
>
> (*FD*, p. 83)

Faulkner's style in this passage emphasizes narrative linking through a rapid series of "ands" that mingles actions and objects and presages future writings that will unfold these souvenirs in other narrations, other novels.[19] There are many stories here.

The dried ink, of course, will fade as it has before on those other "blank" pages marked only by an "occasional brownish penstroke," but as with all ritual actions designed to "apotheosize a name," this fading is an opening of a space for future writing, a writing over previous writing that epitomizes the Faulknerian narrative strategy of revision. Faulkner is not yet fully aware of the significance of his own scene of writing in old Bayard's attic room; the authority of mystified origins remains something of an obstacle to revision or writing over. The fourth generation's First Ancestor is a restrictive model. Yet genealogical narrative, nostalgic and perverse, Faulkner here defines as "significant without meaning," and in a sense this writing for Faulkner is the beginning of an escape from meaning into signification. No longer merely tracing some remote and sublimely authentic origin, nostalgic narration as rewriting loses its interest in beginnings; this first episode in old Bayard's attic initiates the end of the First Ancestor's legitimacy. Bayard recalls his father's ridicule of genealogy, especially in America, labeling it "poppycock." But escape from this powerful sense of family is not so easy for a southerner. Bayard's father also argued that

> the man who professes to care nothing about his forebears is only a little less vain than he who bases all his actions on blood precedent. And a Sartoris is entitled to a little vanity and poppycock, if he wants it.
>
> (*FD*, p. 82)

So old Bayard and Faulkner begin writing in the gap between poppycock and vanity, between repudiation and commemoration. It is an ambiguity at the heart of *Flags in the Dust*, one that Faulkner narratively transcends in his Yoknapatawpha chronicle.

Yet given the discoveries Faulkner made in this first family novel and the subsequent excitement he felt in having opened what seemed an inexhaustible topic with numberless characters, we can easily imagine the anguish he suffered when his publisher rejected the manuscript because it did not "seem to have a story to tell."[20] He had rejected his father's generation in his fictionalization of the Mississippi Falkners because it had "no story," and now his first major attempt to revise his family through genealogical narration had met a similar fate. This denial of his power as Descendant-writer must have seemed especially cruel, for he had believed that *Flags in the Dust* would "make his name as a writer." Clearly he hoped that it would make his name, the transformed spelling of Faulkner, the legitimate name of his Mississippi forebears. Aunt Jenny's claim that the Sartorises were not hers, that she just inherited them, might well describe Faulkner's relationship with his own ancestors, for their name and his sense of his own were still divergent. His narration had not yet made them his family; the authentic past still remained an elusive, repressive, mysterious myth.

CHAPTER 9

Narrative Voice: A Narrated within the Narrator

TWICE IN *Flags in the Dust* Faulkner explicitly links the Civil War and World War I. First, in an argument between young Bayard and Aunt Jenny, the Descendant figure comes into direct conflict with narrative authority; the focus is on the unavoidable comparison of young Bayard's modern wartime experiences with the legendary Civil War exploits of the dual First Ancestor figures, John and Bayard Sartoris. Aunt Jenny speaks:

> "Do you think nobody else ever went to war? Do you reckon that when my Bayard came back from The War, he made a nuisance of himself to everybody that had to live with him? But he was a gentleman: he raised the devil like a gentleman, not like you Mississippi country people. Clodhoppers. Look what he did with just a horse," she added. "He didn't have any flying machine."
>
> "Look at the little two-bit war he went to," young Bayard rejoined. "A war that was so sorry that grandfather [*sic*] wouldn't stay up there in Virginia where it was, even."
>
> "And nobody wanted him at it," Miss Jenny retorted. "A man that would get mad just because his men deposed him and elected a better colonel in his place. Got mad and came back to the country to lead a bunch of brigands."
>
> "Little two-bit war," young Bayard repeated. "And on a horse. Anybody can go to a war on a horse. No chance for him to do anything much."
>
> "At least he got himself decently killed," Miss Jenny snapped. "He did more with a horse than you could do with that aeroplane."
>
> (*FD*, pp. 258–59)

114

The Civil War, which Jenny labels "The War," and World War I are connected by the Sartoris genealogical myth of decline, by the powerful sense of Sartoris fate which reads young Bayard's twin brother Johnny's war death (and young Bayard's failure to kill himself!) as a repetition of the past without the attendant glorification that glosses over the suicidal recklessness of the First Ancestor, the Carolina Bayard. Much of this scene is lightly disguised autobiography recalling Faulkner's futile efforts to attain glory as a pilot in World War I. More interestingly, the passage contains an anticipation of Faulkner's own infamous genealogical error in dropping a generation out of his heritage.[1] Bayard's reference to "grandfather" should read "great-grandfather." Too much psychoanalytical hash has been made of Faulkner's mistake, when the obvious explanation is that a child refers to all ancestors as remote as two generations past by the same designations that the parents use. From Bayard's misstatement in *Flags in the Dust* all that we need infer is an autobiographical link revealing a motive for narrative foreshortening, the author's *desire* to compare First Ancestors and Descendants.[2]

The Civil War and World War I are also linked in the MacCallum episodes of *Flags in the Dust*. The telescoping effect of the Sartoris/ MacCallum parallel, the collapsing of four generations into two, alters the reader's perspective on the conjunction of First Ancestor and Descendant, but the reading of the present in terms of the past, of the present as a repetition of the past, is still the central theme. The discussion here is between young Bayard and Buddy MacCallum, alone at night, talking in the dark.

> "How'd you like the army, Buddy?"
> "Not much," Buddy answered. "Aint enough to do. Good life for a lazy man." He mused a moment.
> "They gimme a medal," he added, in a burst of shy, diffident confidence and sober pleasure. "I aimed to show it to you, but I fergot. Do it tomorrow. . . . I'll watch a chance when Pappy's outen the house."
> "Why? Dont he know you got it?"
> "He knows," Buddy answered. "Only he dont like it because he claims it's a Yankee medal. Rafe says pappy and Stonewall Jackson aint never surrendered."
>
> (*FD*, pp. 367–68)

The comic dimensions of the passage, of course, play upon the stereotype of the Southerner still fighting the Civil War fifty years after Appomattox. But the significant difference between the Sartoris and MacCallum linkings of the Civil War and World War I is the lack of a MacCallum fatedness. That dimension removed, the story is one of humorous misinterpretation, yet here, too, the Old South mythology functions as an ideal knowledge system, as an interpreting machine turned on present experience. We are made aware of an act of misrepresentation which identifies present experience in terms of the past and finds the present a poor imitation of remote, lost glories. The humor reinforces our awareness of this serious issue by echoing Sartoris fatedness. Once again the MacCallums reorient our attitude toward the Sartorises, or more specifically toward the Sartoris myth which we come to see as a powerful narrative device for misinterpretation.

The distance from the "reality" of Faulkner's southern culture to Faulkner's fictional representation of it is problematical. Faulkner's narratives are neither mere reflections of his world nor mere autonomous fictions; the relationship between art and life can only be described as unstable, yet the conflicts and contradictions of a southern reality are recognizably immanent in Faulkner's emerging narrative style. The narrative displacement or revision by which Sartoris and MacCallum linkings of two great wars are juxtaposed opens a space for critical reading. Faulkner's drive to represent his South, a personal, familial history which he extends to a social vision, leads him to experiment with narrative structure and a typifying thematics of relations of present and past. Aesthetically these experiments resemble those of the modernists. The sense of southern fatalism repeats the modernist anxiety of belatedness, of loss of authenticity that accompanies the existential fragmentation of the self. Faulkner's peculiarly southern version of this modernism rests on the compulsion to read the mythical past as an explanation of present social and economic woes. Such an attitude is at the root of all the "New South" schemas which sought to preserve Old South ideals while rejecting Old South failures.

The plot of *Flags in the Dust* reveals this conflict between modernity and an intrusive past. The conflict is so pervasive that it penetrates even trivial details. The modern southern mind refers all experience to the meaning structure of the Old South mythology. Fundamental ideological oppositions like agrarian and urban, or agricultural and industrial, or South and North are subtexts for comic arguments over the relative merits of horses (or mules) and airplanes (or cars). Such arguments are not limited to the South in the 1920s, but they take on a peculiarly southern style when the horse's nobility in battle is pitted against the airplane's efficiency as a mode of self-destruction.

What Faulkner reveals in these moments is the presentness of narrative nostalgia. The opening scene of *Flags in the Dust* romanticizes this nostalgia while also providing an unambiguous comment on the powerful immediacy of the remote and the mysterious.

> As usual old man Falls had brought John Sartoris into the room with him. Freed as he was of time, he was a far more definite presence in the room than the two of them cemented by deafness to a dead time and drawn thin by the slow attenuation of days. He seemed to stand above them, all around them, with his bearded, hawklike face and the bold glamor of his dream.
>
> (*FD*, p. 5)

The southern present is not an effect of a prior (absent) cause; the present repeats a southern lost cause. The remote, mythical trauma of Civil War defeat leaps across Reconstruction and a host of New Southisms, just as genealogical relations in Faulkner's novels leap across generations, collapsing four into two, or omitting one altogether, or mistakenly designating a great-grandfather as a grandfather. Faulkner's narratives give little space and time to Reconstruction and the era of New South planning; the past he portrays is not lost but vital.

Such telescoping of chronology emphasizes the force of the remote past in modern southern mythmaking, in the mind of modern Southerners, in the conversations they have and, most particularly, the stories they tell. Faulkner represents this southern mind through its own narrative style, through the southern narrative strategy which projects the remote past beyond mere history into myth where it is "freed . . . of time." As such the past is made unrepresentable, mysterious, sublime and yet has a "far more definite presence" than mere historical reality. The sublimation of the remote past locates it on the threshold of narrative expression, like a subtext or cultural repressed that insists on being told and retold.

Aunt Jenny is Faulkner's initial effort to create a figure driven by this repetition compulsion. Her story is typical. Her embellishments, Faulkner instinctively recognizes, reveal a strategic sublimation: the intensification of the remote renders it present. Faulkner's effort here, however, is muddled by his authorial irony. Jenny's narrative style is treated as an eccentricity of character rather than as a representative mode of southern self-identification. Jenny is a bit overdrawn. Nevertheless, there are clear indexes of Faulkner's sense of the competence necessary for narrative authority, southern style. In a scene where she berates her servant Simon for telling old Bayard that young Bayard had, without advance notice, returned from World War I, Jenny asserts her rights as principal spokesman in the Sartoris household. Her words, not the third-person narrator's, are unambiguous insinuations of narrative authority.

> She had a fine command of language at all times, but when her ire was aroused she soared without effort to sublime heights. Hers was a forceful clarity and a colorful simplicity which Demosthenes would have envied and that even mules comprehended and of whose intent the most obtuse persons remained not long unawares. . . .
>
> "And the next time," Miss Jenny finished, "you or any section hand or brakeman or delivery boy either sees or hears anything you think will be of interest to Colonel, you tell me about it first: I'll do all the telling after that."
>
> (*FD*, p. 39)

Jenny's skill and authority are not in question, but her motive for seeking possession of "all the telling" remains unclear. This is a fault that Faulkner will correct in the rewriting of Jenny as Rosa Coldfield in *Absalom, Absalom!* Rosa's personal eccentricities are integral to the version of the southern myth she narrates. Through Miss Jenny, Faulkner has just begun to sense the complexity of narrative authority and narrative voice. It is nonetheless an instructive beginning, for Faulkner learned well what was necessary from Aunt Jenny's limitations. Specifically, the existential/phenomenological dynamics of storytelling in *Flags in the Dust* are undeveloped because the context of Jenny's narration is fragmented; the sense of her narration as both a participatory and a revisionary act is muted.

We might argue that Aunt Jenny's narration of the Old South myth is too personal, too clearly an expression of her peculiar character alone. Jenny has an eccentric style that is detached, sarcastic. As a result, Faulkner allows Jenny too much narrative power and young Bayard, the Descendant figure, too little. Young Bayard's voice is stilled. Faulkner's narration of southern narrative style demands a more involved play of pleasure and self-destructive fatalism than is represented in the contrast between Aunt Jenny's authoritative voice and young Bayard's largely silent, neurotic behavior. Again, in *Absalom, Absalom!* Faulkner better integrates the neurosis of the Descendant figure into a dialogue with the authoritative mythmaking of the Jenny-like figure of Rosa Coldfield, although we will see that the road from young Bayard to Quentin Compson first makes an unproductive detour in *The Sound and the Fury*.

The weaknesses of narrative in *Flags in the Dust* derive from Faulkner's uncertain departure from modernist aesthetics, from the crisis of modern ego identity that is reflected in the modernist conception of character development. The form of modernist narrative exposes the anxiety of lost authenticity, the contradiction between aesthetic distance and self-expression. Jean-François Lyotard describes these as characteristics of the modernist consciousness. The function of such narrative, argues Lyotard, is the production of knowledge, what in Faulkner's southern-style narrative is the misrecognition of present experience in terms of a past model of authenticity.

> By way of a simplifying fiction, we can hypothesize that, against all expectations, a collectivity that takes narrative as its key form of competence has no need to remember its past. It finds the raw material for its social bond not only in the meaning of the narratives it recounts, but also in the act of reciting them. The narratives' reference may seem to belong to the past, but in reality it is always contemporaneous with the act of recitation. It is the present act that on each of its occurrences marshals in the ephemeral temporality inhabiting the space between the "I have heard" and the "you will hear."[3]

The modernist emphasis is on performance, on the occupation of the position of the "I" in discursive practice. Temporality is abolished in the irreducibility of present action; the remote past is sublimated on the threshold of the present. Lyotard draws his model of narrative play from ethnological studies of the transmission of Cashinahua stories about remote ancestors and the narrator's role in the storytelling.

> The narrator's only claim to competence for telling the story is the fact that he has heard it himself. The current narratee gains potential access to the same authority simply by listening. It is claimed that the narrative is a faithful transmission (even if the narrative performance is highly inventive) and that it has been told "forever": therefore the hero . . . was himself once a narratee, and perhaps a narrator, of the very same story. This similarity of condition allows for the possibility that the current narrator could be the hero of a narrative, just as the Ancestor was. In fact, he is necessarily such a hero because he bears a name, declined at the end

of his narration, and that name was given to him in conformity with the canonic narrative legitimating the assignment of patronyms [in his or her culture].[4]

Lyotard's model reduces all narration of this style to exemplary modernist form; he makes a series of generalizations that cannot be easily critiqued here. What is crucial, however, is the appropriateness of the model, and of Lyotard's identification of specific characteristics of narrative performance, to Faulkner's sense of southern narrative style (what Lyotard calls "competence"). The subject matter of a story may speak of a remote past, but the link between past and present affirms a sense of identity as descent. Whatever the specific action, whoever the hero, the retold story establishes a genealogical relationship between present teller and present listener on the one hand and the remote past of previous tellings on the other. The form of the storytelling self-consciously acknowledges this genealogy; transmission establishes the legitimacy and authority of the present teller. Yet this is something of a double bind, for that authority originates in an indefinite past. However much the convention may allow for "inventive" performance, an affirmation of a "faithful transmission" is also required. The narrator is poised on the edge of a psychological precipice.

The essentially modernist twist in this narrative style is the assertion of authority over the remote past, motivated by what Harold Bloom has called the anxiety of influence.[5] Faulkner critics have identified this anxiety as the burden of the past, in what is essentially a Sartrean critique of Faulkner's failure to break free of the southern fatalism that he attributed to the Sartorises. Bloom's modernism corresponds to Aunt Jenny's "strong" voice, a commanding voice that emphasizes personal style and self-expression through highly inventive misreadings of the predecessor texts. Lyotard notes that the Cashinahuan model displays a confusion of positions, a transgression of the hero's role by the narrator, a breach of aesthetic distance. The modernist's defense against this breach is the narrative of artistic sensibilities, the novel about the novelist becoming a novelist. This is the tradition of Proust and Joyce. Faulkner abandons this mode after *Mosquitoes* and the unfinished "Elmer." His version of the narrator as hero rests upon a conscious, deliberate breach of aesthetic distance, in a remarkable juxtaposition of telling and being. Faulkner abandons the ego-gratifying self-expression by which the modernist writer allays his anxiety of influence, the aestheticist machismo of Bloom's "strong" voice, in favor of a narration that stresses not his aesthetic distance from the world of his stories but his participation in the reality of the world's discursive practices.

Faulkner produces after *Flags in the Dust* a series of narrations of the Old South myth told not by narrators protected through Aunt Jenny's aestheticist style of ironic detachment but by narrators deeply involved in the subliminal reality of the mythology they perpetuate, renew, and revise. After *Flags in the Dust*, the myth of the Old South promotes not a simple nostalgia but a critique of the present, and it is at this level that narrator and hero merge. From the perspective of later novels we look back on *Flags in the Dust* and read narrators who merely preserve the myth and affirm its authenticity, its authority. Aunt Jenny, removed as she is from participation, nonetheless denigrates all wars in comparison with "The War" and subordinates all Sartorises to the First Ancestor figure she designates "my Bayard." The Sartoris/southern myth of decline reveals a nostalgic desire for half-remembered plenitudes, plenitudes that the later novels dismantle. At base, this narration resembles a fantasy wish for pre-oedipal release from the tensions that modern solipsism, existential thrownness, and oedipal belatedness force upon self-consciousness. The result is Quentin Compson's repetitive obsessions, his death wish, his aesthetic escapism which postpones as it anticipates death with perverse pleasure.

The Old South myth also represents a distorted utopia. After *Flags in the Dust* Faulkner's participant narrators begin to lose their individual voices in a profoundly demystifying narrative strategy. Essentially, two kinds of narrators emerge. Primarily the narrative rests upon the Descendant figure whose double bind of commemoration and repudiation provides the central motivation for narration. All these Descendant figures modeled on young Bayard Sartoris are made participatory in the narrative action. In addition, the detached voice of Aunt Jenny is transformed into an antithetical voice within the genealogical narrative. Neither the author's voice nor that of a disinterested interlocutor, this voice-of-another is participatory no less than that of the Descendant figure. This other voice, however, deconstructs the myth, critically exposes it, releases it (and, could they accept the fall of the sublime Ancestor, might well release its narrators) from the burden of the past. What is at stake here is a reformation of the Old South utopia, a recomposition. Faulkner revises and perverts the Old South myth into a form of conversation. A modernist dialectic of past and present, self and other, fragmented and authentic is rewritten as dialogue, as the telling of the story, not as a genealogy of descent where transmission is a process of legitimation but as a polyvocal delegitimation of the remote, sublime authoritarianism of southern mythmaking itself. Nostalgic desire is politicized, becomes a narrative form of social practice. The authoritarian relationships of class, gender, and race that subordinate voices to the political seats of power are transformed from the mysterious, metaphysical, and private into the familiar, pragmatic, and public sphere of action; the repressive power of sublimation is exposed to critical reading. And, thus, the reader becomes a participant, another voice whose ethical stance enables it to speak for those voices that yet remain silent.

Faulkner's primary interest was not in the Old South but in a modern southern narrative practice. It is this modern southern narrative that he represents. The progress of his career is a continual repositioning of his own voice within southern storytelling; that repositioning revises and perverts in order to reopen a space for further narration, even other voices. As a result the Old South myth with its racist and sexist violence reveals itself in the gaps between revisions/perversions. Admittedly, the positioning of his voice within southern narrative practice never fully succeeds in separating Faulkner from his own sense of a southern (Falkner) fatedness, a genealogical decline. The space for other voices sometimes suggests to him a frightening collapse of narrative order, which in southern narrative discourse is the same as the collapse of social order. The old authoritarian myth too often penetrates his narrative, establishing aesthetic distance, silencing voices, closing narrative form. But never conclusively; for Faulkner inevitably reopens the narrative, repositions another voice or even his own in another relation to his text. Quentin Compson's discovery in *Absalom, Absalom!* that "maybe nothing ever happens once and is finished" (*AA*, p. 261) takes on a double meaning. For Quentin it is a reflection of southern fatalism; for Faulkner it is a declaration of a revisionary narrative strategy that demystifies fatalism, delegitimizes Quentin's Old South mythology at its source in modern southern narrative practice.

The modernist conjunction of aesthetic distance and aesthetic closure forbids representation. The literary work becomes remote and inconsequential. Conflict (Aristotelian plot) is resolved at the level of illusion. This may be the ironic fate of modernist avant-garde art as Peter Burger presents it, ironic because modernism frequently sought a freedom from life in order to preserve a purity of critical expression about life.[6] Faulkner's career is a continual struggle against this modernist inconsequentiality. The aesthetic dualism of closure and distance repeatedly pushes him to an uncomfortable violation of the modernist rules. Southern narrative style could be neither closed nor distanced; it could be represented.

Go Down, Moses is a pure demonstration of Faulkner's mature deconstruction of the idea of aesthetic closure; its "composition" consists of a rearrangement of previously published works. As a result, the stories assert individual unity. For example, the initial story, "Was," defies easy integration into a simple novelesque unity. The events narrated are set in an indefinite past and seem complete in themselves. The story is a comic tale resolved in the refusal of Hubert Beauchamp to call the bluff of Buddy McCaslin in a game of poker where the stakes are the marriage of Buddy's twin brother, Buck, to Hubert's sister, Sophonsiba, against money and slaves. Buddy's legendary abilities at poker bluff Hubert and rescue Buck from Sophonsiba's designs. Yet we learn shortly after this story is concluded that Ike McCaslin, one of the novel's central characters, is the son of Buck and Sophonsiba. There is no error, of course, just the establishing of a revisionary reading, a genealogical breaking through of the aesthetic closure of "Was" that traces the relationships of later stories, set in more contemporary times, to this originary story of a marriage (apparently) prevented from taking place.

Rereading "Was" in terms of genealogical consequences transforms it into a parable. Where the tale once seemed an innocent, metonymic piece of the McCaslin family history, now it functions more like a synecdoche, the fragment that contains the whole.[7] "Was" presents the central terms of the McCaslin history, its twisted genealogical relationships, its patriarchaal structure with its masculine social and economic rituals (hunting and gambling), its tangled structure of exchange value involving women, slaves, money, and property.

So, too, we must rethink what seems a conventional and innocuous narrative occasion in "Was." Technically narrated by an unobtrusive third-person voice, the story recounts a specific set of circumstances for telling and hearing that function as a kind of prologue to the story of Buck's and Buddy's adventures; "Was" begins with a capsule summary of the novel as a whole, a bit of information that is transmitted through genealogical narration. The consequences of this passing down of the story of an authentic experience reside in its repetition and continuation. Ike McCaslin is the recipient of the narration, the one who in turn becomes a narrator of the McCaslin history, an author who, as any modernist would, attempts to write its conclusion. Ike's discovery in the family ledgers of an original McCaslin sin, the incest/miscegenation of the First Ancestor figure, Carothers McCaslin, leads him to seek the missing heirs of Carothers' violations in order to deliver to them a rightful inheritance. His desire is to enact a ritual of legitimation which he can record in the ledgers as a debt paid in full. He is unable to do so, but Faulkner insists that Ike's failure not be thought of as a result of chance, the inability to trace down the descendants of Tennie's Jim. What Faulkner makes clear is that the act of paying the debt for the past merely repeats the sins of the past. The inscription of payment in the balance sheets of the ledgers is an illusion of closure, a purely aesthetic conclusion no less blindly escapist than Ike's dramatic gesture of refusing his inheritance. Ike's effort to resolve the consequences of past actions merely entangles him in those consequences, whatever the cause (noble or selfish) that motivates him to the attempt. Ike passes from narratee to narrator and ultimately to narrated, to hero, the latter a creature under the control of an authorial third person. This omniscient point of view in *Go Down, Moses*, however, must not be thought of as reflecting Faulkner's aesthetic distance from his story, the author's distance from reality. We must remember the autobiographical dimension of Faulkner's family novels. Faulkner has already learned the lesson of narrative participation and involvement that he uses Ike to illustrate.

In *The Hamlet*, published two years before *Go Down, Moses*, Faulkner dramatized the southern narrative style in the story of V. K. Ratliff. *The Hamlet* departs from the typical model of Old South genealogical stories begun in *Flags in the Dust*, and that difference is important for two reasons: (1) it focuses our attention on the immediate social function of storytelling as constitutive of what Faulkner believes to be the modern southern mind; and (2) it foregrounds the "rules" of storytelling, particularly the narrator-text relationship and the relationship between narrative and discursive practice. Thus, by abandoning the specific content of the Old South myth in *The Hamlet*, Faulkner demonstrates the pervasive presence of that myth as a style of narration, a form of thinking, a southern competence. But in *The Hamlet* the narrative voice of Ratliff comes too near discursive reality, disappears into the narration, and suffers for that violation of aesthetic distance.

Faulkner offers us what might be called a Derridian apocalypse. The key is the denial of any privileged perspective on the narrative, the demonstration of the illusion of any "outside" to discursive practice. The author's voice has no authenticity, no discrete presence in the telling. Yet Faulkner would seem to support Derrida's proclamation against resignation to a modernist despair: "It remains, then, for us to *speak, to make our voices resonate* . . . in order to make up for the breakup of presence." [8] The faintly existential admonition here rejects silence (as in Sartoris suicidal fatality); but granted the moral imperative, how to speak? Postmodernism revels in "freeplay," yet for Faulkner play is situated, has limits, has a place, a time, and a motive. Reading Faulkner one might come to see that postmodernism is dialogically located within modernism; the postmodern is a mimetic voice in spite of itself; it is the representation of that which is already voiced and may only be departed from, revised. In *Flags in the Dust* the obsessive repetition of the Sartoris myth merely reappropriates the present; it is that sentimental fatalism that Faulkner departs from in later Yoknapatawpha novels, for in the genealogical narratives that follow that initial experiment the present perverts the past, disperses and reorients the myth by invading the remote with the force of present consequences, immediate effects. We can, therefore, read across Faulkner's career from *Flags in the Dust* to *The Hamlet* and thereby arrive at a juncture where Faulkner is neither mute nor inclined to play word games. *The Hamlet* recapitulates the movement in Faulkner's novels of southern narrative style from mere storytelling to narrative involvement. Faulkner draws modernist (and postmodernist) escapism back to reality, grounds the act of southern narration in the immediate and material conditions of present southern experience.

The style of southern storytelling has, for Faulkner, definite rules. The narrator in *The Hamlet* is V. K. Ratliff. As a traveling salesman he is partly a stereotype, the clever manipulator of words whose travels give him access to information. His function in the community is to maintain a network of exchange among remote areas of Yoknapatawpha County; his profession is gossip as much as anything else. Ratliff, in effect, creates a collectivity tenuously maintained by word of mouth; he is historian and moralist for the community as well as an authoritative voice of legitimation. But these functions rest on two rapidly disappearing conditions: on the lack of other lines of communication (roads and cars), and on a form of trade or barter rapidly being displaced by a system of money exchange. Ratliff is, from the beginning of *The Hamlet*, an anachronism, and this is a crucial factor in his rather spectacular downfall.

Southern-style narration also has an appropriate place in Faulkner's narrative. Ratliff's travels lead back to the hamlet Frenchman's Bend, and more particularly to the places of leisure and talking within the town that provide shelter while remaining open to current transactions of the community. The "normal" place of storytelling is public, affording easy access to participants and an unobstructed view of comings and goings in the town.

> Besides Varner's store and cotton gin and the combined grist mill and blacksmith shop which they rented to the actual smith, and the schoolhouse and the church and the perhaps three dozen dwellings within sound of both bells, the village consisted of a livery barn and lot and a contiguous shady though grassless yard in which sat a sprawling rambling edifice partly of sawn boards and partly of logs, unpainted and of two stories in places and known as Littlejohn's hotel, where behind a weathered plank nailed to one of the trees and lettered ROOMS AND BORD drummers and livestock-traders were fed and lodged. It had a long veranda lined with chairs. That night after supper, the buckboard and team in the stable, Ratliff was sitting here with five or six other men who had drifted in from adjacent homes within walking distance. They would have been there on any other night, but this evening they were gathered even before the sun was completely gone, looking now and then toward the dark front of Varner's store as people will gather to look quietly at the cold embers of a lynching or at the propped ladder and open window of an elopement, since the presence of a hired white clerk in the store of a man still able to walk and with intellect still sound enough to make money mistakes at least in his own favor, was as unheard of as the presence of a hired white woman in one of their own kitchens.[9]

Ratliff is the culmination of Faulkner's several efforts to represent the type of the southern storyteller, but he is not a late conception in Faulkner's career. He traces his origins to the early versions of *The Hamlet*, to "Father Abraham," and to *Flags in the Dust*, where he was called V. K. Suratt. Faulkner's southern novels involved his sense of a southern narrative style from the very beginning, yet Ratliff comes to life finally as a product of the narrative experimentation in Faulkner's greatest work. This distinctive narrative manner is fine-tuned in the early scenes of *The Hamlet*. Appropriate to his authoritative stature, Ratliff does not speak first, waiting to be drawn into the topic which hinges on a current event, the arrival of Flem Snopes to work in Varner's store. It is genealogy again that introduces the occasion for storytelling, although not the cavalier genealogy of the Old South myth. Flem's father, Ab Snopes, has a reputation as a barn burner. The way is opened for Ratliff to assert his authority; he launches into a story about Ab Snopes that casts light on the presence of Flem in the general store. Ratliff also orients the story according to his sense of community values, even to the point of distorting it in order to repress certain obvious conclusions.

Ratliff begins provocatively by asserting that Ab is not "naturally mean. He's just soured" (*HAM*, p. 29). A narrative contract is thereby proposed: to reveal the causes of this particular effect. Following this promise of narrative explanation, Ratliff undergoes a formulaic check of his credentials, of his "competence."

> Once more for a moment no one spoke. Then the first speaker said:
> "How did you find all this out? I reckon you was there too."
> "I was," Ratliff said.
>
> (*HAM*, p. 30)

The occasion and credentials of the storytelling established, we discover that the content of the story is also typical. Ratliff relates the unfortunate events of Ab's horse trading with a legendary horse trader named Pat Stamper. In this masculine domain such a story, like those of gambling and hunting, discloses a set of communal values and behavioral rules that are based on "manly" action, courage, and cleverness. The link to the Old South myth of legendary Civil War exploits is clear enough, but the shift in social context from cavalier to yeoman farmer also reveals Faulkner's class bias. The legendary events of horse trading reflect a code not of idealized honor but of caveat emptor: get away with whatever you can. Ab is swindled by Stamper in a particularly public and, therefore, humiliating manner.

Insofar as this story serves as a parable to account for Flem Snopes's presence in Varner's store, the genealogical relationship is negated. The parallel to be drawn is between Stamper and Flem, not between Flem and his father, for Flem is the victimizer not the victim. Our reading here functions in two registers: (1) we are conscious of the communal meanings and values represented in the story of Ab Snopes's downfall, the use made of the story by Ratliff, and (2) we become increasingly aware of the use made of this story by Faulkner. The former involves a set of necessary conditions or cultural codes. Such codes are the provenance of Ratliff's narrative competence. The legendary Pat Stamper represents not only a challenge to individual pride (Ab sees himself as a clever trader and good judge of horses [*HAM*, p. 31]) but also the "outsider." As such he participates in two discursive dichotomies: he is the slick trader duping the local rubes, and the Southerner's "other," that is, the Northerner. Stamper's origins are unknown, making him inherently suspect to the closed community of Frenchman's Bend. What is at stake in this story of Ab's failure, Ratliff makes clear, is community honor.

> It was them eight cash dollars of Beasley's, and not that Ab held them eight dollars against Herman, because Herman had done already invested a mule and a buggy in it. And besides, the eight dollars was still in the country and so it didn't actually matter whether it was Herman or Beasley that had them. It was the fact that Pat Stamper, a stranger, had come in and got actual Yoknapatawpha County cash dollars to rattling around loose that way. When a man swaps horse for horse, that's one thing and let the devil protect him if the devil can. But when cash money starts changing hands, that's something else. And for a stranger to come in and start that cash money to changing and jumping from one fellow to another, its like when a burglar breaks into your house and flings your things ever which way even if he dont take nothing. It makes you twice as mad.
>
> (*HAM*, pp. 34–35)

Faulkner emphasizes here another pertinent factor: the traditional system of barter has been corrupted by money. The "stranger" and money exchange, and the link to that nongeographical "northern" enemy which combines the two, prove a powerful motive for revenge.

> Ab was coming to town with twenty-four dollars and sixty-eight cents in his pocket and the entire honor and pride of the science and pastime of horse-trading in Yoknapatawpha County depending on him to vindicate it.
>
> (*HAM*, p. 34)

Given this motive in Ratliff's narrative, Ab's clear and unambiguous defeat must be explained away by a bit of obvious narrative manipulation. At the very beginning Ratliff shifts the focus to Ab's wife.

> Because if it was anybody that Stamper beat, it was Miz Snopes. And even she never considered it so. All she was out was just having to make the trip to Jefferson herself to finally get the separator and maybe she knowed all the time that sooner or later she would have to do that. It wasn't Ab that bought one horse and sold two to Pat Stamper. It was Miz Snopes. Her and Pat just used Ab to trade through.
>
> (*HAM*, p. 30)

This odd distortion of the facts ignores at least the Snopeses' loss of the cow that was to provide the milk for that separator. Ratliff's story inclines away from consequences, minimizes effects in the interest of telling a story about one particular effort to defend community honor and pride. Andrea Dimino comments on this narrative move and its effects on the novel's reader.

> Our fascination with Stamper's legerdemain blocks our sympathy for Ab's vulnerability, even though he is now a farmer without a mule or cow; since he tried to beat Stamper, he only receives comic justice when he is whipped. But Stamper has precipitated what Ratliff calls a natural process of "souring" in Ab. At some point after Stamper eliminated Ab from horse-trading, he " 'just went plumb curdled' " and became the mean old man we see at the start of the novel. In order for the story to remain comic, Ratliff must end it here, before the unknown moment of when the curdling actually happens.[10]

Thus the comic elements of Ratliff's story block our attention to certain details, yet Dimino also notes that "under the pressure of economic decline . . . the more traditional comic stories of the first half of the novel are invaded in some way by portents of black humor."[11] The comic misreading of Ab's defeat does not, for example, completely disguise the suffering of Ab's wife or blunt our sense of their poverty.

What is not made clear at first in this example of southern-style storytelling is the implicit narrative breakdown of the aesthetic distance between telling and being. Ratliff's interpretive involvement in his narration of Ab's defeat threatens to overpower the story itself, to displace the "hero" by the narrator whose cleverness is manifest in his narrative skill. Ratliff's defense of Ab becomes a self-defense, and in the course of the novel Ratliff will evolve from authoritative narrator to narrated hero. Ratliff's story of Ab Snopes functions as a parable for his own story, his own defeat in a contest of trading skills with Ab's son, Flem. The occasion of the telling of Ab's story, Flem's presence in Frenchman's Bend, foreshadows Ratliff's concrete experience of a revised version of his own tale. As the narrator becomes the narrated, the consequences of the narrative action are more clearly revealed.

Point of view in *The Hamlet* is that of an unobtrusive third person, and this makes it possible for the reader to shift from early close sympathies with Ratliff to later dismay at his spectacular, self-made downfall. Ratliff's engagement with Flem in a contest of trading skills rests on his admirable desire to set right the wrongs he perceives to have issued from Flem's cruel greed. His moral stature in this crusade, of course, derives more from his role as the narrative voice of the community than from his stereotypical skills as a traveling salesman. Nevertheless, Ratliff seems well armed for his combat; the members of the community express what Faulkner wishes the reader to believe, that Ratliff is the one man who can get the better of Flem. But Ratliff's storytelling authority does not translate into real-life skill because Faulkner presents Ratliff as the defender of an outmoded sense of honor. Ratliff is deluded by his own narrations, by the masculine terms of face-to-face tests of courage and quick wit that Flem Snopes has learned to exploit. In Faulkner's sexist terms, Flem is an unsexed creature who suggests sinister and chaotic forces at work in the destruction of (masculine) modern southern society. Flem remains hidden behind the scenes; he accumulates wealth not through face-to-face tests of wit and trickery, but through blackmail and exploitation of the desperate inefficiency of the local courts of equity. Dimino sees in this a model of the modern corporate state that Faulkner so clearly feared and detested.

> In the horse auction Flem succeeds in evading his individual responsibility by forming a hidden business relationship with the Texan which represents an embryonic stage of the process that Alan Trachtenberg has called "the incorporation of America": the emergence of a changed, more tightly structured society with new hierarchies of control, and also changed conceptions of that society, of America itself.[12]

That there is something alien, newfangled, mysterious, threatening, cowardly, and perverted about Flem Snopes reveals the deep anger Faulkner felt about the changes and "new hierarchies of control" operative in the modern South.

Yet finally *The Hamlet* is not primarily about the emergence of a new and dreaded economic structure; the clash between Flem and Ratliff points to the fall of Ratliff, the fall of the values and codes of behavior he espouses, rather than to the rise of the Snopeses. Faulkner follows Flem's career in the two remaining novels of the Snopes saga, but *The Hamlet* is concerned with the world Flem leaves behind him as he departs from Frenchman's Bend in the novel's final pages. That departure is triumphant and sinister yet not climactic. The reader's greatest moment of surprise and bewilderment has come somewhat earlier when it becomes clear that Ratliff, along with an all too easy mark, Henry Armstid, has been duped by Flem's buried treasure scam. The reader, no less than the citizens of the hamlet, is shocked by this turn of events; Ratliff has been publicly humiliated as was Ab Snopes by Pat Stamper.

Ratliff has been substituted for Ab in a plot no less fantastic and un-believable than the one Ratliff narrated about horses inflated with air and painted by Stamper so as to disguise their identity from Ab.

Ratliff realizes his loss, albeit too late, whereas his partner, Armstid, does not, and this seems like a narrative move to rescue Ratliff from the complete degradation that Armstid suffers. Yet the fall of Ratliff and that of Armstid work in parallel, each spectacular: the former a disquieting example of what Dimino calls "grotesque black humor,"[13] the latter shatteringly pathetic. And it is with the latter emotion that the reader leaves the novel. Ratliff's wounds are at least in part self-inflicted, the result of his living out his own narrative style, the inter-pretive strategy that led him to transform Ab Snopes into a defender of community honor as he related the story of Ab's souring. Ratliff challenges Flem out of necessity, as a futile effort to preserve the nar-rative style and the reality it represents against the encroachment of the modern. Faulkner, for all of his abhorrence of the modern, none-theless unambiguously demonstrates through Ratliff's humiliation the self-destructive consequences of attempting to live through the terms of a nostalgic narrative. More important, we become aware that the stories a culture preserves and tells are not innocent of consequences, whether they are tall tales of horse trading or sublime myths of the Old South. Their status as narratives seems to provide them with aesthetic protection, neutralizing their effects on thinking and behaving; yet if even a Ratliff can talk himself inside his stories, the aesthetic protection functions more as a disquieting subterfuge.

If the consequences of Ab's loss to Stamper appear trivial in Ratliff's interpretive misreading, Faulkner turns the tables on the reader's com-placency at the novel's end. The final section of *The Hamlet* is entitled "The Peasants." It is not an unsympathetic portrait of those whose lives are tormented by outmoded codes of behavior and the unscrupu-lous exploiters of those codes. After all, Flem may represent the new modes of socio-economic relations in the South, but his distance from the old models of these relationships is minimal; Flem repeats both the antebellum social formula as it is figured in Thomas Sutpen and the Reconstruction revision of that figure as it is represented by the good old boy bosses of the hamlet, the Varners.

Myra Jehlen reads Faulkner's tracing of the consequences of these dominantly masculine codes of behavior and narration, the effects par-ticularly on women and children, as excessively sentimental in *The Hamlet*: "Faulkner's sympathy for his poor white characters is here deep enough to evoke their suffering but not quite complete enough to let them speak for themselves. And as long as Mrs. Armstid and her kind remain mute, they cannot at their best behavior really transcend sentimentality." [14] Jehlen, of course, is correct, very much as Sartre was correct in condemning Faulkner for seeing the problem and not then projecting a better way, an alternative world, or utopian solution. Yet we need not draw from Sartre or Jehlen the implication that Faulkner's narrative strategy uses sentimentality to distract attention away from the unvoiced sufferers. Early in *The Hamlet* Faulkner identifies for us, in Ratliff's storytelling, those voices that are usually repressed in this southern-style narrative; then late in *The Hamlet* Faulkner gives these largely mute sufferers perhaps the only voice he could: the masculine voice of a white southern writer come directly into conflict with his own personal project to write himself out of his narrative identity. For Faulkner this is always a hesitating, and at times reactionary, move, yet it also critically opens a space for those who would speak for the unvoiced sufferers, a space for the voice of Professor Jehlen. This is no insignificant accomplishment and is no less important because so many readers of Faulkner before Jehlen and Porter and King and Sundquist and Dimino refused to speak what was necessary or were themselves unheard. What we must see is that Faulkner's novels stand as a profound critique of discursive practices that repress the voices of others, of minorities of class, race, and gender that form the thematic focus of so many of his narratives. Faulkner's project unmasks discursive repression; his narratives break down the powerful southern narrative of legitimation. Faulkner's narrative of narrative projects a need for other voices, for departure and demystification, for a discursive reality in which the Mrs. Armstids and Lucas Beauchamps will be heard. That he does not find an alternative utopian reality is his personal tragedy.

CHAPTER 10

A Writing Lesson: The Recovery of Antigone

E VEN THOUGH *The Sound and the Fury* extended Faulkner's newly begun Yoknapatawpha project into the realm of modernist experiments in narrative form, Faulkner considered the novel a failure precisely because of its modernist aesthetics. The critical tradition, correctly, has been far less willing to acknowledge that he failed to tell the story he wanted to tell, and perhaps this response reflects an understanding that the move from *Flags in the Dust* to *The Sound and the Fury* was a necessary step in the mastery of his narrative technique. Moreover, from the modernist/formalist perspective, *The Sound and the Fury* is a spectacular success. The monologic form of the first three sections; the focus of narrative time in the present and away from the past; the integration of an oedipal symbolic structure into the narrative; and the exposition of the existentialist theme of the loss of the self all recapitulate dominant modernist modes of composition and themes. Remarkably, only the setting of the narrative in the present, a strategy which emphasizes memory and the extraordinary psychosocial pressure of memory on the present, continued to serve Faulkner's emerging narrative of the South in later novels. The rest of the experimental modernist techniques of *The Sound and the Fury* are ultimately rejected, even within the novel itself. The failure of *The Sound and the Fury* arises from the subjectivism the monologic style of modernist stream-of-consciousness technique, and from the antinarrative effects of its oedipal symbolism. Yet it is a most interesting novel simply because it contains a struggle against its own experimental limits; the composition of *The Sound and the Fury* initiates a gradual swerve away from modernist formalism.

The focus of this struggle resides in the relationship among the first three sections of the novel. The second, Quentin Compson's monologue, was written, Faulkner claimed, as the result of his realization that the story he began to tell through Benjy might ultimately be published. The shift from Benjy to Quentin is telling. Benjy's section is purely narrative while Quentin's departs from narrative; Quentin's section is more self-consciously "literary" and, ultimately, lyrical. The shift is not merely one of point of view, a change from the limited consciousness of Benjy to the mature, although neurotic, mind of Quentin. The move from Benjy to Quentin identifies a typical Faulknerian theme: the transition from childhood to adulthood, from innocence to experience. In addition, it represents a decline from authenticity. The composition of Quentin's monologue pivots on a theory of writing embedded in modernist aesthetics, on a dichotomy between an inviolable subjectivity at the core of creative expression and the destructive forces of public dissemination. The reader is reminded of Said's theory of "molestation,"[1] for the intrusion of the outside on the inside is central to *The Sound and the Fury* both as a commonplace psychoanalytic theme and as a career event. Quentin's monologue expresses the modernist anxiety of the loss of subjectivity; his obsessive talking is a case history of resistance to the intrusion of the world on his personal, private self. The section is appropriate in every way to Faulkner's own reluctant step toward publication of a story he had wished to keep private.

Quentin's section also represents a retreat into fashionable oedipal symbolism, a transition which accounts for the fact that it has become the interpretive epicenter of the novel. Benjy's section represents the experience of a loss of innocence. The hero is Benjy himself, whose innocence is violated by desire, not his but Caddy's. Benjy's consciousness is invaded by time, loss, and aloneness, although in a nonsymbolic mode, a repetitive experience linked to a rudimentary memory of a state of plenitude. Quentin's monologue expresses the utopianism of a wish to recapture such a lost innocence, a wish that grows naturally in the soil of the modernist anxiety of belatedness. Benjy, unlike his brother, Quentin, takes aggressive action against those who threaten the expression of his desire for Caddy, and as Faulkner describes Benjy's responses to Caddy's meeting with one of her lovers, we read through a consciousness, diametrically opposed to Quentin's, that has yet to be acculturated by Oedipus.

"Benjy." Caddy said. "It's just Charlie. Dont you know Charlie."

"Where's his nigger." Charlie said. "What do they let him run around loose for."

"Hush, Benjy." Caddy said. "Go away, Charlie. He doesn't like you." Charlie went away and I hushed. I pulled at Caddy's dress.

"Why, Benjy." Caddy said. "Aren't you going to let me stay here and talk to Charlie awhile."

"Call that nigger." Charlie said. He came back. I cried louder and pulled at Caddy's dress.

"Go away, Charlie." Caddy said. Charlie came and put his hands on Caddy and I cried more. I cried loud.

"No, no." Caddy said. "No. No."

"He cant talk." Charlie said. "Caddy."

"Are you crazy." Caddy said. She began to breathe fast. "He can see. Dont. Dont." Caddy fought. They both breathed fast. "Please. Please." Caddy whispered.

"Send him away." Charlie said.

"I will." Caddy said. "Let me go."

"Will you send him away." Charlie said.

"Yes." Caddy said. "Let me go." Charlie went away. "Hush." Caddy said. "He's gone." I hushed. I could hear and feel her chest going.

"I'll have to take him to the house." she said. She took my hand. "I'm coming." she whispered.

"Wait." Charlie said. "Call the nigger."

"No." Caddy said. "I'll come back. Come on, Benjy."

"Caddy." Charlie whispered, loud. We went on. "You better come back. Are you coming back." Caddy and I were running. "Caddy." Charlie said. We ran out into the moonlight, toward the kitchen.

"Caddy." Charlie said.

Caddy and I ran. We ran up the kitchen steps, onto the porch, and Caddy knelt down in the dark and held me. I could hear her and feel her chest. "I wont." she said. "I wont anymore, ever. Benjy. Benjy." Then she was crying, and I cried, and we held each other. "Hush." she said. "Hush. I wont anymore." So I hushed and Caddy got up and we went into the kitchen and turned the light on and Caddy took the kitchen soap and washed her mouth at the sink, hard. Caddy smelled like trees.[2]

This passage hinges on the contrast between Benjy's lack of language and the repetition of the word "said." Everyone else can talk. Benjy's world is not verbal but sensual, a complex of sights, sounds, and smells. The dominant sensation is visual, reinforced by repetitive references throughout the first section to Benjy's fascination with mirrors. The paradigm is neo-Freudian, Lacanian; Benjy's pre-oedipal desire for Caddy is set against the realm of the oedipal symbolic that names, describes, and directs cultural behavior. Language is associated with lacking ("He cant talk"), lies (Caddy does not "come back" to Charlie that night just as she does not keep her promise to Benjy: "I wont anymore, ever"), and absence (the magic name "Caddy" ceases magically to present the object of Benjy's desire). Language, in this passage and throughout Benjy's section, is associated with naming, with the identity of the speaker in verbal exchanges, and above all with narrative convention, the indication of the direction of speech, the place of the speaker in relation to the hearer.

Moreover, we read in this passage a distinction between Benjy's desire and Charlie's. While Charlie's desire is strictly gonadal, Benjy's desire is specifically not that. As a result, Benjy's desire remains inaccessible to us because it is also mysterious for the characters in the novel, and he cannot articulate it for us; it is, therefore, subject to interpretation, to the imposition from without of that language which Benjy lacks. For one who cannot express his desires, all desires in the oedipal symbolic become one. Benjy is castrated because he frightened some schoolgirls walking by his house.

> They came on. I opened the gate and they stopped, turning. I was trying to say, and I caught her, trying to say, and she screamed and I was trying to say and trying and the bright shapes began to stop and I tried to get out.
>
> (*SF*, p. 64)

Benjy is victimized by oedipal language throughout his narrative; surrounded by words he cannot use, he is used by words. Deprived of his uncle Maury's name, he is verbally banished from the family. Because he cannot speak, others speak for him; an interior monologue, Benjy's narrative nonetheless is predominantly the voices of others he hears and transmits to us without a trace of distortion. He is confused by the supplemental play of language which distinguishes between "Caddy" and "caddie" because he cannot displace signifieds from signifiers. He exists consciously in a world with which he cannot communicate, repeatedly violated by that world in words he cannot utter.

What is curious is the absence of Quentin's voice in Benjy's consciousness, although our curiosity arises only as an afterthought to reading Quentin's monologue. Quentin seems, in effect, to be recreating in his mind a consciousness of time-innocence modeled on Benjy's imprisonment in the continuous present, but Quentin is far more than a mere repetition of Benjy in a different psychic register. The shift from pre-oedipal to oedipal consciousness changes everything. While Benjy's desire is sensual, bodily, for warmth, touch, and a kind of nurture, Quentin's desire is an aesthetics of disinterested interest. Quentin's desire is schizophrenic, an incestuous desire for the other of himself, Caddy, the completion of the self to the end of eliminating desire, hence, a death wish.

> I held the point of the knife at her throat it wont take but a second just a second then I can do mine I can do mine then
> all right can you do yours by yourself
> yes the blades long enough Benjys in bed by now
> yes
> it wont take but a second Ill try not to hurt
> all right
> will you close your eyes
> no like this youll have to push harder
> touch your hand to it
> but she didnt move her eyes were wide open looking past my head at the sky
> Caddy do you remember how Dilsey fussed at you because your drawers were muddy
> dont cry
> Im not crying Caddy
> push it are you going to
> do you want me to
> yes push it
> touch your hand to it
> dont cry poor Quentin
> but I couldnt stop she held my head against her damp hard breast I could hear her heart going firm and slow now not hammering and the water gurgling among the willows in the dark and waves of honeysuckle coming up the air my arm and shoulder were twisted under me
> what is it what are you doing
> her muscles gathered I sat up
> its my knife I dropped it
> she sat up
> what time is it
> I dont know. . . .
>
> I got in front of her again
> Caddy
> stop it

I held her
Im stronger than you
she was motionless hard and unyielding but still
I wont fight stop you better stop
Caddy dont Caddy
it wont do any good dont you know it wont let me go
the honeysuckle drizzled and drizzled I could hear the crickets watching
us in a circle she moved back went around me on toward the trees
you go on back to the house you neednt come
I went on
why dont you go on back to the house. . . .

(*SF*, pp. 188–191)

The parallels between this scene and the one where Benjy draws
Caddy away from her lover are obvious. Yet Faulkner here uses a different language, a too obviously Freudian one with its doubled phallic
symbol in the knife that is both the object and the instrument of castration. It is a powerful scene emotionally, concentrating with lyric
economy themes of incest, suicide, castration, and the intrusion of time,
yet as this "literary" style breaks through we read seemingly beyond
Quentin's voice, hearing in his fantasy or remembrance a coldness in
Caddy's responses to him. Caddy seems to taunt Quentin, daring him
to murder or rape her. Her "poor Quentin" is without emotion, and
she teases him about his virginity before sending him home like a small
boy. This is hardly the partner for a romantic union of souls, and it
contrasts directly with the genuine sympathy Caddy exhibits for Benjy.
Caddy's sexuality, which is not at issue in Benjy's consciousness, is,
for Quentin, "hard" and "unyielding"; Faulkner's peculiar ideal of the
little girl with muddy drawers has long since been lost.

If we read Quentin's section back on Benjy's we link Benjy's castration with Caddy's sexuality; after all, it is Caddy's lie to Benjy that
seems to explain his seeking for young schoolgirls as supplements for
her absence. If we read forward from Quentin's monologue, we discover that Jason Compson as well is obsessed with Caddy, although she
is present to him in the figure of her young daughter, Quentin. Caddy
serves Faulkner as the link between all of the Compson brothers, and
that link would provide a formal structure of containment for the novel.
The effect is that Caddy becomes a signifier for incestuous desires, and
both Jason and Quentin suffer a symbolic castration, a linguistic repetition of Benjy's very real castration, as a consequence of their illicit
transgressions. Thus the authority of Quentin's oedipal symbolism is

affirmed. This forgets, however, the pre-oedipal sentiment of Benjy's section, an innocence arising from Benjy's victimization by oedipal violence. For Benjy, Caddy is no empty signifier. Yet the idea of going into print, the writing of Quentin's section, seemed to spark in Faulkner a retreat into convention, the abandonment of Benjy's insistent dwelling in Caddy's presence and a reworking of her into a metaphor that would provide unity for his novel.

In recognition of the impossibility of his task, however, Faulkner passed through monologue, and the transformation of Caddy into a free-floating signifier, to the final section of his narrative which is initially focused on Dilsey; there he abandoned first-person narration in favor of authorial omniscience. The change in point of view, nevertheless, reflects a move toward just another type of ruling metaphor, one designed to encompass extremes rather than signify original, forbidden desire. This metaphor is Dilsey. Dilsey is not a Compson, although she has served the family for many generations. Dilsey inevitably compels the narrative away from the Compsons into the symbolism of an Easter Sunday at an all black Protestant church. The subject of Reverend Shegog's Easter sermon is resurrection, but here in particular the symbolism simply does not work. Faulkner's narrative balances precariously between the Compsons and the black worshipers who rapturously listen to Shegog, between an end to the Compson family and the promise of salvation for those still repressed by the same paternal myth Quentin Compson longed to resurrect. This contrast finds a parallel in Shegog's sermon, in his *voice* which modulates from one which "sounded like a white man" to another voice that "consumed him, until he was nothing and they were nothing and there was not even a voice but instead their hearts were speaking to one another in chanting measures beyond the need for words . . ." (*SF*, pp. 366 and 367).

Shegog's voice, the reader recognizes, hovers between individuality and stereotype. Yet it also suggests, perhaps inadequately, a context beyond the Compsons, one that does not merely observe and interpret the Compson world. It is no more than a moment of the otherness of an outside in this novel, for the narrative returns, in search of a conclusion, to Jason, "the first sane Compson since before Culloden and (a childless bachelor) hence the last" (*SF*, p. 420). But Jason reprised is not so much a conclusion as a stopping point. The symbolism has not contained the narrative; Benjy remains outside Oedipus, the one wholly sympathetic Compson who finally has more in common with

Dilsey and the black congregation listening to Shegog's sermon than with his brothers. The story that Faulkner wants to tell cannot be contained within the monologic points of view of the three brothers or even within the Compson family itself. It cannot be symbolized in a ruling metaphor. In writing *The Sound and the Fury* Faulkner learned that monologue and oedipal symbolism were not adequate for his narrative project to write about the South.

In a letter to Malcolm Cowley in 1949 Faulkner proposed that it was his "ambition to be, as a private individual, abolished and voided from history, leaving it markless, no refuse save the printed books."[3] Here, on the eve of his greatest fame—his reception of the Nobel Prize— Faulkner lapsed into sentimentality; his work would live beyond him, conferring on him immortality and allowing him the pleasure of having created himself in and through his books. In this we can read his final revenge on old W. C. Falkner, for in abolishing himself as "private individual" he also abolishes his family history, the reality that always lurks as a guarantee beneath the claims of authenticity in all narrative representation. But that reality never meant much to Faulkner who located the real inside narration, and the juxtaposition of "ambition" and abolition, "private" and "printed" sets off peculiar resonances in the context of Faulkner's novels. To void or abolish, to leave anything "markless" is a rather un-Faulknerian style. Faulkner revises and explores, dislocates and expands; he writes over rather than erases. The private individual was never what concerned him, for it was the public figure of legend and story that he set out to revise in "print."

There is a significant pattern in Faulkner's life from the youthful pretense of World War I heroics to the grand manner of the master of Rowan Oak in his later years. Faulkner measured himself in the public sphere in images; he was constantly about recreating himself, and in the process he seemed to stumble upon an insight that fascinated and frightened him. Writing, as it displaces the merely private, drives toward dispersal, toward the breaking down of authority, priority, even the grand genealogical dichotomies of First Ancestors and Descendants. It is this latter breakdown that is crucial, for the genealogical order of patriarchy formed both the private (familial) and the historical discursive contexts out of which and against which Faulkner composed a printed self. Faulkner consciously adopted the role of the rebellious child, of a minor breaking open a space in the continuous order of discourse so that he might speak. He revises as a minority;

perhaps it was the only position he could take as a modern southern writer, as a descendant of W. C. Falkner, writing in the shadow of The Defeat, after the fall. All the old voices of authority and authentic heroic stature had ceased to speak, although their words reverberated within his voice, threatened to silence him.

There is, therefore, too easy a sentimentality in the romantic desire to live only in books, and it is a desire figured in Quentin Compson, a character many critics simplistically identify with Faulkner himself when they hear Keatsian aesthetic escapism in Faulkner's wish to abolish himself from history. But Quentin evolves throughout Faulkner's career, evolves in reverse, "progresses" from the isolated figure of interior monologue in *The Sound and the Fury* to the revised figure of a discursive "commonwealth" in *Absalom, Absalom!* The transition from the earlier to the later work jars us; we read against career chronology, forward from *The Sound and the Fury* to discover in *Absalom, Absalom!* Quentin's public voice as it was prior to his private monologue in *The Sound and the Fury*. Here Faulkner transgresses modernist limits, making a bold move out of the private world of the aesthetic displacement of the real and into the public domain of social, historical discourse, from monologue to dialogue. It is in part a turning back to history, not to a simple nostalgic recreation of an authentic past but to the past as it functions in the present. It is the past in a dialogue with the present which forms the narrative structure of a novel like *Absalom, Absalom!*

This move reflects a self-destructive rift within modernism. Alice Jardine describes the rift in a particularly Faulknerian tone: it is the unleashing of a powerful force which is

> terrifying, *unnameable;* it can engender itself; it has no need of a mother or father. It is beyond the representation that Man has always presented himself with and controlled. It is . . . an indistinctness between the inside and the outside, between original boundaries and spaces. To think this indistinctness in the twentieth century has been to think a crisis of indescribable proportions, to throw all of the Big Dichotomies into question: for if the exterior is interior, then the interior is also exterior; Man's soul is outside of himself; history is but the exterior of his own no longer interior imagination.[4]

Jardine's language is melodramatic like Faulkner's. She describes a postmodernist vision glimpsed from inside modernism, which is, perhaps, the only place one may see it. The crucial emphasis rests on the power unleashed by the transgression of boundaries, a power that opens spaces of articulation which hitherto had been silenced. Just as the splitting of the atom dispersed a primal unity, so this transgression of limits, she says, is a form of "delegitimation," a "loss of the paternal fiction, the West's heritage and guarantee."[5] It is a call to arms: for Jardine it is a feminist manifesto; for Faulkner it began as the opening of a narrative space for the voices of children, especially for the male Descendants of First Ancestors. Yet soon it came to embrace other minorities repressed in the paternal fiction: blacks, and, admittedly, all too infrequently, women. The question in reading Faulkner is not so much whether a mature white male southern writer can speak for others, can give a legitimate voice to children, blacks, and women, for Faulkner found this task always beyond him. The question is whether he wanted to undertake the task at all, and this he most certainly did. In transgressing the boundaries of his personal paternal fiction he discovered its social and political pervasiveness. The insight was frightening, for Faulkner's effort to represent the voice of the other, the dispersing, deconstructive voices within the paternal model of meaning, led him to venture into strange languages, those Jardine rightly notes he would have considered "mad, unconscious, improper, unclean, . . . profane."[6] Yet he did raise these voices more often than one would expect, and the inaugural event of this venture was *The Sound and the Fury* or, more precisely, the "failure" of that novel.

Faulkner's deconstruction of the South's cavalier mythology parallels the modernist crisis of delegitimation. The paternal order of meaning that supports this mythology had to be unmanned in order to damage it at the place of its regenerative power, but this symbolic act of oedipal revenge threatened, Faulkner sensed, to bring down the mythic ground of society itself. Faulkner's project does not, contrary to the claims of most of his Freudian critics, simply affirm oedipal authority. Faulkner's transgression is to bring this authority into question, to dare to speak, and through speaking to demythologize Oedipus. The Old South cavalier myth had been little more than an oedipal schema; to destroy one destroyed the other. Thus Faulkner's position within oedipal modernism intensified his anxiety, yet he insistently traced the Oedipus within the cavalier throughout his career. It is this testing of limits, the transgressing of the forbidden, that his most perceptive biographer, David Minter, isolates as a central motivation in Faulkner's writing. In daring to speak Faulkner expressed a taboo against speaking.

Within normative oedipal structure, the fall of the father, a wish symbolically accomplished, is coordinate with the rise of the son, the opening of the future, but Faulkner's thematizing of Oedipus as the southern cavalier, a historicizing of Oedipus, seems to portray no future. This is the locus of the Sartrean quarrel with Faulkner; it is also the source of Faulknerian melancholy and pessimism, which Sartre, among others, reads as nostalgia. Faulkner is never simply nostalgic; his interest in the past is truncated, for the Faulknerian past is always a palpable presence. What is undercut in the translation of Oedipus from the personal/familial to the social/historical are the oedipal guarantees: the repetition which legitimizes, mythologizes, symbolizes oedipal universality. Faulkner looks beyond good and evil without a trace of Nietzschean (or Derridian) gaiety. What remains is a Freudian apocalypse, a life after Oedipus which is neither oedipally secure nor regression to savagery. Neither is it utopian, and it is shot through with modernist anxiety, a sense of loss that is not merely nostalgic.

The historicizing of Oedipus narrates it. In *Totem and Taboo*, Freud also risked this temporalizing of the atemporal oedipal law in his effort to narratively reconstruct the mythic origin of oedipal authority. It is a peculiar text which seems to strain against its purposes. The story that Freud wants to tell, has to tell, is postponed, delayed, even disclaimed, yet that story triumphs in his writing. It is a spectacular tale that overwhelms Freud's scientific posing and, more important, threatens to disperse the lyric elegance of oedipal law into the limitless supplementarity of narrative. Similarly, narratizing the repressed is a tactic that Faulkner turns on the oedipal authority of his personal world, the symbolic father, W. C. Falkner. He narrates him; better stated: since the Old Colonel was already a narrative, Faulkner renarrates him, revises him, perverts him. Hence the myth is demythologized into history, the hero dispersed into multiple voices. There is no room for nostalgia here, and in this sense Faulkner is more radical in his transgression of repressive limits than is Sartre. Sartre's existential freedom rests on his at least half-serious claim that his father's early death left him with no "superego," with "a most incomplete Oedipus complex."[7] Thus absolved from the repressive past, from history, he berates Faulkner for dwelling too lovingly in it, but Sartre spent much of his life trying to reintegrate an unsentimentalized history into his existential thought. Faulkner's autobiographical narratives are utterly different as they subject the terms of oedipal legitimacy to historical demythologizing; Faulkner, unlike Sartre, begins with the stifling presence of the oedipal Father and disperses him into dialogue.

It is not a sustained effort, yet we are aware of its moments. We detect it in broad patterns. The revising of young Bayard into Quentin Compson deepens the central figure of Faulkner's modernism: the anti-hero suffering the agony of obsessive self-analysis, the suicidal guilt that affirms oedipal authority, the nostalgic mythology of better men and more heroic times. Quentin is an important figure of genealogical decline for Faulkner, yet Faulkner clearly took a wrong direction in *The Sound and the Fury,* and therefore in *Absalom, Absalom!* he revises his central figure, who becomes invaded by dialogue, by voices other than the father's, by subversive voices that cannot be silenced. In *Go Down, Moses* he is revised again. This time, as Ike McCaslin, he possesses the social consciousness that Quentin so clearly lacked in *Absalom, Absalom!* but still has Quentin's fatal flaw: the nostalgia for a utopian, pre-oedipal state. Then he is revised once more; as Chick Mallison in *Intruder in the Dust* he enters into a collective, minority voice that overthrows masculine authority, that itself revises paternal discourse. We can document the rise of the son, the emergence of the Descendant, the voicing of the unvoiced in this series of revisions.

The contrary motion of the fall of the oedipal father is even more dramatic in the chain of revisions that links the Sartoris, Sutpen, and McCaslin patriarchs in a decline from legend to the corruption of the flesh old Carothers McCaslin exhibits in his repugnant act of incestuous miscegenation. More radically, in *Intruder in the Dust* all of the genealogical pretensions of the oedipal/cavalier myth are conspicuously absent. It is as if by that time neither Faulkner nor the reader needs those guarantees. And yet they are not so distant that we are likely to forget them, for the presence in the novel of Lucas Beauchamp, the black descendant of the white McCaslin patriarch, reminds us of what we have passed through, perhaps been liberated from.

What is extraordinary in the Faulkner critical tradition is that so few critics have noted the sustained and powerful attack on Oedipus that drives Faulkner's narrative. His narrators are mostly members of minorities; *The Sound and the Fury,* for example, rests on the point of view of children. This does not, of course, necessarily produce anti-oedipal strategies. It does pitch the narrative voice in the register of social and political concerns, for the writer's selection of the gender, race, and class of his narrator cannot be protected from judgment behind a veil of aesthetic innocence. Who speaks and who does not is a matter of political importance, and the social implications are complex and sometimes contradictory. It is a device of mystification when the First Ancestor is given no direct voice in the narrative; John Sartoris remains remote and sublime in *Flags in the Dust* until he is revised into the dialogic structure of *The Unvanquished*. The figure of legend needs to be narrated into heroic stature by others who commemorate and preserve the myth. For this particular figure of the symbolic father, to be given a voice is to be brought into the presence of discursive practice, which familiarizes that which had been defamiliarized into symbol.

Yet Faulkner is very little interested in exposing the "true" nature of his great patriarch figures; the revision of John Sartoris shows rather the disillusion of his son Bayard, the son's refusal to repeat the heroic codes of behavior that the symbolic father expressed. How different is this son from Quentin Compson who longs to resurrect the symbolic order of Oedipus. *The Unvanquished* is possible only after the failure of Quentin, that is, after the failure to order the narrative of *The Sound and the Fury* under an oedipal symbolic. Faulkner's concern is not to present the authentic version of the Old South but rather to follow the consequences of Old South mythmaking. He traces the manner in which the commemorators and preservers trap themselves in their own stories, involve themselves as victims of the oedipal structures they help create. Such is Quentin's fate, although this is not clearly worked out until *Absalom, Absalom!* reprises Faulkner's most pathetic Descendant figure. The inheritors of Oedipus occupy Faulkner's attention. Here again his strategy is complex, even contradictory. The oedipal model is essentially Sophoclean rather than Freudian, and in Faulkner there is an unexpected anti-Freudian recovery, an unleashing of an oedipal repressed. The children of Oedipus were four, two sons and two daughters. The fates of three are clear; one daughter, Ismene, seems forgotten, eclipsed by the heroic and tragic end of her sister, Antigone. If there is any real sense in which Oedipus is redeemed from his tragic fate, it must be through Antigone, whose death questions the foundations of law and authority, but does so honorably, heroically.

Antigone's fate in Western culture, particularly in the nineteenth and twentieth centuries, is especially revealing. For George Steiner it is the eclipse of Antigone that marks the transition from romanticism to modernism.

> Between the 1790's and the start of the twentieth century, the radical lines of kinship run horizontally, as between brothers and sisters. In the Freudian construct they run vertically, as between children and parents. The Oedipus complex is one of inescapable verticality. The shift is momentous; with it Oedipus replaces Antigone.[8]

Steiner's genealogical trope of the vertical displacing the horizontal is particularly appropriate to the authoritarian, paternal meaning structures that are derived from Freud's repression of the genealogical consequences of Oedipus' transgression: that is, his children, particularly Antigone. Such a consequence would call oedipal order itself into question through the voice of the other. In Faulkner's later novels this voice undermines patriarchal authority, subverts the social order of the Old South mythology, and rewrites the legend of the First Ancestor. The "other" voice assumes a broad function in this narrative model; it is the voice of the minority whether this minority be one of gender, class, or race. It finds its most remarkable exemplar in Thomas Sutpen's black daughter, Clytemnestra, in *Absalom, Absalom!* Mr. Compson argues that she is misnamed, should have been called Cassandra, and she is appropriately a virtually silent presence who nonetheless without any voice reveals the fatal flaw in Sutpen's dynastic design. Clytemnestra/Cassandra foretells, as she doubles her half-brother, Charles Bon, the fall of the Sutpens, and thereby she also betokens the fall of the Old South. In herself she embodies, as symbol of presence itself, the racial contradiction of marketplace and family values that corrupted the Old South from within. She is the voice of voiceless minorities, more powerful as a symbol in that she merges the two strongest themes of Faulkner's novels: gender and race. That cultural perspective is still absent from the rather narrow and ahistorical oedipal mythology of *The Sound and the Fury.* There we read: modern Oedipus must have no daughters, or, at the least, they must remain silent.

Faulkner's sister/daughter figure, Caddy Compson, stands in the place of Antigone/Ismeme; that is, she is outside the narrative, no place with no voice. In *The Sound and the Fury,* as we have seen, Caddy seems no more than a symbol of the brothers' incestuous desires, a "fiction within the fiction": "One might even argue that Caddy is little more than a blank counter, an empty signifier, a name in itself void of meaning and thus apt to receive any meaning."[9] Caddy is such a symbol, and Bleikasten's reading here is clever, but such a reading reflects Quentin's symbolizing turn of mind, not Faulkner's. Faulkner only seems to be dramatizing the full implications of what Steiner labels as modernism's momentous shift from Antigone to Oedipus. In crucial moments of the novel Caddy does not function as a blank counter; rather she emerges as a fully developed character whose voice threatens to break through the aesthetic (oedipal) defenses of Quentin's monologue. Perhaps this is the irrepressible consequence in Benjy's section, but it also shows itself in textual ambiguities in Quentin's repressive oedipal monologue. The scene of Quentin's failed suicide/incest with which we began this chapter contains an instructive example. The tangled style of the narrative constantly frustrates the reader's desire to know who is speaking; wholly distributed within an interior monologue, narrative dialogue (remembered, fantasized) is reduced to the play of conventional symbols, to lyric. Yet here in the ambiguity of a single line, dialogue threatens to disrupt monologic authenticity and authority. We first sense it in Caddy's tone, which does not fit Quentin's idealizing fantasy of suicide/incest, his romantic tempting of oedipal authority in order to affirm oedipal power. Caddy suggests another point of view: "it wont do any good dont you know it wont let me go" (*SF*, p. 191). The literal, dramatic reference in this line is to Quentin's apparent effort to prevent Caddy from meeting her lover in the woods by physically holding her back, yet the "it" also refers to Quentin's romantic ideal of incest/suicide. We read this line in two ways. On the literal, dramatic level it has three clauses: (1) it wont do any good (2) dont you know it wont (3) let me go. The lack of punctuation also allows us to read the line as two clauses: (1) it wont do any good (2) dont you know it wont let me go. This second reading intrudes otherness into Quentin's monologue. The line says: what may provide release for Quentin will not work for Caddy, "me." Freedom for Caddy does not reside in Quentin's fantasy, in his holding her or possessing her.

Caddy's voice contains a primal sense of denial, and, therefore, of an-other kind of strength, but Faulkner's representation of this female otherness gives it the shape of perversity and promiscuity. The feminine becomes for him a weapon to challenge the hegemony of the oedipal father, the symbol of authority, but our primary sympathies are clearly supposed to go with the male Compson children, those Descendant figures repressed by the First Ancestor, by the symbolic father in Quentin's oedipal monologue. Caddy's degradation, her fate in becoming the mistress of a Nazi army officer, as Faulkner wrote it in the appendix to *The Sound and the Fury*, merely solidifies her function as metaphor of dissolution and perversion, brings her again under oedipal hegemony. Faulkner is bound by oedipal symbolism even as he struggles against it. Yet the narrative of other voices emerges here as a tool of deconstruction, as a challenge to the monologic authority of the paternal structure of meanings and values in the southern culture Faulkner was concerned to represent in his Yoknapatawpha novels.

The repression of Antigone is a repression of one portion of genealogy, a repression of certain consequences that would play themselves out across time and history, a repression of narrative. In that spirit, Faulkner's narration of the oedipal/cavalier myth uncovers progeny, traces the consequences of myth upon history, allowing for at least the momentary return of the repressed. This is the central theme of *Absalom, Absalom!* but the process is initiated in *The Sound and the Fury* with the exposing of Quentin's modernist nostalgia for a romantic ideal. Steiner unknowingly describes Quentin Compson's neurotic desires.

> There is only *one* human relationship in which the ego can negate its
> solitude without departing from its authentic self. . . . It is a relation
> between man and woman, as it surely must be if primary rifts in being are
> to be knit. But it is a relation between man and woman which resolves
> the paradox of estrangement inherent in all sexuality (a paradox which
> incest would only enforce). It is the relation of brother and sister, of
> sister and brother. . . . It is here, and here only, that the soul steps into
> and through the mirror to find a perfectly concordant but autonomous
> counterpart. The torment of Narcissus is stilled: the image is substance,
> it is the integral self in the twin presence of another. Thus sisterliness
> is the ontologically privileged beyond any other human stance. In it, the
> homecomings of Idealism and Romanticism are given vital form. This
> form receives supreme, everlasting expression in Sophocles' *Antigone*.[10]

Such a golden ideal has no trace of romantic innocence in Faulkner's recovery of it; it signals in Quentin merely neurosis. Coming after the oedipal eclipsing of Antigone, it questions not the biological primacy of the oedipal father but his authority; it questions the universality, the mythic stature, of mere repetition, the son who images the father, by opening the space for others, for the schizophrenic dislocation of identity in the horizontal genealogical link between brother and sister. It is radical and, therefore, frightening, mysterious, monstrous; it is the perversity that underlies all revisionary narrative strategies, the undoing of knots, the dispersing of collectivities. For Faulkner the voice of the recovered Antigone figure is the expression of delegitimation, and because of this it is a weapon powerful enough to deconstruct the oedipal/cavalier myth.

This voice is female. Yet we cannot name Faulkner's recovery of it feminist. Nor is it clear that Antigone, restrained as a consequence of the rise of Oedipus, as the dutiful daughter and sister of genealogical narrative possesses metaphoric power sufficient to embody the anti-oedipal. Can the voice against oedipal repression issue from the repressed, or must it speak from some more privileged position? We are far from having resolved this dilemma; the question has only been approached, not even well stated. My purpose here is more modest; for Faulkner does not want to recognize even the possibility of the anti-oedipal question, and yet his deconstruction of the oedipal/cavalier mythology of the modern South forces that question on him in the voice of the repressed. He deflects the feminist implications of that voice, seems not to know the legend of Antigone. In that way he is a Freudian modernist. The female voice of repression is transcribed, dispersed into the voices of male children (the Descendant figures) or into slaves and descendants of slaves. The female voice is filtered, distanced, disrupted, finding perhaps its most powerful expression in *Go Down, Moses* in Molly Beauchamp and especially the unnamed black woman of "Delta Autumn." *Go Down, Moses* begins in a strictly masculine world—the antebellum South, although certainly not the South of aristocratic splendor—and concludes in a world Faulkner defensively presents as subverted by women. This feminine presence in *Go Down, Moses* marks the final deconstruction of the oedipal/cavalier myth, the last revision of the legend of the great-grandfather. It is the recovery of the female voice, a recovery that is often accidental or unwanted, that Faulkner's central character responds to with disease. Nevertheless, the female voice of the recovered Antigone does emerge in Faulkner's narratives, often in the midst of the most firmly oedipal, paternal monologue. In these moments the potential for dialogue appears within a monologic text deeply resistant to the dialogic voice of the other.

Most immediately, Faulkner's failure to control the monologic narrative of *The Sound and the Fury* produced another version. *As I Lay Dying* seems to be motivated by a desire to establish authorial mastery, to risk everything and then rescue the narrative at the last moment. That risk comes in the form of Faulkner's most powerful female voice yet; this time it is not that of the sister, the romantic Antigone figure. This time it is the voice of the mother whose power over her sons almost allows her to overthrow the father's authority. By putting down this figure of perversion, Faulkner affirms the oedipal once more. It is, however, an affirmation of narrative skill that only momentarily shores up modernist Oedipus against his destruction. *As I Lay Dying* is a major work in the evolution of the Yoknapatawpha narrative, a work that continues to test oedipal order at its limits.

CHAPTER 11

A Writing Lesson: *As I Lay Dying* as tour de force

T HE ENDING of *As I Lay Dying* is outrageous. The narrative is resolved by a deus ex machina. A new character is introduced in the final pages; a crucial character materializes as if by magic. Who would marry Anse Bundren on the day of his first wife's funeral, on the spur of the moment with no previous introduction? Of course, Faulkner gives us some hints. Kate Tull tells us on the day of Addie's death that Anse will "get another one before cotton-picking" (*ALD*, p. 32), and Cash lets the matter slip in his reference to a "Mrs. Bundren" several pages before the novel's conclusion (*ALD*, p. 225). But Anse's new wife is a narrative surprise, a punch line, a violation of "realistic" narrative by a device more typical of allegory.

There is an explanation; Faulkner concludes *As I Lay Dying* with authority, as a demonstration of his narrative skill, an answer to those who doubted his formalist talents in the earlier Yoknapatawpha novels. The novel as tour de force aestheticizes, narratizes oedipal law, and myth thus becomes a model form for storytelling, for representation of social action. The ending is inevitable because Anse's remarriage is a natural extension of his oedipal authority to confer his name. The family needs a new mother; Anse provides a new "Mrs. Bundren." The ambiguities of authentic experience are glossed over. Faulkner is very modern here; the Bundrens are unencumbered by genealogy, by history. The novel focuses exclusively on the present, highlighting the dynamics of the structure of the family. The family is the principle of order for the

150

narrative; the plot traces a movement from the threatened disintegration of family unity resultant upon Addie's death to the resurrection of
the family through Anse's remarriage. Oedipal authority in an oedipal
society provides a natural conclusion to the family narrative.

But to judge *As I Lay Dying* a tour de force performance has specific
negative implications: that the novel is marked by unjustifiable, inartis-
tic authorial manipulation. Such a narrative is merely clever. It is this
cleverness that is important, of course, if we are to place the novel in
the developmental sequence of Faulkner's career. Although it has much
in common with *The Sound and the Fury*, *As I Lay Dying* departs
significantly from the narrative experimentation of the earlier work.
Faulkner's "failure" to tell the complete story of the Compsons led him
to the focus necessary to tell the whole story of the Bundrens. If *The
Sound and the Fury* lacks a sense of an ending, *As I Lay Dying* asserts
finality in a well-made comic ending: a marriage. Surprisingly, the fragmenting effect of the isolated monologues of *The Sound and the Fury* is
overcome in *As I Lay Dying* by fragmenting the monologues even more
radically. Instead of three monologues and a desperate third-person
narration designed to bring order out of chaos, *As I Lay Dying* juggles
fifty-nine monologues in what appears to be a random sequence so that
the highly distinct personalities of individual characters are blurred
through an overlap, an interpenetration of interiorities. The Bundrens
think alike to the extent that they often know what other family members are thinking without conversation. The issue here is a blending
of individuality into a collectivity within the oedipal structure of the
family. The smallest unit of identity is the individual; the largest is the
community. Between these two is an elastic zone named "Bundren"
where boundaries are unclear and individual and community meet.

The outrageous ending of the novel also displaces bodies of experience, affirms the priority of words. "Addie" can be rewritten as "Mrs.
Bundren"; "mother" surrenders priority to "wife"; biology (childbirth)
is subject to the conventions of exchange, of autonomous symbolic
meanings. The ubiquitous signifier covers over, buries, its signifieds.
Faulkner seems on the threshold of postmodernist freeplay, abandoning altogether the seductive allure of the modernist vision of authentic
experience. Real power, social and aesthetic, resides in the authority of
the one who confers names, the modern Adam who is Oedipus' double.
But there are substantial reservations in Faulkner; the cavalier displacement of the mother fails to erase Addie Bundren's powerful hold on our
readerly consciousness. It is she who affirms for us the consequences

of symbolic authority on the body of experience, in feelings of pleasure and pain (mostly the latter in this instance). This is what makes the ending outrageous, our sympathy for the woman, a sympathy staged by Faulkner in his representation of the reprehensible man, Anse Bundren. It is as though the ending deliberately controverts the force that flows throughout the novel up to the final page; there Faulkner concludes what he had, through Addie's lingering, made inconclusive.

The title of *As I Lay Dying* locates the narrative in a continuous present which problematizes aesthetic closure, but closure can be found in the modernist updating of Keatsian frozen moments where process replaces product and mere labor is idealized as self-expressive work. Process art is pure art, capturing the flow of present experience within a metaphoric unity. The journey to Jefferson to bury Addie provides a motif that promises a conclusion, but the narrative continually defers this ending. "Death" is rewritten as "Dying," implying the processes of decay and disintegration of the narrative itself. Process, plot, narrative structure reveal their affinities with desire. Addie's presence decomposes family and narrative order by delaying a proper conclusion, but this delay, as the expression of desire, is also the space of narrative; it is the opening of a world that is peopled with individuals struggling to escape the loneliness of the loss of the central defining figure (metaphor) of their lives. Their story lacks a mother.

Conclusions, therefore, are at issue on every level. Conclusions even define character; in particular, Addie strives to conclude the Bundren story in her way, through a lingering presence that extends beyond death, beyond the grave. She does so by occupying the consciousnesses of her children, particularly her sons. She attempts to drive Anse out of her narrative into the background. She makes an impression; she is a felt presence and is remembered.

> I knew that it had been, not that they had dirty noses, but that we had to use one another by words like spiders dangling by their mouths from a beam, swinging and twisting and never touching, and that only through the blows of the switch could my blood and their blood flow as one stream.
>
> (*ALD*, p. 164)

She claims: "My children were of me alone . . ." (*ALD*, p. 167). Consciousness for Addie is of the body, sensual, experiential; the mind is formed around feelings of pleasure and pain, and writing begins as a lasting inscription on, into the flesh, in a releasing of a flow of blood like the flow of ink on the blank page, like the flow in menstruation. Does Faulkner hint at an *écriture féminine*? I think not, in the strictest sense of that designation, for Addie's writing turns out to be simply a negative of masculine authority, an "other" of the male author, an unnaming, a delegitimation.

Addie's power resides in an extended process of reproduction which merges gestation, parturition, and nurture; hers is the enduring power of touching which precedes, displaces, and deconstructs language. Giving birth to her first child, Cash, is a revelation.

> That was when I learned that words are no good; that words dont ever fit even what they are trying to say at. When he was born I knew that motherhood was invented by someone who had to have a word for it because the ones that had the children didn't care whether there was a word for it or not.
>
> (*ALD*, p. 163)

Identity is experiential, for names have no effect on reality.

> And when I would think *Cash* and *Darl* that way until their names would die and then fade away, I would say, All right. It doesn't matter. It doesn't matter what they call them.
>
> (*ALD*, p. 165)

Lurking in the background here is Freud, the child as completion of the woman, the child as phallus: "My aloneness had been violated and then made whole again by the violation . . ." (*ALD*, p. 164). Her children are extensions of her body, of her personality, and of her consciousness. They are her phallic power as an autonomous reproductive machine.

Addie's existential faith, however, becomes entangled in Faulkner's conventional appropriation of childbirth as a metaphor for writing; her dismissal of words, naming, and the authority that accompanies mastery of language makes her a threatening figure. Faulkner represents Addie not as a woman excluded from masculine language but as a woman who challenges the authority of masculine symbolic order. Addie is militant. She delegitimizes Oedipus in the production of an illegitimate son, Jewel. She is, from the oedipal perspective, from Faulkner's point of view, evil, not merely a unity challenging another unity but an incomprehensible plurality: "I was three now," she says after the birth of her third child (*ALD*, p. 165). She is chaos, a "natural" force for dispersal. The unfaithful wife and domineering mother are linked to promiscuity, to Faulknerian characters like Caddy Compson and Temple Drake. Addie's obsessive cleaning of her house is both defensive and repressive, an erasing of names that delegitimizes and castrates.

Faulkner's representation of Addie is so conventionally and narrowly oedipal that it seems hardly in need of explication. The woman as wife/ mother is a necessary evil defined by a reproductive capacity that is inherently anti-authoritarian. Addie's power to regenerate herself in and through her children gives her a lingering presence that defies narrative authority, postpones an ending through the infinite extension of the body, the infinite multiplication of experiences. Addie is Faulkner's metaphor of the body of otherness which he must contain in an assertion of the primacy of the symbolic order. Reproductive potency must be recaptured on the level of textual play; that is, the extension of the narrative, the multiplication of its parts, the fifty-nine monologues, must seem an adequate form for Addie's experiential resistance to language. Aesthetic closure is all the more convincing when it encloses a serious challenge to its authority.

The assertion of narrative authority, therefore, resides in the disposition of bodies; the conclusion is as inevitable as death, for the patriarchal myth of Oedipus is nothing more than a disposing of bodies, a burial of the dead. Yet, in an odd postmodernist twist, putting Addie in her place rests on a freeing of the narrative from its bondage to presence, on the unleashing of freeplay. Aesthetic closure in *As I Lay Dying* erases personality, individuality; "Addie" is rewritten as "Mrs. Bundren" in order to translate the particular and unique into the conventional. Even the personalities of the children seem less distinct at the novel's end. But difference as supplementarity on the level of the signifier alone grows pale and reveals its kinship with formalism, aestheticism, and tour de force performance. There is, then, an inevitable modernist reaction in Faulkner's writing, for the body, once disposed, returns to haunt the narrative. References to the body do not disappear but are obsessively multiplied. Thus writing is continually disrupted by the body in the form of metaphor, the birth metaphor which marks the masculine appropriation of the feminine, the symbolic appropriation of reality.

This uncovering of anti-Oedipus within Oedipus, of course, merely reflects modernist antinomies: narrative authority as opposed to experiential authenticity, form as opposed to content. Nevertheless, in its thematic exploration of the symbolic appropriation of reality, *As*

I Lay Dying contains the point of departure for Faulkner's strategy of narrative revision. Recognition of a feminine presence within the masculine symbolic order, a presence that accounts for both desire and the writer's productive power, also uncovers an otherness rooted in revenge, the revenge not of the son against the father, nor of the Descendant against the First Ancestor, but of the mother/sister against the father/brother.

It is appropriate, therefore, that revenge is the theme of Addie's monologue in *As I Lay Dying*. Addie's revenge is a haunting, the return of the voice of the "(m)other" from the grave, the metaphor of continuous, inescapable presence. This is Addie's crucial ambiguity; she is the most vital character in the novel, yet we do not hear her voice until long after she has been pronounced dead. Faulkner is experimenting with Addie's voice, with the voice of the "(m)other." He is not yet ready to employ its revisionary power, for the modernist (oedipal) will-to-conclusion is still too strong in him. As a consequence, Anse never knows of Addie's revenge, and he appropriates her death for his own purposes: new false teeth and a new wife. Faulkner's symbolism has grown bold here. Anse suffers very little as the narrative progresses; he remains aloof and reserved, as if he knew all along the proper conclusion of this cautionary, oedipal tale. Addie's revenge is silent, and Faulkner's text is unclear at the crucial moment of her annunciation of it. Is this revenge her wish to be buried in Jefferson, or her affair with Whitfield, or her symbolic murder of Anse as she dismisses his presence in the emptiness of his name? The revenge of the "(m)other" is unspeakable unless it can be appropriated as another form of revenge, revenge against the great-grandfather's legendary authority and authenticity, against the better man of a better, more heroic time in Faulkner's genealogical myth of the Old South. This is the myth that he will go to any length to deconstruct.

We must begin, therefore, with the observation that *As I Lay Dying* is a novel about the separation of language and the body, a narrative about the loosening of the functional and ontotheological bond between the proper name "Addie" and the body of her presence. The novel conventionally represents the "feminine" as a limit of the (masculine) norm (a limit of the symbolic), as hysteria (as the womb or body). We may go even further, for modernist aestheticism, with its emphasis on formal closure, has its roots in the effort to drive a wedge between words and their meaningfulness, in the formalist ideology of self-referentiality which violently orders words at the expense of the world. And, finally, the particular case of Addie Bundren puts us at the crossroads between the Oedipus myth and modernist language theory. The triumph of oedipal conclusions in the novel follows directly from her theory of language, her separation of words and experiences, and the reader recognizes in this her complicity in her own repression. Of course, we also recognize that we are reading from inside Oedipus; Faulkner locates Addie's power in her lingering presence, in her body, and that is her narrative weakness. The conclusion is inevitable because Anse's contrary power is in words. Addie's chapter, with its division of doing and saying, establishes the terms of the dramatic reversal which reveals itself in the conclusion to the novel.

The result is that Addie's chapter must be read as doubled. The immateriality of the word is the locus of Addie's power over Anse within her monologue, but the separation of language and the body puts words and things into a reversible relationship. Language can (and will) be used to deconstruct presence. Within Addie's monologue we do not immediately see the end coming. Addie's revenge rests on what she thinks is her secret.

> He did not know that he was dead, then. Sometimes I would lie by him in the dark, hearing the land that was now of my blood and flesh, and I would think: Anse. Why Anse. Why are you Anse. I would think about his name until after a while I could see the word as a shape, a vessel, and I would watch him liquefy and flow into it like cold molasses flowing out of the darkness into the vessel, until the jar stood full and motionless: a significant shape profoundly without life like an empty door frame; and then I would find that I had forgotten the name of the jar. I would think: The shape of my body where I used to be a virgin is in the shape of a   and I couldn't think *Anse*, couldn't remember *Anse*.
>
> (*ALD*, p. 165)

Addie's transformation of a name into a thing allows her to cut Anse out of her consciousness, out of her personal experience. But the freeing of words from things also empowers Anse's concluding repression of Addie, his depersonalization of her name into "Mrs. Bundren." The point is that the separation of language and the body allows Addie's personal identity as mother/wife to be rewritten as an encoded set of symbolic functions. If Addie's name, like Anse's name, can be collapsed into materiality, the name can also be interred with the body and another name, "Mrs. Bundren," supplemented. Addie's forgetting of Anse's name takes the form of a symbolic castration. But, then, the blank on the page is nothing more than a sexist cliché, the representation of the female as lacking. The place of the feminine in this representation is other-than-language, a place of desiring. Here, too, the female-other is merged with the "land" to which it must be summarily returned, and because of this naturalization, the female-other simply comes to represents the threat of castration/death, the breakdown of oedipal symbolic order. The ambiguities of Addie's chapter, particularly this crucial passage of sexual/textual violence, contain the threads of the narrative's conclusion.

In *As I Lay Dying*, therefore, the limits of oedipal authority are defined by the female body, what Alice Jardine terms *jouissance*, the play of the child/savage which suggests mystery and chaos, the realm of nonknowledge which is a "space coded as feminine."[1] The blank in the text represents absence, the condition of lacking, the missing phallic term. It is not so much that something here is censored but rather that the space of the feminine is forbidden; Jardine uses the term *inter-dit*. The place of the encoded, repressed, woman is between speaking, in the silences between words and letters, the between of interdiction wherein "inter" has an uncanny link with the latinate verb *to inter*. Thus the space of the feminine is always after death, always from an enforced absence, from a covering over, from out of taboo. The female body is not the proper subject of oedipal conversation. Citing Lacan, Jardine says: the "between words, between-the-lines, provides an access to what is perhaps the most important discursive limit . . . , the Real."[2]

Addie is unknowingly forced to speak against herself, against her will. She cannot easily rid herself of the power that resides in words. Her presence is easily metaphorized; "the Real," which is a limit of language's representational force and not reality, is expressed tropologically in the novel as a feminized landscape. Everything is gathered into a grand symbolic pattern that rests on an elemental composition of the world. Bleikasten notes this pattern in his reading of the novel.

> Everything happens as if the elements were disputing Addie's corpse: air (the possibility of the body being left prey to the buzzards), water (the coffin immersed in the river), fire (cremation narrowly avoided in the fire scene), and earth, in which the dead woman is eventually buried, none of the "four countries of death" is missing from the novel. For Addie, the passage from life to death is not just a matter of a moment but a long

quest strewn with ambushes and perils, like the funeral crossings of myth and legend.[3]

It is more precise to say that the elements dispute the unnatural lingering of Addie's corpse; Faulkner writes as if reality, as oblivion beyond the encoded world, was merely reclaiming its own.

The encoding of reality as a female body recurs repeatedly in the novel. Perhaps most dramatic is how Darl's madness can be traced through his monologues in the widening gap that develops in his consciousness between words and things. Dewey Dell's violent hatred of Darl results in part from his detachment from real experiences, his lack of sympathy for her own "female" troubles; she metaphorizes this in the statement: "The land runs out of Darl's eyes; they swim to pinpoints" (ALD, p. 115). Darl's retreat from the land, from the body, into pure freeplay parallels his retreat from Addie. The child of Addie's rejection, Darl is put by his efforts to rid himself of Addie's corpse in ironic league with the primordial forces of nature, that extension of the feminine which touches the uncoded earth, marks the limits of the symbolic order. Yet Darl moves away from the body, rejects the body; his response to Dewey Dell's pregnancy is scornful, insulting. He watches her as she waits on the bank of the flooded river while Jewel and Vernon Tull retrieve Cash's tools from the water: "Squatting, Dewey Dell's wet dress shapes for the dead eyes of three blind men those mammalian ludicrosities which are the horizons and the valleys of the earth" (ALD, p. 156). The horizon he speaks of here is that which defines the very edges of meaningfulness, locates an extreme that presents itself as ludicrous. From Darl's perspective the representational strain of language merely reinforces the separation of language and bodies; metaphor reveals reality's absurdities.

Darl's responses are extreme but characteristic. For example, Addie's lingering presence is metaphorically associated with the elements, the weather, by Peabody, the doctor in attendance at her death.

> That's the one trouble with this country: everything, weather, all, hangs on too long. Like our rivers, our land: opaque, slow, violent; shaping and creating the life of man in its implacable and brooding image.
>
> (ALD, pp. 43–44)

The cliché expresses the oedipal encoding of mother-country, and the representational dimension of Faulkner's narrative emphasizes the rural setting as a mind-set, as a cognitive structure of knowing and expressing. Tull, commenting on the absurdity of the Bundrens' journey, finds the elemental symbolism natural, ready-to-hand: "They would risk the fire and the earth and the water and all just to eat a sack of bananas" (*ALD*, p. 133). And Lula Armstid, complicitous by her own affirmation of the symbolic order in the oedipal law which displaces the female body from proper discourse, charges that the lingering of Addie's corpse is obscene, unnatural, even illegal: Anse, she says, "should be lawed for treating her so" (*ALD*, p. 178). Addie is of the earth and must be returned to the earth; the fault, according to Lula, is Anse's, but the motives for Anse's prolonged journey to Jefferson are unknown to her. Perhaps under oedipal law the expediency of obtaining a new Mrs. Bundren would excuse the impropriety of Addie's delayed burial. The conclusion of the novel suggests that this is so.

We must not, however, reduce this novel to a simplistic oedipal theme of clichéd castration fears. The association of the female body with the land emerges in a more specific discursive practice. The narrative is mythic, but localized in space and time, intersecting with historical discourse. Bleikasten recognizes the myth when, extending the association of Addie with the elemental structure of the world, he characterizes the flooded river as "a symbol of cosmic motherhood."

> Mixed with the earth—the water is muddy, black or yellow—and therefore doubly feminine, it represents the primordial matter . . . in which all life is made and unmade. And the fact that Addie's coffin is swallowed up and almost carried away by the current (Vardaman says his mother moves like a fish in the water) confirms, if confirmation is needed, its maternal character.[4]

Yet this is not enough, or perhaps it is too much. The flooded river like all nature, like the female body, is, according to Faulkner's consistent imagery, that which must be subdued and controlled by men. The land is a source of nurture and death, just as Faulkner represents women, particularly mothers, as ambiguous symbols of good and evil. The journey is, as Anse says, "a trial" (*ALD*, p. 156), a test of manly courage and cleverness in the subduing of nature, the female, in the slaying of the dragon that is accomplished only at the cost of bearing a permanent scar. Masculinity must overcome its origins in the body/earth; masculinity is belated, an adding to the female body. Masculinity, linked to the accession to language in the Freudian schema of Lacan, merely mimics the genetic process which adds a Y chromosome to what is the priority of the female X. It is a triumph that must be won anew with each generation, in each individual male child's triumph over the mother.

Although myth is the form of this journey of masculine trial, we must not read the courage and cleverness on exhibit in it as simply heroic. Bleikasten classifies such a reading as "Humanistic" and quotes Cleanth Brooks as an example, but the passage from Brooks is curiously ambivalent.

> As a commentary upon man's power to act and endure, upon his apparently incorrigible idealism, the story of the Bundrens is clearly appalling —appalling but not scathing and not debunking. Heroism is heroism even though it sometimes appears to be merely the hither side of folly. . . . For a summarizing statement on *As I Lay Dying*, one might appeal to one of the choruses in *Antigone*: "Wonders are many, and none more wonderful than man." *As I Lay Dying* provides a less exalted but not unworthy illustration of Sophocles' judgment.[5]

The claim that "heroism is heroism" is surely as outrageous as applied to *As I Lay Dying* as the ending of *As I Lay Dying* itself. And the analogy from *Antigone*, with its repression of the feminine in the burial of the female, is startling in its unconscious appropriateness.

What is apparent is that the mythic/tragic reading of *As I Lay Dying* is in itself inappropriate, for Faulkner's narrative represents not pure consciousness but collective discursive practice. Myth is operative at the level of consciousness as an encoding of immediate experience. We must follow the conversations carefully. On one page talk shifts easily from Cash's fall from the wet roof of a barn to the fragility of the farmer's existence. And all of this occasional matter comes to rest in the oedipal mythology of the feminization of the land. In the middle of this discussion we discover an italicized passage wherein the identities of the speakers are insignificant, although the conversation before this passage had carefully named each one.

> *I dont mind the folks falling. It's the cotton and corn I mind.*
> *Neither does Peabody mind the folks falling. How bout it, Doc?*
> *It's a fact. Washed clean outen the ground it will be. Seems like something is always happening to it.*
> *Course it does. That's why it's worth anything. If nothing didn't happen and everybody made a big crop, do you reckon it would be worth raising?*
> *Well, I be durn if I like to see my work washed outen the ground, work I sweat over.*

(*ALD*, p. 85)

This discussion fades out behind Cash's angry protest: "It's them durn women" (*ALD*, p. 85). Cash's victory over elemental nature in the construction of Addie's coffin has been thwarted, appropriately, by the women who prepare Addie's body for burial. In the service of some reasoning beyond Cash's rationality, a reasoning that he can only label as perverse, they place Addie backward in her coffin, undoing what his masculine skill had accomplished in the balancing of natural forces in order to neutralize them. Balance is Cash's skill; as mastery of nature it is also a masculine skill. It is the limit of that mastery that Cash tests on the wet planks that cause his fall and injury, an event which occasions the community's condemnation of the rain that washes up the crops the men labor to harvest.

There is great dignity in the elemental struggle of these farmers, a struggle for survival, but it would be a mistake simply to read that dignity back on the Bundrens. The oedipal family that the Bundrens represent is superimposed on that struggle, and that particular family is appalling, without humanistic redemption. And since the novel tells their story, the novel is appalling; it is outrageous. Nevertheless, it is not a work easily dismissed, for in it Faulkner explores a rather radical theory. The superimposition of Oedipus on nature symbolized in the encoding of a feminine Real is set upon another layer of primordial nature that is continuous with the feminine and yet outside the limits of the symbolic order. This is the elemental nature that would reclaim Addie's body, and it is against this primal force, a nature that resists feminization, defies encoding, that Oedipus must defend itself. Oedipus cannot see this primordial nature in any other way than as female, as perverse, and as a readiness for symbolization, but Faulkner's narrative balances on this threshold without resolution. It is a countervoice within oedipal speaking that arises along with and as a consequence of Addie's complicity in her own repressive symbolization. It aligns the reader with Addie and not Anse in the recognition of the outrageousness of the conclusion. Above all, it is a voicing of a priority that defies oedipal appropriation, thus bringing down upon itself an oedipal condemnation. It is not clear whether it is real or imagined; it is just there.

We have arrived at the center of our reading of Faulkner. *As I Lay Dying* contains the intersection of three lines of force: personal psychology, literary technique, and social history. If, as so many say, the signature of Faulkner's novels is revenge, revenge against the South, against the First Ancestor (old W. C. Falkner), then the choices of subject matter and form are deeply significant. Beneath these choices is the primary one: the choice to be a writer. The tour de force characteristics of *As I Lay Dying* reveal much about these choices; in particular they reveal that revenge within Oedipus is not simply "manly," admittedly a bitter pill for Faulkner to swallow. The decision to subvert a social system constructed upon the oedipal symbolic order puts the writer on the side of the other, the beyond of the feminine.

Within this career struggle Faulkner also tests the limits of modernism, subverts its aesthetic principles in conjunction with his questioning of Oedipus. There is a pushing beyond modernist monologue, beyond the obsession with authentic self-expression, beyond experience and the body into the realm of discursive practice, dialogue. Concomitantly, there is an unraveling of the monologic, authoritarian voice of Oedipus in the insistent presence of a haunting repressed, in the voice of an-other. This is the voice of the authentic, of the body revealed in the gaps between words, a voice previously silenced by Oedipus' monologue of monologues, a voice looking for a place from which to speak. Faulkner, therefore, locates for us a threshold which he expresses most clearly in Addie Bundren's image of the "empty door frame." She describes this emptiness as a "significant shape profoundly without life" (*ALD*, p. 165). The anteriority of this profundity makes the emptiness signify the before of life, or, better, the outside ("without") of life. The phenomenology reminds us of Heidegger, for we are defining horizons or limits, limits we call "life." In the literary register life is contained within an Aristotelian plot: the beginning-middle-end form. Yet the beyond of life is not a mere regressive logical beforeness, for this profoundly significant outside has infinite extension beyond symbolic play; after symbolic action ends it doubles back as the ground, the beginning, of symbolization. What Faulkner plays upon is the link between the mortality of the body and matter, matter which can be neither created nor destroyed, only transformed, harnessed, controlled, made useful by and for man.

The threshold is not a paradox. It is the infinitely divisible gap between language and experience, the source of the problem of mimesis. Trapped within modern oedipal boundaries, the threshold is encoded as loss, as lacking, as castration. Faulkner represents this modernism as a passage from innocence to experience, the young boy's the accession to the oedipal symbolic order. It is traumatic, for it is accompanied by a realization of the corruption of the body which, in Faulkner, is always figured as a young girl's concurrent accession to maturity. Quentin and Caddy are the models. Quentin's accession to masculinity violently divides him from Caddy; it is a transition that can be represented only as isolation, aloneness, impotence, monologue, suicide. Quentin's monologue wallows in modernist nostalgia, a looking backward to a time of innocence, a return to the past that overshoots the mark and passes into oblivion, like Freud's fantastic death wish. It is crucial that we understand here that Freud's death wish can be projected only from with oedipal discourse; it too is an encoding of the beyond of the symbolic order that merges before and after into the infinite extension of the female body, the oblivion out of which life emerges and to which it returns. Hence we grasp that oedipal monologue can only end its own life in blindness, castration, or death.

Faulkner's sense of failure in *The Sound and the Fury* leads him in *As I Lay Dying* to break through that monologue on the way to another aesthetic principle that locates monologue in social discourse, in narrative rather than in lyric. I am tempted to argue that this aesthetic principle is a beyond of the beyond of the pleasure principle, but only because it involves not simply the opposition of life and death. Narrative is capable of a continuation beyond the grave, of resurrection, ghostlike presences, above all, revision. There is, therefore, a ghost, the already spoken, within every closed narrative text; there is also always the one more voice to say again what has been said before, to beg to differ, to contradict, to silence yet in that silencing to speak more loudly than before. It is no wonder that we hear other voices within even the strongest personal voice; perhaps we hear them more in that strong voice. Dialogue absorbs monologue at the risk of being repeatedly interrupted by it.

The threshold between authority and authenticity, between symbolic action and the body of experience, marks a continuum mediated by the marginalized body we call "the feminine." The issue for Faulkner, as it must be for all theorizing of gender, is the determination of the consequences of symbolic practice on actual bodies. What is said can hurt. Why does Addie's body keep on talking after her death? Why will she not (conveniently) go away? Why does she intrude, her rotting corpse stinking in the nostrils? She must be put out of sight because her body corrupts the symbolic order; her presence is stronger even as she is absent. It is Addie in the coffin, for all of the members of her family, not just a clod of earth. So she exposes the other side of the limits of symbolic order, and the horror and the dark comedy rest on the postponing of the end, on a resistance to death in the reluctance to stop talking.

The novel's outrageous ending is imposed upon the extensive narration of the journey to Addie's burial, imposed as a reassurance. The postponing of an ending reminds us of the limit of language, a limit we would like to forget. There is, moreover, no word for this state of being (Addie's lingering) that is not life or death, which has presence within the consciousness of all the other characters in the novel who are merely living. That which can be symbolized and that which cannot marks the gap between writing and   —what? Not living, not experiencing, for what is represented in the significant emptiness of the blank is beyond symbolizing. Modernism defined the limits of mind in refining the famous Cartesian dualism; what remained a mystery was the limit of the body. The journey, the narrative, postpones a destiny, the orderly return of the body to its home (Addie's burial with "her people"). Or is it a return of the home to order (Anse's provision of a new "Mrs. Bundren"), a replication of bodies, or a resurrection of the body? Does symbolization here cross the boundary between words and things? Does Anse's authoritative voice matter?

There are two essential motifs in the journey in *As I Lay Dying*. The first is a masculine test, Anse's "trial," his attempt to gain mastery of nature, to suppress the female body. We read this not so much in the rescue of Addie from flood and fire, those events that she prophesied as her resurrection from death, as a prolonging of her presence beyond the grave (*ALD*, p. 160), as in the relatively low-key passages that describe at length the efforts of Jewel and Vernon Tull to retrieve Cash's tools from the flooded river (*ALD*, pp. 153–56). The struggle, which rescues civilization from nature, involves a rudimentary test of courage (to dive into the swollen river) and skill (to measure, or rationalize, the natural forces of gravity and flowing water in order to locate the lost items). The oedipal dimensions of these acts are certainly clear. Cash's tools, the symbols of his masculine, rational mastery over nature, are rescued and returned to their rightful place.

The second motif of the journey involves Dewey Dell's effort to obtain an abortion. That she fails reflects Faulkner's and his culture's attitudes about her right to choose whether to have a baby, but the dramatization of that failure also forms a pattern of masculine commentary on the feminine. Dewey Dell is never much more than an image of mindless potency, but the real interest is in the men who deny her control over her own body. The first is Moseley, who, on conventional moral grounds, refuses to help her.

> But it's a hard life they have; sometimes a man . . . if there can ever be any excuse for sin, which it cant be. And then, life wasn't made to be easy

on folks: they wouldn't ever have any reason to be good and die. "Look here," I said. "You get that notion out of your head. The Lord gave you what you have, even if He did use the devil to do it; you let Him take it away from you if it's His will to do so. You go on back to Lafe and you and him take that ten dollars and get married with it."

(ALD, p. 192)

The second is a drugstore clerk named Skeet MacGowan who tricks her into having sex with him.

> "You come back at ten oclock tonight and I'll . . . perform the operation."
> "Operation?" she says.
> "It wont hurt you. You've had the same operation before. Ever hear about the hair of the dog?"
> She looks at me. "Will it work?" she says.
> "Sure it'll work. If you come back and get it."

(ALD, p. 237)

The final scene is with her father who takes her ten dollars. She calls him a "thief."

> "It's just a loan. God knows, I hate for my blooden children to reproach me. But I give them what was mine without stint. Cheerful I give them, without stint. And now they deny me. Addie. It was lucky for you you died, Addie."
> "Pa. Pa."
> "God knows it is."
> He took the money and went out.

(ALD, p. 246)

Here three dimensions of oedipal control are clearly expressed: oedipal morality, rape, and authority. The last, Anse's taking of the money, interprets the other two, for the purpose of these three interlocked events is to reinforce symbolic authority, the masculine right to encode the feminine, that is, to use the female body.

That the final, and summary, event should be Anse's taking of Dewey Dell's money also locates the novel's social order in a modern economy. Oedipal morality here is not feudal, is not simply a revision of the Old South's economics of slavery. The economy of the modern oedipal family eschews ownership; the wife/mother, as well as the daughter, is granted an inviolable private self, but the masculine order retains control of the mechanics of exchange. What is owned is not the body but its productivity, the right to encode and thereby profit from that productivity. Power rests on skill rather than on strength; power remains behind the scene, hidden in the strategies of manipulation and control legitimized by Oedipus.

Faulkner knows the difference between the economies of New South and Old South symbolic structures, for the link between *As I Lay Dying* and *Absalom, Absalom!* emphasizes it. The New South is modern, the Old South located in an ill-defined space between feudal and early-capitalistic schemas. The Civil War forms the historical threshold in Faulkner's narrative of these economies. Thomas Sutpen is a literalist of the imagination; his "design" is a reflection of the oedipal symbolic order, of modernist strategies of power and manipulation, but his motive is to achieve possession by strength rather than by behind-the-scenes manipulation. Sutpen is a figure of dramatic presence, posing and posturing for all to see. He seeks confirmation of his power in the visible manifestations of his sense of self. He must, therefore, have an audience; he is a man of actions, not words. Yet even within *Absalom, Absalom!* he is recognized as an anachronism. His struggle is personal, motivated by wealth or power not for themselves but as a proofs of self-worth, as means to prestige. His masculine trial is in one sense not unlike the efforts of Jewel and Tull to retrieve Cash's tools from the flooded river, but the symbolic import of Sutpen's courage and skill is far different. Sutpen raises his plantation out of virgin wilderness so that it will be known as "Sutpen's Hundred," a personal possession. On the contrary, the modern capitalist finds personalized ownership too much a burden. The modern capitalist will not be seen fighting his own slaves in a bloody test of personal strength and individual will. For Faulkner, the modern capitalist avoids confrontation, like Flem Snopes in *The Hamlet*. Business is depersonalized, anonymous, measured by profits and losses and the control of money and of productivity. It is, for Faulkner, unmanly.

Yet for all of his distaste for the modern and his frequently nostalgic and idealistic characters, Faulkner's orientation is always toward the "now." The modernist economy of control and manipulation is at the base of the struggle between Addie and Anse in *As I Lay Dying*, and the opposition between authentic experience and symbolic authority is no real contest when contained within the oedipal symbolic. So too, the old ways, the honorable and heroic ways are no longer viable in the New South. Faulkner never doubted this. Addie challenges patronymics with her own personal version of matronymics. Hers is an alternative story to the strictly patriarchal narrative of Anse's authority; Addie's story, which must be told by others, is an allegory. Olga Vickery was among the first of Faulkner's readers to note the pattern: "Through an unconscious identification with her, they [her children] faithfully reproduce, though in varying degree, her very moods as well as her attitude to the external world."[6] Vickery goes on to identify this pattern with a particular narrative form, one that contrasts directly with the narrative that features Anse: "Centrifugally, each section establishes the relationship between Addie and the character whose thoughts and observations are being recorded. Linearly, each section contributes to the sequence of actions and events which constitutes the plot."[7]

The conflict here between centrifugal and linear plot forces is a brilliant insight. Addie's plot is centrifugal because her children, most of them, are extensions, both positive and negative, of her personality. Cash is her pragmatic side, Jewel her passionate self (he has a reputation for sexual promiscuity [*ALD*, p. 32]). Darl, whose name is distorted, represents all that she hates about words and those who hide behind them. Dewey Dell is a projection of her reproductive potency, but much like Darl she is a negative integer. Anse, as Vickery claims, "lives by words alone"[8] and is, therefore, beyond Addie's influence. But, as we have seen, this is the crucial conflict of the novel. The last words of Anse's narrative are concluding remarks: "Meet Mrs. Bundren." Anse's narrative is linear and closed, bound within oedipal words, oedipal symbolic play. Addie's centrifugal narrative is little more than a delaying action, a holding off of the inevitable before the allegory of names breaks apart.

Addie is something more than a domineering mother who emasculates her sons (see the curious remark by Eula Tull at the time of Addie's death: "I reckon Cash and Darl can get married now" [*ALD*, p. 32]). The allegory of her children also reflects her economics of the family.

> I gave Anse Dewey Dell to negative Jewel. Then I gave him Vardaman to replace the child I had robbed him of. And now he has three children [Cash, Darl, and Vardaman] that are his and not mine. And then I could get ready to die.
>
> (*ALD*, p. 168)

Given her violent rejection of Anse only a few pages earlier one wonders why she feels she owes him anything. What is important about the number three—that is, about Vardaman whose birth Addie uses to settle her accounts and close the books on Bundren reproductivity—

at least insofar as Anse's expectations are concerned? She can cancel her guilt for the illegitimate Jewel with the "negative," Dewey Dell. Why Vardaman? He seems superfluous, an overproduction, an excess. Appropriately enough, we read the answer in Anse's words, the only character who is directly quoted in her monologue. Anse's voice alone penetrates her privacy: crucially, in his misunderstanding of her request, after the birth of Darl, that she be buried in Jefferson when she dies:

> "Nonsense," Anse said; "You and me aint nigh done chapping yet, with just two."
>
> (*ALD*, p. 165)

Anse's voice carries into her monologue his patriarchal authority, a demand that she recognizes and fulfills. Vardaman is the one more than "just two."

Three, of course, is also the oedipal number, and here Vardaman's being in excess returns us to oedipal economics. As a symbolic machine for harnessing reproductive power in the service of the father, the oedipal triad can be rewritten as $2 + 1 + x$ where x is an infinite series of one more. The value of x depends on natural resources (scarcity) and artificial factors of regulation (the marketplace), in other words, on the relationship between the reproductivity of the female body and the symbolic code, or between the aesthetic and the political dimensions of Faulkner's narrative. Addie's one more demystifies Oedipus, deconstructs the imposing mythology of Oedipus read as $3 + 1$ where 1 is a transcendental guarantee of oedipal authority and conclusiveness; 1 is the One.

Vardaman's excessiveness seems confirmed by the relation of most of the other characters to him; he is largely ignored. Moreover, his name, borrowed from a well-known Populist politician in Mississippi in the 1920s,[9] fractures Addie's personal allegory by introducing into it a themes of class relations and social history. Vardaman is the only Bundren with a clearly expressed class consciousness, and as such he is less a revision of Benjy Compson than an anticipation of Thomas Sutpen, the young boy on the threshold of socialization violently thrust into adulthood by a rejection at the door of the mansion or by the death of his mother. If the mythical $3 + 1$ of oedipal order represses, encodes the $2 + 1 + x$ as the "proper" Oedipal family, Vardaman's presence is disruptive, forces us to read the oedipal code as economic and political, not mystical.

So we read Vardaman as another of Faulkner's threshold children at the traumatic point of accession to the symbolic order. His entry is blocked, however, by his excessiveness; he is not a replication of the father but an integer in Addie's economy somehow related to Addie's personal allegory of the self. Vardaman is learning symbolic language, learning metaphor, a trope central to the oedipal mythology of 3 + 1. It is doubly traumatic for he is acquiring symbolic thought against the background of his mother's death, and he is learning not from the proper oedipal authority but from his brother, Darl. He learns from the most distorted oedipal figure in the Bundren house. The metaphor he picks up from Darl, a metaphor which defines the son's relationship to his mother, is extended by analogy to a personal expression of identity.

> "Jewel's mother is a horse," Darl said.
> "Then mine can be a fish, cant it, Darl?" I said.
> Jewel is my brother.
> "Then mine will have to be a horse, too," I said.
> "Why?" Darl said. "If pa is your pa, why does your ma have to be a horse just because Jewel's is?"
> "Why does it?" I said. "Why does it, Darl?"
> Darl is my brother.
> "Then what is your ma, Darl?" I said.
> "I haven't got ere a one," Darl said.
> "Because if I had one, it is *was*. And if it is was, it cant be *is*. Can it?"
> "No," I said.
> I am. Darl is my brother.
> "But you *are*, Darl," I said.
> "I know it," Darl said. "That's why I am not *is*. *Are* is too many for one woman to foal."
>
> (*ALD*, p. 95)

Darl articulates oedipal legitimacy—"pa is your pa"—suggesting that the identity of the mother is irrelevant, a matter of symbolization. Darl's disintegration, his madness, is already evident here; the play of language drives out the body, the authentic, the personal presence of Addie. What is most important, however, is the demeaning, dehumanizing reference to female reproductive excess: "*Are* is too many for one woman to foal." That excess of productivity leaves Vardaman to align himself with his brothers. Still outside oedipal symbolic order, Vardaman does not yet place himself in the masculine role of replicating the father, but Darl's cruel teasing metaphorically, symbolically displaces the young boy from his mother, from Addie. His identity is derived from serial relationships, from the flow of one metaphor of kinship to another, rather than from descent. Vardaman's confusion at this symbolic play exists against his presymbolic tracings which make death so difficult for him to understand. He remains linked to images of the body; he drills holes in Addie's coffin so she can breathe. He merely supplements Darl's metaphor of Jewel's oedipal obsession with Addie, adding one more and thereby establishing an infinite series that links him metonymically with his brothers. Anse's symbolic authority seems inadequate to stem the flow of this symbolic reproductivity, the legacy of Addie's economics of the family. Nor, ironically, can Addie's personal allegory contain the infinite series of supplementations set in motion here. The threshold once again proves to be an opening onto the beyond of the symbolic order, onto that which Oedipus cannot explain away, repress, or symbolize.

The radical verticality of oedipal genealogy has been invaded by a counterforce that cuts across descent, bisects its lines of force, interrupts its authoritative voice. Here *As I Lay Dying* opens up a revisionary practice that links all the dynastic novels from *Flags in the Dust* to *Go Down, Moses*. We need only look at the printed genealogical charts of the Sartorises and McCaslins to grasp the difference. The radical verticality of the Sartoris line emphasizes descent, masculinity, oedipal repression, all of the factors in the Sartoris fatedness and sense of decline. The McCaslins, however, represent very different lines of force. Their genealogy emphasizes collateral relationships, shows a fracturing of verticality that deemphasizes descent, displaces masculine authority, and reveals a fundamental transgression, the combined incest and miscegenation that undermines oedipal law and social order. In the McCaslins we read again of the fall of the Old South, but also of the fall of old W. C. Falkner. There is an unmasking here, a delegitimizing, a deconstruction, a historicizing of Oedipus.

That unmasking is demanded by a woman, a black woman who commands language, writing even though she cannot read or write. The last story of *Go Down, Moses*, the title story of the novel, focuses on Lucas' wife, Mollie Beauchamp. Mollie has come to town, drawn by some mysterious understanding and not by any certain knowledge of the facts, in order to arrange a funeral for her grandson, a murderer to be executed in Illinois. Mollie's mourning is contained within a largely female world, one defined not by race so much as by gender. Most significant, however, is the effect of Mollie's presence on the citizens of

Jefferson, particularly on Gavin Stevens, a white lawyer who takes care of all the arrangements for her, even collecting money from the men around the town square to cover the costs. Gavin persuades the editor of the newspaper to bear a large share of the financial burden, and together they achieve Mollie's wishes. After the ceremony, the editor tells Gavin of his own experience with Mollie.

> "Do you know what she asked me this morning, back there at the station?" he said.
>
> "Probably not," Stevens said.
>
> "She said, 'Is you gonter put hit in de paper?' "
>
> "What?"
>
> "That's what I said," the editor said. "And she said it again: 'Is you gonter put hit in de paper? I wants hit all in de paper. All of hit.' And I wanted to say, 'If I should happen to know how he really died, do you want that in too?' And by Jupiter, if I had and if she had known what we know even, I believe she would have said yes. But I didn't say it. I just said, 'Why, you couldn't read it, Aunty.' And she said, 'Miss Belle will show me whar to look and I can look at hit. You put it in de paper. All of hit.' "

> (*GDM*, p. 383)

Perhaps there is no better representation of the feminine power to demystify Oedipus than this command articulated by an illiterate black woman to the masculine figure of symbolic authority and literacy, the editor of the local newspaper. Since she is unable to read, language becomes for Mollie merely graphic, the marking of a space where symbolization takes place, the message of that symbolic act reduced to utter triviality. The obituary is a mark of presence and absence; confined wholly to the level of personal experience, the only authentic dimension to language: its dependence on the marriage of black ink and white paper. Through Mollie the symbolic order once again seems to cross its own limits, to reach into that beyond of symbolization, and to do so only at the insistence of the feminine voice pitted against the suppressive authority of the masculine law. Gavin and the editor had already decided not to "put it in the paper"; they seriously misread Mollie's will.

An Interlude on Signatures

There are two crucial letters in *Absalom, Absalom!* and both serve as framing devices. One of those letters will occupy our attentions later;

relevant here is the letter that frames chapter 4, a chapter concluding Mr. Compson's long narration. Mr. Compson gives the letter to
Quentin, noting that it is "without date or salutation or signature" (*AA*,
p. 129). He assumes, and the reader concurs, I believe, that the letter
is from Charles Bon to Judith Sutpen, that it is, for all its eccentricity,
a "love" letter, and that the very existence of this letter, to say nothing
of the lack of salutation and signature, indicates that there were "other
letters" (*AA*, p. 128). This letter is, then, part of a larger dialogue.

The circumstances that put this letter in the possession of the Compsons are also curious and exemplary; it was given by Judith to Grandmother Compson. Mr. Compson recreates for Quentin the conversation between the two women as it was transmitted to him. That
conversation, for Mr. Compson, is an incomplete explanation of Judith's motives; there is no record of whether or not Grandmother
Compson found it so puzzling. The crux of what Judith says is as
follows:

> And so maybe if you could go to someone, the stranger the better, and
> give them something—a scrap of paper—something, anything, it not to
> mean anything in itself and them not even to read it or keep it, not even
> to bother to throw it away or destroy it, at least it would be something
> just because it would have happened, be remembered even if only from
> passing from one hand to another, one mind to another, and it would
> be at least a scratch, something, something that might make a mark on
> something that *was* once for the reason that it can die someday.
>
> (*AA*, p. 127)

A conflict between masculine and feminine is reflected in Mr. Compson's incomprehension. Just as Mollie demands that her grandson's
obituary be printed in the newspaper even though she cannot read, so
the message of Judith's extraordinary gift is simply the gift itself. It
institutes a mystery, promises more than any master text can deliver;
it is exclusive, a countermessage that must be accounted for. To Mr.
Compson the letter is at the limit of comprehension, the indication, as
he repeatedly says, merely that "something is missing" (*AA*, p. 101).
That which is incomprehensible is the feminine which can be appropriated only as that which does not make sense. To appropriate the
feminine in this way is a desperate act of interpretation, textualization,
domestication. The gift of the letter pushes us beyond convention to
that which cannot be encoded.

Because of this we cannot separate the letter from its genderized lines of transmission. The gift of the letter foregrounds the act of communication, contains, therefore, the act of writing the letter in the first place. Rather than distract us from the contents of the letter, Judith's act calls attention to the letter as a complex act of composition and interpretation. From the point of view of convention, the letter, lacking a date, a salutation, and a signature, also lacks authority, or truth. It is a peculiarly detached bit of writing offering itself up for appropriation for whatever purposes, perhaps for Mr. Compson's theory of "other letters." Yet it remains inconclusive, incomplete, without legitimate credentials. What it does have, however, is the uncomfortable aura of the authentic, a gift, a mark, that something "*was.*" It is that sense that invades the writing itself, emerges as the subject matter of the letter, the some-thing that remains beyond the grave as well as beyond convention.

> *You will notice how I insult neither of us by claiming this to be a voice from the defeated even, let alone from the dead. In fact, if I were a philosopher I should deduce and derive a curious and apt commentary on the times and augur of the future from this letter which you now hold in your hands—a sheet of notepaper with, as you can see, the best of French watermarks dated seventy years ago, salvaged (stolen if you will) from the gutted mansion of a ruined aristocrat; and written upon in the best of stove polish manufactured not twelve months ago in a New England factory. Yes. Stove polish. We captured it: a story in itself.*
>
> (*AA,* p. 129)

The peculiar first sentence introduces a denial, a refusal of an "insult." The reference is to "this" letter itself, to its written form and material presence; the denial rejects the link between "voice" represented in this writing and death. This writing is both "commentary on the times and augur of the future," but not in the mere contents of the letter, rather in the materiality of paper and ink, that which can be held in the hands, which has been and is being held in the hands: Judith's, Grandmother Compson's, Mr. Compson's, Quentin's, the reader's. The legacy is long. I am not, of course, simply buying into a fiction. This letter is no more than a part of a text written by William Faulkner and published in 1936. It is, nevertheless, a curious part. It forges a link between things and symbolic meaning. The paper and ink are more than inert materials, without significance; here they have a history that stands as a warning to philosophers who overlook the obvious. If the letter lacks the convention of a date, the paper does not. The ink, here stove polish, can likewise be dated. And the black ink which mars the pure, white, virgin surface of the page is more than a mere metaphor. The paper and the stove polish represent the very conditions of the letter's composition, its occasion. They not only date its composition but personalize the act of composing.

And they do much more; the paper and the stove polish unleash symbolic play from its binding to convention. The writing of this letter is a transgression, a misappropriation and misuse of materials. The violation of paper by ink repeats a series of interlocking violations: of the old by the new, the South by the North, the aristocratic by the commonplace, the agrarian by the industrial, the white by the black. The letter is written near yet before Gettysburg, after Sherman's devastating march, at a moment when the outcome of the Civil War can no longer be in doubt even among the most faithful partisans of the Lost Cause. But this letter is written not by a partisan but merely by one who recognizes beforehand the South's postwar plunge into the role of the victimized. The writer knows also the victim's increasing vulnerability the more the victim affirms the old values as those values are destroyed. Therefore, out of the story of its own material composition the letter proposes: "*We have waited long enough*" (*AA*, p. 131). And that waiting, concurrent with the war itself, ends with the war. A letter, the very material existence of which reproduces the defeat of the Old South, proposes that as a consequence of that defeat, no barriers remain to some unnamed, and perhaps heretofore forbidden, act. Why would we not, therefore, simply supply the absent salutation and signature? Judith's giving of the letter seems to establish her rights to it as receiver; the circumstances of its composition seem to identify only Charles Bon. We can never be sure, but the indications are no less strong than in any act of historical interpretation. The mystery seems solved as we imagine Bon, knowingly motivated by revenge or unknowingly motivated by love, finalizing a proposal of marriage that was legally impossible before the war and now seems a violation of a universal taboo.

We cannot be satisfied, however, with this simple reading. The lack of date, salutation, and signature is wholly fictional, as are Judith and Bon and the placing of the communication near the end of the Civil War. The letter is more than fictional as we react to the text we hold in our hands. It is actually addressed to the reader from William Faulkner, but how can we supply such a signature; how dare we under the powerful restrictions of poststructuralism which always deconstructs the author's signature? The answer, of course, is to recognize the production of texts, to read writing, in a radically different manner from that of the poststructuralists. Writing does not proceed out of freeplay; it originates in specific material conditions which engage freeplay. The validity of a signature is denied by freeplay philosophies even more hysterically than the personal is opposed in modernist formalism. There is something of a straw man here; a signature damages freeplay at its heart only if it signifies personality, individuality, an inviolable self. Yet it never does that. A signature is, certainly, a part of the text, and like the text, the signature is contextualized in the sense that personal expression cannot exist outside of collective discursive practice. There is no true monologue. A signature, therefore, marks a place of violation; in Faulkner it also marks a place of revision. Judith's letter, without date or salutation or signature, is Faulkner's proposal to write, to revise, to violate the Old South myth, to demystify the legendary history of the Falkners of Mississippi. Faulkner may not know the future of his enterprise any more than does his fictional character, Charles Bon, in proposing that he and Judith have waited long enough. Writing is not prophecy; it is a struggle against convention, against what has already been said, against all the voices that would appropriate the writer's personal voice, and against the material conditions of composition, that is, against life. This last is not simple facticity, but the encoded Real that establishes limits for what may be said. Bon's proposal strikes against the boundaries of the possible; it is not abstract but located in history, grounded in time and place. Faulkner's proposal is no different.

CHAPTER 12

The Narrative Scene: The Voice of the Body

R OSA COLDFIELD'S narrative in *Absalom, Absalom!* contains all of the terms of Faulkner's autobiographical dismantling of Old South cavalierism, but Rosa does not speak for the author. Like those of all of Faulkner's female characters, Rosa's voice is disruptive, marginal, and oppositional with regard to traditional masculine narrative authority. She functions as a certain type of the southern woman, although she is not stereotypical. Her individuality (she is one of Faulkner's most memorable characters) emerges within and against the narrative structure or context of *Absalom, Absalom!*—within and against the discursive practices of Faulkner's Jefferson, Mississippi. In her eccentricity she is, nevertheless, a typical participant in the patterns of community behavior; her story of Thomas Sutpen is, according to Quentin Compson,

> part of his twenty years' heritage of breathing the same air and hearing his father talk about the man, Sutpen; a part of the town's . . . eighty years' heritage of the same air which the man himself had breathed between this September afternoon in 1909 and that Sunday morning in June in 1833 when he first rode into town out of no discernible past. . . .
>
> (*AA*, p. 11)

More important, the collective and individual forces of her narrative encompass a second duality. Within the context of a traditional Lost Cause apologetics she creates her own version of Sutpen. For her he is both a chthonic son of the Old South (having "abrupted" from its native soil) and not of the South (a demon who "wasn't even a gentleman," was not truly human) (*AA*, pp. 8 and 11). Though he established the grandest plantation in Yoknapatawpha County and fought courageously in the Civil War, Rosa excludes him from the list of cavalier gentlemen she celebrates in her poems about Confederate "cavalry heroes" (*AA*, p. 171). Her story of Sutpen is not a celebration. It does not belong to her "literary" production, to her public voice as the unofficial "poetess laureate" of the town and county (*AA*, p. 11). This story is personal; she tells it to Quentin Compson instead of writing it down. This shift from written to oral performance, moreover, initiates narration in *Absalom, Absalom!* yet the context remains southern fatalism, an explanation of "why God let [the South] lose the War" (*AA*, p. 11). Rosa's traumatic and heretofore private memory of Sutpen is of a man who mocked the genteel codes of antebellum cavalier culture. He represents Lost Causism's last defense, submerging southern racism, classism, and sexism beneath his own inexplicable evil and self-destructiveness. Sutpen is the Old South's noble ideal perverted, gone mad for no apparent reason other than capricious demonic intervention in the affairs of man.

Rosa's narration reveals regret for her belatedness; the Old South glory is her wish rather than her authentic experience. She belongs to the postwar South, to the New South's initiatory narrative struggle to come to terms with the past. Her confessional story of longing intersects with and revises the narrative of Sutpen that has been in public circulation since his arrival in Mississippi seventy-six years earlier. Rosa's narrative corrects, she believes, what "they" will have already told Quentin. Her monologue (Quentin makes only polite and empty responses) is designed to foreclose further discourse, to write an ending to the story of Sutpen. She moves toward a final discovery and revelation, a last accounting of Sutpen's fallen dynasty; in her personal version of the story she would contain Sutpen within her autobiography. Her narrative adapts Lost Cause defensiveness to her motive of self-justification.

By linking her personal motives to this communal narrative practice Rosa takes a bold risk whose payoff Faulkner undoes with genealogy. First, the limits of her eyewitness knowledge of the events she relates blind her to the hidden ("not obvious") possibilities of the Sutpen genealogy (*AA*, p. 370). She misrecognizes Sutpen's "heir," the idiot black man named Jim Bond (*AA*, p. 371). Second, and most significant, she confronts a narrative genealogy that traces from Sutpen's first-person recitation of his story through three generations of Compson men to Quentin Compson, making him the most recalcitrant audience Rosa could have selected to hear her tale and judge her honor and her rightness (*AA*, p. 167). Rosa's monologue appropriates the Sutpen story only to have it reappropriated by the Compsons, they who consider themselves the possessors and trustees of Sutpen's personal history, aggrandizers of and apologists for a man they conceive to be a tragic figure in the South's cataclysmic fall from grace. Yet neither do the Compsons have the last word; nor do they all revise Sutpen's story under the same motive forces. Rosa's appropriation initiates a series of revisionary strategies, a struggle for authority and comprehension that ultimately decenters authority and disperses narrative voices, while also exposing the repressed motives of Lost Cause apologetics. In all of this heterogeneity of voices no one speaks for Faulkner, yet the narrative of dispersal accomplishes Faulkner's revisionary autobiographical designs. The demystification of Sutpen traces its genealogy back through Sartoris to the "model" First Ancestor of Faulkner's dynastic novels, his great-grandfather, W. C. Falkner.

Rosa Coldfield traces her genealogy to both Aunt Jenny in *Flags in the Dust* and Addie in *As I Lay Dying*. She is less naive than either prototype. Rosa's cleverness manifests itself in the appropriation of the central theme of Lost Cause apologetics, the theme of "innocence," for her personal defense. Rosa's innocence, like the innocence of the Old South defenders, depends on establishing the outrageous guilt of someone, or something, else. In the novel hers is a preemptive narrative move, although its wisdom is debatable. Her demonizing of Sutpen elevates him into the rhetorical sublime, distances him from the realm of particular and personal experience, and threatens to trivialize her very real encounter with him. Sutpen, she argues at a moment of high emotion, "was not articulated in this world" (*AA*, p. 171), and yet it is his very real presence on the threshold of physical contact with her that motivates her storytelling. Rosa's narrative balances precariously between mythical narration (Sutpen the symbolic figure of the Lost Cause) and a recounting of authentic experience (the man she has just cause to consider no gentleman). She begins her narrative of personal experience with a series of "I saw" assertions (*AA*, p. 18), but during her monologic performance she slips imperceptively (how else?), under the force of Lost Cause sublimation, into a regretful admission that she did not see everything (*AA*, p. 30). Her narrative strives to link the symbolic with the intimate, with insistent images of the body as the locus of pleasure and pain.

The feminine body, as we have seen, is no neutral ground in Faulkner's novels. His focus is always on the threshold between masculine symbolic order on the one hand, and, on the other, feminine (or the female) otherness that links language to a beyond of language. This linkage is a strictly feminine project among Faulknerian characters (which does not mean that these characters are always women), and Rosa expresses this crossing of barriers better than any of his previous narrators. Moreover, she reveals Faulkner at a rather acute moment of balancing on the modernist fence between legitimacy and authenticity. Narration, language, has its sources for Faulkner; storytelling, as we have seen with Ratliff in *The Hamlet*, obeys culture's rules while it also recreates particular, lived experiences within culture, as it recreates Addie's presence in *As I Lay Dying*. Rosa's autobiographical monologue dwells between the what-it-was-like and the what-it-means.

The key to this narrative is memory. As a figment of Faulkner's modernist sensibilities, Rosa defines memory as visceral, in contrast to the simplistic imagistic conception of memory as a storehouse of pictures in the metaphorical space of the mind's eye. Memory is rudimentary, primitive, Proustian sensuality, instinctual response to pleasure or pain.

> *That is the substance of remembering—sense, sight, smell: the muscles with which we see and hear and feel—not mind, not thought: there is no such thing as memory: the brain recalls just what the muscles grope for: no more no less: and its resultant sum is usually incorrect and false and worthy only of the name of dream.—See how the sleeping outflung hand, touching the bedside candle, remembers pain, springs back and free while mind and brain sleep on and only make of this adjacent heat some trashy myth of reality's escape: or that same sleeping hand, in sensuous marriage with some dulcet surface, is transformed by that same sleeping brain and mind into that same figment-stuff warped out of all experience.*
>
> (*AA*, p. 143)

Yet Rosa's insistence here on the priority of experience over the "figment-stuff" of myth, dream, and narrative must not be read simplistically any more than the same division articulated by Addie can be seen as a simplistic divorce between saying and doing. That words cannot, for any modernist, adequately express personal experiences does not exclude another sort of interaction between saying and feeling, does not mean that words can't hurt. The focus of Rosa's narrative is on a personal insult, Sutpen's outrageous proposal that she bear him a male heir before he consents to marry her. His words, which she cannot bring herself to repeat, break free of propriety and conventionality, inflict an unforgettable wound. Her pain, which is not merely metaphorical, rests on the suggestive literal meaning of the word "insult": a leaping upon.

It is unlikely that any reader of *Absalom, Absalom!* would argue that Sutpen's proposal was not insulting to Rosa, yet it is not self-evidently so. What Faulkner searches for in Rosa's monologue is the basis of the insult in a morality of the encoded body. Were Sutpen's proposal prompted by romantic love, or even lust, an impatience with ritual and formality, Rosa admits she would have acquiesced. But it is not. The proposal violates conventional, honorable behavior with its established approach to the body through ritual verbal performance. What the social code creates is personalization, individuation in the union of bodies, a naming and identifying of bodies. Rosa's sense of herself as a "presence" is destroyed by Sutpen's proposal. She has become for him, she thinks, mere physicality, a reproductive function without identity, an integer, a signifier without a signified, without any indication of the personal. There is in Sutpen's proposal nothing civilized and, hence, everything monstrous and strange, violent and destructive. Words, proper and improper, touch, define, arrange, and identify (name) the body.

Sutpen's design acts upon bodies without passion or concern; the breach between the symbolic and the imaginary is complete. Sutpen's extraordinary blindness to the consequences of his verbal acts may be traced through that infamous design, that rigid model of Old South cultural order he attempts to articulate in the frontier world of Mississippi, to the devastating consequences of Lost Cause apologetics that Faulkner exposes in the modern South's obsessive mythmaking. Southern storytelling is a mode, a style, a form of being in the world for Faulkner's figures of southern discursive practice. In explaining why Rosa tells her story of Sutpen rather than writes it, Faulkner privileges orality, but not for the sake of narrative authenticity, romantic-modern self-expression, simple presence. Orality best models for him the performative nature of narration, the binding together of what J. L. Austin labeled illocutionary and perlocutionary forces in language.[1] Intentionality and affectivity are indivisible components of communal discourse, of cultural narrative projects. To tell one's own version of the common story is an aggressive act of breaking into and controlling the circuit. David Carr proposes a more polite term for this, "negotiation," which defines the exchange among members of a community for rights to different versions of the common stories.[2] But Faulkner depicts the appropriation of the Sutpen story by Rosa as a dislocation designed to displace other versions, to silence other voices through the refocusing of the story on her irreducibly personal experience. Hers is a narrative of words that hurt. The lesson is that all narratives do so.

Barbara Hardy defines narrative as a "primary act of mind," as a placing of the self in time and space;[3] for Faulkner that involves a displacing as well. Perhaps we must read Hardy's "primary act of mind" in terms of Maurice Merleau-Ponty's phenomenology of language acquisition in the child, and thereby invest narrative performance with what he calls the "quasi-magical" function of signs.[4] Language competence for Merleau-Ponty derives from our rudimentary mimetic effort not to represent things but to imitate the behavior of others. Narrative acts, therefore, are rooted not in simple ontotheological assertions but in social transformations, appropriations, and revisions, designed to produce results for the self similar to those produced by and for others. Rosa makes Sutpen's story her own, not simply as revenge (a form of character assassination) but far more significantly to assert (insert) her presence into the Sutpen/Compson narrative tradition of male exclusivity. It is a formidable task in Faulkner's world. Yet language does things. Narrative directs imaginary bodies through entrances and exits "dramatistically," to use Kenneth Burke's suggestive term;[5] a novel about propositional discourse insistently focuses on proposals of marriage, the union of bodies within a cultural code of identity and naming. *Absalom, Absalom!* returns again and again to this theme initiated by Rosa, raising always in the echoes of her voice the image of her pain, of her real presence in the Sutpen myth.

The language of storytelling in Faulkner, therefore, is manipulative and not descriptive. Words may fail to represent authentic personal experience adequately, but Faulkner is concerned with the more rudimentary aspects of narration as social performance and as autobiography. For Rosa, Sutpen's proposals, the insult, have extraordinary consequences measured not merely in terms of social impropriety but in more personal terms; they are an outrage against the socialized body. There are, we should remember, two proposals, and they define the inside and the outside of the social. The form of the first may be eccentric and abrupt, but it is within the bounds of propriety; it initiates a familiar narrative sequence of actions that normally would move from verbal performance to sexual union.

> *"You may think I made your sister Ellen no very good husband. You probably do think so. But even if you will not discount the fact that I am older now, I believe I can promise that I shall do no worse at least for you."*
>
> *That was my courtship. That minute's exchanged look in a kitchen garden, that hand upon my head in his daughter's bedroom; a ukase, a decree, a serene and florid boast like a sentence (ay, and delivered in the same attitude) not to be spoken and heard but to be read carved in the bland stone which pediments a forgotten and nameless effigy. I do not excuse it. I claim no brief, no pity, who did not answer "I will" not because I was not asked, because there was no place, no niche, no interval for reply.*
>
> (*AA*, p. 164)

Rosa's interpretation here overwhelms a literal reading of the proposal. Sutpen's words, quoted directly, are unremarkable, as easily self-deprecating as sinister. What Rosa conveys is her experience of his persuasive authority, a real power over her will and consequently over her body.

> *Yes. I sat there and listened to his voice and told myself, "Why, he is mad. He will decree this marriage for tonight and perform his own ceremony, himself both groom and minister; pronounce his own wild benediction on it with the bedward candle in his hand: and I mad too, for I will acquiesce, succumb; abet him and plunge down."*
>
> (*AA*, p. 165)

Yet she tells us that no date is set for the wedding, and three months elapse between the first and second proposal. Despite her fears or desires there is no evident haste to consummate the contract, no evident passion driving Sutpen. Her rereading of a sinister intention in the first proposal as she relates the events to Quentin, of course, derives from the perspective of the second experience, from the insult. It is, she tells us, only after that outrage that she understands what Sutpen means, grasps his perception of her:

> *there are some things for which three words are three too many, and three thousand words that many words too less, and this is one of them.*

It can be told; I could take that many sentences, repeat the bold blank
naked and outrageous words just as he spoke them, and bequeath you
that same aghast and outraged unbelief I knew when I comprehended
what he meant; or take three thousand sentences and leave you only that
Why? Why? and Why? that I have asked and listened to for almost fifty
years.

(*AA*, pp. 166–67)

It is important that Rosa this time does not choose to give us Sutpen's
words "just as he spoke them." She represses his voice, projecting it
outside of her three thousand sentences, and his unspeakable words
are all the more monstrous and demonic for her refusal to articulate
them. What Rosa does give us is an analogy, the what-it-was-like. The
insult dehumanizes her, denies her not only an interval of reply, a verbal space, the authority of her own self-expressive voice, but also the
dignity of personal presence, even the circumscribed identity of the
properly feminine within a paternalistic discourse. She is not even a
woman.

He had not even waited to tether his horse; he stood with the reins over
his arm (and no hand on my head now) and spoke the bald outrageous
words exactly as if he were consulting with Jones or with some other man
about a bitch dog or a cow or a mare.

(*AA*, p. 168)

The lack of interval for reply becomes the space of her fifty years
of writing poems of celebration of Confederate heroes. The failure to
reply is motivation for her confessional recitation to Quentin Compson. The poems compensate for Sutpen's outrageous impropriety, but
only the autobiographical monologue expresses the personal pain, the
lingering wound, the sense of humiliation, and the inescapable memory
of the way his words hurt. In neither of these forms of reply does she
reject the paternalistic codes that repress and marginalize her; instead
she blames Sutpen for the destruction of cavalier honor and with it her
chance for fulfillment as a proper southern lady, as a woman according
to the only model she knows and accepts, that encoded within the narrative of the Old South myth. In this tangled web of social myth and
personal experience Faulkner identifies the threshold between symbolic
action and the encoded body. Rosa's language is as often sensual as it
is sublime; it is earthy, even crude for so proper a southern lady. She
describes her sexual awakening in terms of the fairy-tale metaphor of

the sleeping beauty who needs a man to unleash her sexuality and bring her to her proper feminine role in the paternalistic social schema.

> *It was a vintage year of wistaria: vintage year being that sweet conjunc-*
> *tion of root bloom and urge and hour and weather; and I (I was fourteen)*
> *—I will not insist on bloom, at whom no man had yet to look—nor*
> *would ever—twice, as not child but less than even child; as not more*
> *child than woman but even as less than any female flesh. Nor do I say leaf*
> *—warped bitter pale and crimped half-fledging intimidate of any claim to*
> *green which might have drawn to it the tender mayfly childhood sweet-*
> *heart games or given pause to the male predacious wasps and bees of later*
> *lust. But root and urge I do insist and claim, for had I not heired too from*
> *all the unsistered Eves since the Snake? Yes, urge I do: warped chrysalis*
> *of what blind perfect seed: for who shall say what gnarled forgotten root*
> *might not bloom yet with some globed concentrate more globed and con-*
> *centrate and heady-perfect because the neglected root was planted warped*
> *and lay not dead but merely slept forgot?*
>
> (*AA*, p. 144)

In what she calls the "miscast summer" of her "barren youth" she exists as neither female nor male, living more as a man than as a woman but in both unfulfilled, lacking. It is the summer of Charles Bon's courtship of Judith Sutpen, a time of voyeur pleasures, the material of fairy tales and romantic dreams; as she recounts this moment in her life on the way to the climactic insult, she prepares us for the permanence of her lacking, the failure of her final awakening into womanhood, into the comple- tion and defining of her femininity. Sutpen's "outrage" condemns her unfulfilled desires to sublimation in writing poems of cavalry heroes, in fantasy. In the failure to reply, in her acquiescence, she is stained and condemned to the outer fringes of society: the poverty-stricken old maid, "*Rosie Coldfield, lose him, weep him; found a man but failed to keep him*" (*AA*, pp. 169, 170). She is the victim of a form of shunning, of systematic exclusion from proper society. At this most personal level of her monologue she demystifies her demon Sutpen:

> *a certain segment of rotten mud walked into my life, spoke that to me*
> *which I had never heard before and never shall again, and then walked*
> *out; that was all.*
>
> (*AA*, p. 171)

What she will never hear again, of course, includes the proper first pro- posal as well as the insult; "that was all" is portentous, for she will have no more proposals. She will remain barren, obsessively supplementing her bodily lacking with poetic symbols of cavalier honor.

Yet within three sentences of this personal moment of demystification Rosa returns to the sublime, retreats from the images of the feminine body, albeit the marginalized body of lacking, to the symbolic realm of Lost Cause apologetics, to the demon.

> *He was the light-blinded bat-like image of his own torment cast by the fierce demonic lantern up from beneath the earth's crust and hence retrograde, reverse; from abysmal and chaotic dark to eternal and abysmal dark completing his descending.*

(*AA*, p. 171)

And here we must anticipate what our reading of the novel in its entirety will dictate. Rosa's Lost Causism is self-deluding, the proving of an ideal against its demonic corruption. What was and would have been all glorious if not for the incomprehensible irrationality that destroyed it: Romance, Camelot. Her defense of herself is turned by Faulkner into a representation of a social failure, of defeat and fatalism. Her appropriation of Sutpen for her personal defense inverts to Faulkner's appropriation of Rosa as a symbol of the mind of the modern South which obsessively preserves within its self-conception its self-condemnation.

The telling of a Sutpen story never proves innocence. Rosa implicates herself, or is implicated in Faulkner's revisionary strategy. That Faulkner begins *Absalom, Absalom!* with Rosa's narration has thematic and structural pertinence for a novel about the destructive consequences of Old South mythmaking, but is it impertinent as well? Faulkner uses Rosa Coldfield, uses the conventional myth of masculine verbal power figuratively, as a trope or a metaphor. The technique is reminiscent of a Nietzschean strategy that used Jews and women tropically, with the difference that this symbolic use of reality is put into question here. Reading Rosa's narrative of personal pain we cannot treat the symbolic as "literary" privilege; no use of language is innocent. Rosa is not for Faulkner merely a hysterical female, nor is she simply a desexualized old maid. Her moral and personal outrage dominates her monologue, and the ambiguities in her defense of the Old South code and in her demonizing of Sutpen, who symbolizes the self-inflicted collapse of the code, are the terms of Faulkner's critical dismantling of that code. The link between Sutpen's two proposals embodies one such ambiguity, for these propositions exist as a chiasmus, not canceling one another but as mirror images, inverse repetitions, of one another. The outrageous insult is a distortion, the dark side of what the Old South myth presents as light and reason. There is a rigid binarism in these propositions by Sutpen that forces Rosa to affirm the symbolic order of the code over its alternative: the improper, the chaotic and the monstrous. She speaks wholly within the confines and in celebration of that which, in its dark-side manifestation, has violated her.

Our reading of Rosa's narrative fixes our reading of the novel as a whole; her voice, the insistent tracing of real consequences attendant upon verbal performance within a determinative discursive context, does not cease with her departure from the novel's present action. Even though Faulkner subjects her narration to the extraordinary power of masculine reappropriation, to the Compsons' narrative of innocence and Quentin's particular shift of focus from Sutpen to Sutpen's children, we continue to hear Rosa's narration and read within it a powerful argument against innocence. This is not to privilege her monologue as closure, a modernist privileging of her eyewitness authenticity. Her version has no more claim to "truth" than Mr. Compson's, Quentin's, or Shreve's; all are, to extend the third-person narrator's intrusive comment, "probably true enough" (*AA*, p. 335). Faulkner insists on a revisionary performance; we read narratives as a Foucauldian "series" without an original,[6] as moments in a collective discourse which mark the place of the individual.

So again we return to the question of innocence, to the sense that any interpretive use of the term in reading Faulkner is itself risky. John T. Matthews rests the burden of his reading of *Absalom, Absalom!* on "Sutpen's innocence." He submits this innocence, borrowed from the Compson narrative, to a Derridian revision in order to argue that Sutpen's failure rests on a linguistic naiveté, on a speech "impediment" that gives it full oedipal suggestiveness.[7] Sutpen's innocence, therefore, becomes a deconstructive blindness, foreclosure of Derridian freeplay. The argument has appeal. Matthews observes that *Absalom, Absalom!* "dismantles Sutpen's statement of dynastic sense because [that statement] disregards the complexities of language."[8] This is insightful but misrecognizes that the "statement of dynastic sense" is not merely Sutpen's. Matthews is forgetful of Rosa Coldfield's narrative statement, and her innocence is of a different order from Sutpen's.

Rosa's narration does not fit well in Matthews' Derridian strategy. Much of his analysis of *Absalom, Absalom!* argues Faulkner's retreat from representation, and here he echoes a conventional approach to the novel, one the New Critics also employed to justify its purely symbolic character, its thematics of the "literary," its unconcern with questions of morality and politics. Focusing on the passages where Rosa defines memory as visceral, as below the level of language's differential functioning, Matthews concludes that, for Faulkner, the representation of "substance" is impossible.[9] Yet Faulkner has no interest in this limited mimesis. Rosa's visceral memory expresses by means of verbal play an analogy, the lingering of pain consequent upon the outrageous violence of Sutpen's verbal behavior. No-thing is represented here; Faulkner searches for the threshold between body and mind. The modernist division between authenticity of experience and the legitimizing power of language (a dualism Derrida resolves into supplemental freeplay) is challenged in *Absalom, Absalom!* The play of language is not innocent, has effects on bodies, on the world of real human relationships, behavior, sensual contact.

We must not read Rosa as we read Quentin, whose appropriation of her narrative translates Rosa's insistent threshold experience of speaking and feeling into symbolic play. Recalling his visit to the Sutpen graveyard where, guided by his father, he decipered a narrative in the messages carved on the Sutpen family tombstones, Quentin exclaims: "If I had been there I could not have seen it this plain" (*AA*, p. 190). The "it" and "there," however, are empty functions without reference. The "seen" indicates a point of view of omniscience and authority since the *what* of this seeing is a panoramic narrative that traces the route of the marble stones from Italy, through the Civil War battle lines, to Yoknapatawpha County, Mississippi. What Quentin sees is not "substance" but narrative as explanation, legitimacy; he perceives nothing; he comprehends. The thrust of Quentin's narrative elevates Sutpen above the plain of social/political action, above the Civil War. It is an act of aggrandizing that trivializes the human consequences of Sutpen's actions. In some sense here we have that Sutpen who is without passion, ideology, or commitment, the Sutpen who refuses to join the KKK after the War not because he sees it for what it is, a morally repugnant idea, but because he has no cause at all that might enlist him. Sutpen is a hollow man of designs, symbolic patterns. Quentin's Sutpen is neither Rosa's demon nor the "certain segment of rotten mud" that marked her life forever.

Marked her life by means of supplemental freeplay, the perverse inversion of the proper, the outrageous utterance of the unspeakable.

Rosa's Sutpen is more Derridian than Matthews admits. Quentin, following the Compson line, traces Sutpen's innocence to his boyhood in the West Virginia mountains. There, he surmises, Sutpen heard "tales" of "Tidewater splendor," but had "nothing in sight to compare and gauge the tales by and so give the words life and meaning" (*AA*, p. 222). What would seem here a very un-Derridian prioritizing of authentic experience over language does not work out that way in Quentin's depiction of Sutpen's sense of his grand symbolic design. Two factors are crucial. Sutpen's attempt to transplant "Tidewater splendor" to the Mississippi frontier disregards experience altogether. More important, Quentin recounts what he claims to be Sutpen's own words on his design: "Whether it was a good design or a bad design is beside the point." Here reality becomes a set of "ingredients" for Sutpen's symbolic dream: "money, a house, a plantation, slaves, a family—incidentally, of course, a wife."

> It was that innocence again, that innocence that believed that the ingredients of morality were like the ingredients of pie or cake and once you had measured them and balanced them and mixed them and put them into the oven it was all finished and nothing but pie or cake could come out.
>
> (*AA*, p. 263)

Sutpen's design raises moral issues that cannot be dismissed as "beside the point" or disguised behind a speech impediment. The "incidental" wife reference returns us to Rosa's narration, for it is the ingredient of a wife that becomes the focus of morality in Sutpen's design. Matthews' description of Sutpen's innocence oddly repeats Sutpen's outrageious moral disclaimer. For Matthews, Sutpen's failure to comprehend the flaw in his design evidences a blindness to the deconstructive freeplay of all closed systems, to the Gödel-like loops that de-sign, break down, open up all narrative legitimations. Yet this does not prevent such systems from exercising a repressive force in human relations, or guarantee that we will not articulate such repression against ourselves. Matthews rightly classifies Sutpen's design as a dynastic order based on an oedipal model: a "phallic, paternal model of meaning."[10] Yet Sutpen's innocence of morality and history (recall his extraordinary idea that he can restore Sutpen's Hundred to its full splendor even after the Civil War) echoes the drift of Derridian freeplay toward the ahistorical, amoral, and apolitical.

Matthews' error, a Derridian misconstruction, is in reading Sutpen's design as a metaphysical project. Sutpen is no metaphysician; he repeats what he hears and thinks he sees: the phallic, paternal model of meaning. That model deconstructs under the force of translation into propositional action, into performance. Rosa's narrative, whatever its eccentricities, insistently puts Sutpen's design into action as a sequence of outrageous verbal acts that violently distort the nature of human relationships. Her only model for such relationships is itself distorting, but to recognize that fact does not make Sutpen's proposals any less outrageous. Sutpen's innocence, which for Rosa is his guilt, and for Matthews is Derridian blindness, actually runs in another direction.

Matthews follows both the Compson approach and much of the novel's interpretive tradition by overemphasizing Sutpen, yet clearly Faulkner's narrative design here raises the very question of why Sutpen should be the focus of obsessive celebration and condemnation. The narrative structure of *Absalom, Absalom!* continually drifts away from Sutpen, as Quentin's primary effort at reclamation, recovery of the original, disperses into Shreve's imaginative play. What *Absalom, Absalom!* dismantles is not Sutpen's "statement of dynastic sense" but the entire "phallic, paternal model of meaning" that is the subtext of southern mythmaking, a subtext of southern narrative practice, storytelling. This critique is accomplished within the revisionary narrative form that moves from Rosa's personal story to a generalization about the mind of the South.

The novel's climactic moment is in chapter 7. There the central motivating event of Sutpen's life is revealed; it is the moment of emergent social, even class, consciousness caused by the boy Sutpen's rejection at the front door of the grand Tidewater plantation where his father worked (*AA*, p. 232). Faulkner marks here a transition; Sutpen's initial response is merely childish; he has been insulted and must give reply, a form of revenge. Yet that reply suddenly opens a new realm of thought for the boy.

> It was just there, natural in a boy, a child, . . . because it was what a boy would have thought, and he knew that to do what he had to do in order to live with himself he would have to think it out straight as a man would. . . .
>
> (*AA*, p. 237)

Sutpen's transition from childhood to maturity is sudden and traumatic; it is characterized by a move from an instinct for direct action to a reflective consciousness, from unself-conscious being in the world to a self-conscious desire to master the world. Here we read another of

Faulkner's critical threshold stories, one of a genealogy of stories from the legendary tales of the boyhood of old W. C. Falkner to short narratives like "What's to Be Done," their protagonists ranging from the Sartoris men to Sutpen, to Ike McCaslin, to Chick Mallison. Faulkner's fascination with such transitions, sometimes as arrested development in characters like Benjy Compson, Boon Hoggenbeck, or Ike Snopes, pivots on cataclysmic departures.

Young Sutpen's thoughts move from direct action *("I can shoot him* [the owner of the plantation]. . . . *No. That wouldn't do no good")* to an extension of this physical aggression into "analogy" (*AA*, p. 234). The former is linked to childish behavior, the latter to thinking like a man.

> It was like that, he said, like an explosion—a bright glare that vanished and left nothing, no ashes nor refuse; just a limitless flat plain with the severe shape of his innocence rising from it like a monument; that innocence instructing him as calm as the others had ever spoken, using his own rifle analogy to do it with, and when it said *them* in place of *he* or *him*, it meant more than all the human puny mortals under the sun that might lie in hammocks all afternoon with their shoes off: He thought "If you were fixing to combat them that had the fine rifles, the first thing you would do would would be to get yourself the nearest thing to a fine rifle you could borrow or steal or make, wouldn't it?" and he said Yes. "But this aint a question of rifles. So to combat them you have got to have what they have that made them do what the man did. You got to have land and niggers and a fine house to combat them with. You see?" and he said Yes again. He left that night.
>
> (*AA*, p. 238)

Faulkner describes in this passage a paradigmatic transition from childhood to maturity; crucially, the latter obliterates the former like an explosion that leaves no trace, opening "a limitless flat plain" that signifies accession to the symbolic register of verbal play, of writing on the whiteness and two-dimensionality of a blank page ready for inscription. Faulkner details here the move from physical action to "analogy," from the intensive focus on "things" and bodies, from a remote world of romanticized personal combat, personal contact, to a depersonalized and paranoiac *"them,"* to a realm where things become symbols of prestige, power, and economic exchange, where "land and niggers and a fine house" are signs of abstract value, signs that "do" things.

Yet what intrudes into this flat plain is a "severe shape" that is "like a monument." Faulkner's language is straining after an image of the body, the image of such an image. The explosion is not without some "refuse"; it is not the case that "nothing" remains beyond that transition from childhood to maturity, from images of the thingness of bodies to the pure symbolic play of exchange values. Nor is it the case that nothing of the presymbolic touches upon or anticipates the symbolic, as the analogy strives to suggest. The two registers interpenetrate, according to Faulkner. And that is Sutpen's mistake; he fails to see that the link between saying and doing implicates symbolic order in the affairs of real men and women. The "monument" he speaks of is the image of his "innocence," of his presymbolic state of imaginary being among bodies, of the aggressive drive of the imaginary which displaces, appropriates, consumes. It is the "severe shape," not the thing itself which the shape represents, that refuses to be nothing, that cannot be forgotten. Sutpen's innocence becomes at this moment a repression of the imaginary, of the personal, of that which represents the body, of the effect of words on the body. Sutpen's explosive accession to the symbolic is traumatic, an end to innocence which haunts him in the form of innocence. Sutpen is innocent not of the complexities of language so much as of reality.

The devastating effects of Sutpen's design are the result not of the flaw within the oedipal model of meaning but of his own unnatural misrecognition of reality, and this explains a central mystery in the novel: Sutpen's refusal to acknowledge Charles Bon as his son. Recognition is visual in Faulkner's dynastic novels, beginning with the McCallums of *Flags in the Dust*, in whom the replication of physical traits is a proof of legitimacy. The force of the visual leads Quentin to speculate about Bon's resemblance to Sutpen. He recreates a meeting between Bon and Sutpen from Bon's point of view:

> Then for the second time he looked at the expressionless and rocklike face, at the pale boring eyes in which there was no flicker, nothing, the face in which he saw his own features, in which he saw recognition, and that was all.

> (*AA*, p. 348)

Because it is a second meeting the "recognition" is ambiguous; what is certain in Quentin's story is that the recognition is not a public act of acknowledged paternity, is not legitimizing.

Sutpen's refusal to make this act of social recognition fascinates both Quentin and Shreve. Sutpen represses the images of the past; he is "shocked," according to Shreve, when Bon, long forgotten, returns. It is a past he has written off, a debt paid, cancelled as if it had never existed or had no force on the present play of his symbolic design.

> Listen, dont you remember how your father said it, that not one time did he—the old guy, the demon—ever seem to wonder how the other wife managed to find him, track him down, had never once seemed to wonder what she might have been doing all that time, the thirty years since that day when he paid his bill with her and got it receipted, so he thought, and saw with his own eyes that it was (so he thought) destroyed, torn up and thrown to the wind; never once wondered about this but only that she had done it, could have and would have wanted to track him down?
>
> (*AA*, p. 296)

What is curious about Sutpen's refusal to recognize Bon as his son is that it is unnecessary in terms of the paternal model of meaning he appropriates as his design. That model delegitimizes Bon, insofar as Bon might make a claim against Sutpen's estate, because Bon is black. We know this to be Bon's impediment because it is the only reasonable explanation of Sutpen's abandonment of his first wife. And here again Matthews' Derridian schema breaks down, for it cannot acknowledge the force of Faulkner's representation of a southern discursive practice. Matthews misreads Sutpen's refusal as a reflection of a contradiction within Sutpen's "dynastic speech." He thinks Bon must have some sort of prior claim based on entail, which would disenfranchise Sutpen's legitimate son, Henry.[11] But Sutpen's design voids Bon's prior claim. His recognizing Bon as his "black" son would not change this, and such a recognition for one who is, like Sutpen, a blind follower of the dynastic model of meaning presents few problems. Faulkner understood this and nowhere in the novel raises the issue of Bon's legal priority. The redundancy of the refusal of recognition, however, is important, for it portrays again Sutpen's symbolic innocence as a blindness to reality. Bon's presence is a surprise, a shocking return of the repressed image of the body (*AA*, p. 265).

Sutpen's design deconstructs in performance; for Faulkner deconstruction is not an act that has always already happened but a historical event, a trauma. Matthews' reading of Faulkner would be served by thinking through Derrida's somewhat surprising announcement that he is "quite close to [J. L.] Austin, both interested in and indebted to his problematic."[12] The "interest" here expresses Derrida's cautious and severely restricted effort to account for the "other side" of the Saussurean paradigm that is the subtext of Derridian supplementarity, that other function of language that Saussure called "executive." For Saussure, the executive function of language is subsumed by freeplay. Austin's theory of "how to do things with words" proposes too narrow a range of motives or intentions for Derrida; for Austin such motives include felicity, sincerity, competence, and execution. Such motives, Derrida rightly argues, are less explanations of speech as action than a set of open-ended questions, and Derrida quickly dispatches dogmatic defenses of Austin's theory, like John Searle's. And yet the dimension of language "use" is of primary significance, as Derrida realizes, if we are to respond to the ethical and moral implications of what people say. Much of the narration concerning Sutpen in *Absalom, Absalom!* strives for an understanding of intention, strives to reconstruct the context of Sutpen's propositional discourse. The novel is an extraordinary sustained effort to situate speech acts in a specific discursive practice, to situate the individual in history.[13]

The performative nature of Faulkner's storytelling, in conjunction with the proposals of marriage and the dynastic implications of the replication of images of the body, emphasizes the centrality of Bon's presence in the novel. It is Bon who cuts across all of the narratives. The return of Sutpen's repressed precipitates the novel's most dramatic event: Henry's murder of Bon. Yet even that violent effort to absent Bon fails. Bon endures beyond the grave through a replication of bodies that mocks and deconstructs Sutpen's dynastic design, through a genealogy of illegitimacy that will not go away. Jim Bond remains beyond the limit of Rosa's misrecognition of genealogy and beyond Sutpen's refusal to recognize his son. Bond remains an elusive but insistent presence to be accounted for, not only an abstract symbol of southern racial guilt but also a fact, an experiential reminder of that which cannot be forgotten, rendered invisible. This "scion" and "heir" of Sutpen's design, of the southern myth that Sutpen articulated in his world, is the "one more" that defies narrative comprehension. It is not far from the fact of Bond's presence to the dissolution of the southern myth, the morally outrageous southern discursive practice. He is Shreve's last word on southern guilt: its real presence that defies symbolic repression.

> "You've got one nigger left. One nigger Sutpen left. Of course you can't catch him and you dont even always see him and you never will be able to use him. But you've got him there still. You still hear him at night sometimes. Don't you?"

"I think that in time the Jim Bonds are going to conquer the western hemisphere. Of course it won't quite be in our time and of course as they spread towards the poles they will bleach out again like the rabbits and the birds do, so they won't show up so sharp against the snow. But it will still be Jim Bond; and so in a few thousand years, I who regard you will also have sprung from the loins of African kings. Now I want you to tell me just one thing more. Why do you hate the South?"

(*AA*, p. 378)

Absalom, Absalom! represents the unraveling of narration before the fact of presence. To ignore this representational force vitiates the novel's power, for it is presence that must be faced in the South not absence. It is the enduring fact of racism, classism, and sexism that *Absalom, Absalom!* reveals. The authority of genealogical origins, that is, legitimacy, and the names which order and authenticate the proper replication of bodies, bind symbolic play to resemblances. These are the motives of southern mythmaking, storytelling, motives intensified by the modern South's migrational disruptions, by the unsettling of the South's social structure during the Depression era. The genealogical/historical structure of this narrative transforms recognition (which includes misrecognition) into naming; the performative dimension of symbolic play rests on counting in its double sense of reckoning one's economic worth and being powerful. The language of storytelling in Faulkner exposes the sinister motives of accounting practices. The Constitution of the United States granted the South the right to count: to not count black slaves on the same value scale as white men, to count white women but not allow them to count. Sutpen's design implements the spirit of these constitutional rights; he refuses to count blacks or women, to recognize them as anything more than signs of wealth, as necessary ingredients in his recipe for prestige. So any presence, like Bon's or Rosa's, must be accounted for according to some scale—or rendered no count. An unwanted presence must be "negatived" just as Addie cancels Jewel's illegitimate presence with the female body of lacking, her daughter, Dewey Dell. Henry negatives Bon but cannot, does not, will not negative the replications of Bon which are the insistent presence of Bon in his images.

A deconstructive misreading of *Absalom, Absalom!* eventuates in a dismissal of the moral and historical importance of the final exchange between Shreve and Quentin. This is a trap that catches John Matthews despite his otherwise insightful reading of the novel.

"Why do you hate the South?"

"I dont hate it," Quentin said, quickly, at once, immediately; "I dont hate it," he said. *I dont hate it* he thought, panting in the cold air, the iron New England dark; *I dont. I dont! I dont hate it! I dont hate it!*

(AA, p. 378)

Matthews is compelled by his Derridian approach to rewrite Quentin's agonized lines as "functions," contentless bits of mere grammatical repetition "significant" only in their stylistic typicality.[14] His argument here rests on his effort to solve the formalist puzzle of Henry Sutpen's only direct speech in the novel, the same passage that so obsessed Cleanth Brooks.

And you are—?
Henry Sutpen.
And you have been here—?
Four years.
And you came home—?
To die. Yes.
To die?
Yes. To die.
And you have been here—?
Four years.
And you are—?
Henry Sutpen.

(AA, p. 373)

Unlike Brooks, Matthews sees no mysterious meaning here, no further dialogue perversely or forgetfully omitted by Faulkner. What Matthews grasps is the deconstructive surface of signifiers repeated without purpose, a pattern that "confirms," for him, the novel's "processes." This is, of course, quite true, only not for the empty reasons Matthews adduces. The passage is not simply repetitious; it is another chiasmus which echoes the rhetorical effect of Sutpen's two proposals. The repetition forms a pattern: "Henry Sutpen," "Four years," "came home," "to die," "been here" (home), "Four years," "Henry Sutpen." It is a pattern of name, time, place, place, time, name which pivots on a presence, not an absence: to die. Henry Sutpen is not dead yet, whatever his anticipations or desires. This verbal vortex, surely Faulkner's implementation of a modernist trope of self-assertion, focuses genealogical legitimacy—conferred by the name, which performs Sutpen's dynastic design—on the here and now. The past, with its mythic sublimity, traces genealogical effects in the immediate present, loses its remoteness in this climactic moment of Faulkner's narrative.

This insistence on the real presence of the Old South in New South mythmaking, storytelling, anticipates Shreve's devastating question only five pages later: "Why do you hate the South?" Because of Henry Sutpen's presence in the novel, because his words, elicited in Quentin's catechismic interrogation, contain the novel's "truth," the full weight of southern history is brought to bear on Quentin's response. We cannot, as Matthews does, dismiss Shreve's last words on the Sutpen narrative, on the accountability of Jim Bond, as a "feeble, false summary," or as a "racial calculus" that distorts the novel. Jim Bond's presence remains beyond the immolation of Clytie and Henry as a proof against false summaries. The dramatic and thematic power of the novel is concentrated in these final two dialogues; they form no aesthetic closure to Faulkner's narrative representation of southern discursive practice; quite the contrary, they insist on the continuing presence of the conditions of southern experience that produce such discourses. Yet there is also no retreat into the empty sophistication of freeplay. Discourse is, for Faulkner (and can it be otherwise?), articulated in the world. If we do not always say what we mean or even mean what we say, what we say does mean and does do things.

CHAPTER 13

Dialogue

S HREVE'S REFERENCE to Sutpen as "the old guy, the demon" (*AA*, p. 296) contains a contradiction. It also links Shreve's narrative to other narratives, for the difference between "demon" and "old guy" measures the distance from Rosa's style to Shreve's style, thereby encompassing the novel. We "hear" in this linking two distinct voices, but we are aware of much more. Faulkner's narrative is dialogic, like that style Mikhail Bakhtin describes as the essential narrative technique in the novels of Dostoyevsky:

> Dialogue has penetrated inside every word, provoking in it a battle and the interruption of one voice by another. . . .
> Thus, at the very beginning of the novel the leading voices in the great dialogue have already begun to sound. These voices are not self-enclosed or deaf to one another. They hear each other constantly, call back and forth to each other, and are reflected in one another.[1]

The effect is to extend the present moment of conversation (the moment of reading) outward toward the novel's horizon, to deepen the immediate through a layering or over-sounding. Neither cacophony nor close harmony, dialogue is nevertheless many-voiced, simultaneously expressed and reexpressed in each utterance, even in a single word: "demon." Each narrator's speech references or revises the others, and, hence, each revision rests on "quotation." What distinguishes Faulkner is his intensification of this dialogic webbing into a sense of community. This rendering of what Quentin calls a "commonwealth" of talking and listening (*AA*, p. 12) rests on a poverty in common language, on repetitious styles, plagiarisms, willful distortions (misreadings), and impolite interruptions. Individual members of a community sound alike, yet they do not speak with a single voice, not even the author's. The poverty of common language defines a reality, restricts perception, even thought. It resists change but does not prevent it; it is conservative yet very fragile. Individuality—that is, difference—is defined within the poverty of common language; the majority (not a number but a trope) limits the discourse of minorities. Faulkner's writing is from the perspective of minorities.

According to Deleuze and Guattari minority writing is revolutionary,[2] but Faulkner is no revolutionary. His perspective is revisionist. The issue here is not one of prestige, for in canonical terms Faulkner is no minor writer despite early reviews that categorized him as a minor regionalist. The idea of a minority writing is very complex, perhaps more so than Deleuze and Guattari claim, for the position of a minor writer with regard to the majority is ambiguous.[3] Faulkner's regionalism, his Yoknapatawpha narrative, reflects a conscious choice of a minority position both as a rejection of formalist aestheticism and in the promotion of a rebellious thematics. As we have seen, Faulkner was reappropriated by the establishment aestheticism of the Fugitive/ New Critics, but this legitimation was something he responded to ambiguously. He sought fame, in large part as an oedipal challenge to the legendary fame of his great-grandfather. Yet he also disclaimed the status of "writer," preferring to identify himself as a farmer. He even went so far as to claim that there is no true southern "art," and his persistent role-playing creates an image of eccentricity. The link between his oedipal challenge and these disclaimers is central to his narrative style. *Absalom, Absalom!* is a prime example of the minor writer's tactic of fragmentation of authority through the dispersion of the majority voice into dialogue.

Faulkner's narratives are a struggle to find a voice within the dominant discourses of his southern society. His rebelliousness is childlike, and his sympathies with children, a minority on the threshold of majority, at the moment of initiation into a dominant discourse, are the strongest sympathies in his novels. Quentin Compson, Ike McCaslin, and Chick Mallison are central voices in Faulkner's southern narrative where the most memorable figures are frequently minorities: blacks and women as well as children. They narrate or act out, in fact create, the fragmentation, the polyvocity, the collapse and disintegration of majority culture: the deconstruction of the myth of the Old South. This fatality can be narrated only from within a community of narrations, from within a dialogue of southern mythmaking which ambiguously preserves as it critiques and disperses, but it is also always articulated from the margins, at the threshold, on the limits, of that communal discourse.

There are a host of issues arising here. We have great difficulty today defining a "community"; to define it reifies it, and a community is not a thing but a conglomerate of familiar behaviors, many of which, but not all, are language behaviors, ways of talking. A community, therefore, has style; perhaps that is all that it has. Style, on the other hand, is a manner of presenting subject matter. Style has occasion and location, time and place. Style represents something to someone for some purpose. A novel might be said to resemble a community, which is not to say that a novel always represents a particular community, although in Faulkner's novels this is the case. Implied in all of this is an old dilemma; we tend to define a community as an individuality, but a community is not like an individual writ large; community is not outside individuals but inside each individual's discrimination between the familiar and the strange. Community depends upon memory and recognition. Individuals are different, distinct, in greater or lesser degree, but each recognizes in the behavior of others a familiar pattern or a departure from a familiar pattern. If there is such a thing as a collective unconscious, it is not the exotic or unique but the familiar. The style of a community, its dominant and residual relationships, and its majority and minority voices, reside in its familiar expressions, in the poverty of its common language.

Community is a game infused within language games, like the ones described by Wittgenstein.[4] These games have rules that are goal oriented; the rules are repetitious to the point of being unconscious. They define "positions" for users (speakers) within the common game. The problem is how to explain departures from the rules, true change and not mere play or virtuosity; game rules are conservative, like communities. Richard Rorty answers that change is the manifestation of "contingency," treating "everything—our language, our conscience, our community—as products of time and chance."[5] Insofar as the metaphysics of the rise and fall of communities is concerned, "chance" is a satisfactory explanation. But ground-level motion, the experience of change within a community, requires more than the positing of "contingency." The effects of change on lives are a measure of the flow of the strange into the familiar. Change alters style and language in a way that defies

Rorty's disguised metaphysics of "chance." Change rarely appears as a purely unmotivated happenstance to those experiencing a fundamental alteration in "reality." Change is recognized as oddly familiar, as part of the pattern of the common, and philosophical glibness about contingency is a poor commentary.

Rorty knows this and shifts his ground from the covert metaphysics of contingency to the poetics of metaphor.

> We call something "fantasy" rather than "poetry" or "philosophy" when it revolves around metaphors which do not catch on with other people— that is, around ways of speaking which the rest of us cannot find a use for. . . . Conversely, when some private obsession produces a metaphor which we *can* find a use for, we speak of genius rather than eccentricity or perversity. The difference between fantasy and genius is not the difference between fantasies which do not lock into something universal, some antecedent reality out there in the world or deep within the self, and those which do. Rather, it is the difference between fantasies which just happen to catch on with other people—happen because of the contingencies of some historical situation, some particular need which a given community happens to have at a given time.
>
> To sum up, poetic, philosophical, scientific or political progress results from the accidental coincidence of a private obsession with a public need.[6]

Rorty's casual universe begs a lot of questions: what are these private and communal needs; what forces produce them; how determinative is a historical situation with regard to a particular change of metaphor within a particular community; what qualifies as a legitimate meaning of "change" or "use" within a particular historical situation; what is the sense of a word like "progress" in the universe of contingency? Rorty illustrates only one of the issues he sets out to explore in his essays on contingency: the inability of philosophy to explain change.

"Change" has more than one meaning in common usage. Phrases like "a change of heart" or "a change of mind" are metaphoric, although they are common enough to have lost their "poetic" gleam, if they ever had any. Phrases like "a change of address" or "a change of plans" are not usually metaphoric, nor do they trace to some previously poetic state. In any case, not all metaphors are poetic, and many metaphors are quite useful. The difficulty we have defining "change" is very much the same difficulty we have defining "community"; these are terms that function sometimes as metaphor and sometimes as literal description. Both change and community are matters of individual recognition within the context of a historical situation. So, too, we must acknowledge the contextual meaningfulness of "use." Change and use are intimately involved in the individual's perspective on/within the community. Change and use raise questions about the nature of need or desire to produce satisfactions, and desire is expressed in an imitative style within community. Here pragmatic motivations come into contact with reality principles, at some level with materiality, for use is a manner (style) of change that produces material satisfactions for someone's needs. The individual reproduces familiar, communal patterns (styles) of behavior to reach a goal (prestige, power, survival, etc.). To some extent needs are themselves produced, and changes in needs are internal to the community, although the dilemma here is an old one since changes in the community produce new senses of community, new realities, and consequently new needs.

This tangled discussion of community and change unravels as long as we pursue any such approach as that proposed by Rorty. It is possible to argue for or against change in a community (is it progress or regress?), to evaluate it according to some representative first principle (a narrative), but it is not possible to explain it by a single universal—except "contingency," an empty term if we wish to understand a particular historical instance of communal change. And particular instances are what we do wish to understand. Metaphor is certainly not the explanation of change, at least not the lyric metaphor of the romantic poets and New Critics that Rorty borrows. Narrative is an explanation. Faulkner's efforts to represent a community in transition reflect the complexities of the issue of change far more sensitively and adequately than does a metaphysics of contingency. Faulkner's South rests on the interpenetration of past, present, and future; it exposes the dialectic of residual and emergent meanings and values. For Faulkner change and community are produced within dialogue as a complex divergence/convergence of voices forming a familiar communal style.

Rosa's monologue opens the dialogue in *Absalom, Absalom!* On the dramatic surface Quentin's response is passive and polite, but in fact Quentin hears more than Rosa; he hears other voices that at times completely repress her voice. Rosa's narration is interrupted for three chapters in which Quentin's recollection brings together the voices of his father and even the community of Jefferson, Mississippi. The reader adds to this the voice of the author as narrator. Rosa's story, therefore, is almost immediately contextualized.

It was a part of his twenty years' heritage of breathing the same air and hearing his father talk about the man, Sutpen; a part of the town's— Jefferson's—eighty years' heritage of the same air which the man himself had breathed between this September afternoon in 1909 and that Sunday morning in June in 1833 when he first rode into town out of no discernible past and acquired his land no one knew how and built his house, his mansion, apparently out of nothing and married Ellen Coldfield and begot his two children—the son who widowed the daughter who had not yet been a bride—and so accomplished his allotted course to its violent (Miss Coldfield at least would have said, just) end. Quentin had grown up with that: the mere names were interchangeable and almost myriad. His childhood was full of them; his very body was an empty hall echoing with sonorous defeated names; he was not a being, an entity, he was a commonwealth.

(*AA*, pp. 11–12)

No passage is more central to our reading of the novel than this one; it is typically Faulknerian, summarizing the whole narrative and thereby focusing the reader's attention on those particular voices which exist as variations on one another. These narratives of individual lives, of existence itself, emerge within the webbing of an ongoing communal discourse that proceeds without Aristotelian beginning or ending.

Hearing in any one voice the many voices of the community of narrations, we must develop an acute ear for differences. We are trained by the multiple interruptions, interruptions within interruptions like the infamous Faulknerian parentheses within parentheses. There are critical moments of interruption. At one point in Rosa's long monologue Quentin's thoughts drift toward crucial associations. He stops listening: "But Quentin was not listening, because there was also something which he too could not pass" (*AA*, p. 172). There is a distinction to be made here between "listening" and "hearing," for Quentin's inattention to Rosa's voice does not mean that he no longer hears her. He hears more than her voice. Later in the novel, in an entirely different context, Shreve couples this "not listening" with an echo of the earlier passage on the community of voices.

But you were not listening, because you knew it all already, had learned, absorbed it already without the medium of speech somehow from having been born and living beside it, with it, as children will and do: so that what your father was saying did not tell you anything so much as it struck, word by word, the resonant strings of remembering.

(*AA*, pp. 212–13)

Hearing displaces listening as dialogue intrudes upon monologue. Vernon Lee distinguished between listening and hearing in an essay on music appreciation written in 1933. Lee determined that listening was more "active," for the listener must pay attention to the details of composition. Listening reflects a "sense of an interest, an importance, residing in the music and inseparable from it." Hearing, on the other hand, is less concentrated, marked by a moving in and out of reveries and daydreams.[7] Lee's bias in favor of listening is formalist; he describes an aesthetic experience in the Kantian mode, or something like the "rapt intransitive attention" of Eliseo Vivas which blots out all external voices in its focus on the formal properties of the composition.[8]

However, it is not listening but hearing that is active, for the drifting in and out of rapt attention, in and out of reveries and daydreams, is what marks the disruptive intrusion of dialogue into monologue. Hearing breaks down the barriers of the composition and disperses voices. This model of interruptive hearing dominates *Absalom, Absalom!* and it never results in either the production of mere noise or the reduction of several voices to a single voice. This latter merging of dialogue into an authorial monologue has been often attributed to Faulkner's narratives, but this is a misreading, even in that famous passage in *Absalom, Absalom!* where the third-person narrator describes a "marriage" of voices.

> "And now," Shreve said, "we're going to talk about love." But he didn't need to say that either, any more than he had needed to specify which he meant by he, since neither of them had been thinking about anything else; all that had gone before just so much to be overpassed and none else present to overpass it but them, as someone always has to rake the leaves up before you can have a bonfire. That was why it did not matter to either of them which one did the talking, since it was not the talking alone which did it, performed and accomplished the overpassing, but some happy marriage of speaking and hearing wherein each before the demand, the requirement, forgave condoned and forgot the faulting of the other—faultings both in the creating of this shade whom they discussed (rather, existed in) and in the hearing and sifting and discarding the false and conserving what seemed true, or fit the preconceived—in order to overpass to love, where there might be paradox and inconsistency but nothing fault nor false.
>
> (*AA*, p. 316)

This marvelous passage does not resolve difference into sameness, erase distinctness of voices in a Faulknerian style. It is, after all, an authorial intrusion into the dialogue of Quentin and Shreve, a momentary disruption of their ongoing exchange. Nor does this moment of mutuality dispense with "paradox and inconsistency." More important, the "happy marriage of speaking and hearing" cannot be limited to the dualistic exchange of Quentin and Shreve alone, for in the very act of "overpassing" to the theme of "love" (a theme Quentin, by the way, never accepts), they are "conserving" as well as inventing, revising the common narrative of Thomas Sutpen. What is extraordinary about this "marriage of speaking and hearing" is that it regresses "before the demand," a regression that is a forgetting of the faults of the "other." Faulkner's language strains to locate a mutuality that is no ordinary exchange, and which will not only merge speaking and hearing but also defy the authorities of prior narrations through aggressive narrative play. This marriage, homosexual in the tradition of great American novels from Cooper to Melville to Twain, representing a masculine bonding, is fundamentally anti-oedipal, once more a threshold of oedipal order. It tells us that the narrative game is serious, an overpassing that disperses legitimate, oedipal love into all of its forbidden othernesses: incest, homosexuality, and miscegenation. What diverse voices we hear in this passage!

This marriage with its supposedly egoless freeplay links the two passages we have already noted where Quentin is said not to be listening to another speaker. The first is an interruption of Rosa which raises Quentin's obsession with incest to consciousness: that "something which he too could not pass." The second is specifically anti-oedipal, the overpassing of his father's voice, of his authority as narrator, as speaker of the law. Mr. Compson's voice is distinctive, yet he also dwells on the topics of marriage and love, so that this passage on the marriage of speaking and hearing reprises his narration, revises it. Most important of all, Mr. Compson's voice is profoundly disruptive. It is the hearing of his father's voice that fills most of Quentin's not listening to Rosa; Mr. Compson explains her narration to his son. The effect is to limit Rosa's authority, to restrict her voice by dwelling on what she did not know (particularly about Bon). Mr. Compson speaks with the authority of one possessing privileged information, although that information is also inadequate. The effect of his interruptions, via Quentin's reverie, is to dismiss Rosa, to paint her as an eccentric and pathetic figure. Mr. Compson places her in the minority, as a woman, as one of those whom he sees as either whores or ladies (*AA*, p. 117), or about whom he says: "Yes. They lead beautiful lives—women. Lives not only divorced from, but irrevocably excommunicated from, all reality" (*AA*, p. 191). The tactic is designed to reappropriate the narrative of Thomas Sutpen for the legitimate Compson genealogy of masculine descent.

Reality in Mr. Compson's narrative is masculine; the authority of the possession of the real is masculine. It is also "tragic." Mr. Compson locates his narrative authority in a central tradition of Western literacy. Appropriately for a genealogical novel, the focus is on naming, or mis-naming, which leads Mr. Compson to rename Sutpen's black daughter "Cassandra" rather than "Clytemnestra" (*AA*, p. 62). It is also a name Rosa appropriated for herself at the beginning of her monologue, one of the echoes that allows Quentin to superimpose his father's narrative on Rosa's (*AA*, p. 22). Sutpen's misnaming, according to Mr. Comp-son, is a reflection of his innocence, by which he implies an ignorance of culture, an ignorance that helps to determine his fate. But the double naming of Clytie has further implications. Clytie is not the murderer of an Agamemnon; she is, however, a particular kind of prophetess. She does not speak the truth only to be ignored, but she is silently the pres-ence of a truth that few can interpret: a black child of Thomas Sutpen who represents the inescapable fate of Sutpen's design, the return of the repressed "other" within the house of Sutpen. She is the prophetic image of Charles Bon.

We hear in Mr. Compson's voice a classical and modern oedipalism. The dominate mode of reference is drama, and we read through the epic references to Clytemnestra and Cassandra to the primary story of Cadmus, to a climactic dramatic conflict that is contained in the tragedy of Oedipus. Yet this is a search for first principles, primal laws and explanations that are far more modern than Greek. The appropria-tion of Rosa's story in Mr. Compson's narrative reestablishes masculine narrative authority in the voice of the father, the man of law, the lawyer with all of Western culture at his command. The range of reference is encyclopedic, from Sophocles to Oscar Wilde. Even the Faulknerian intertext is caught up in the multiple references to drama; *Macbeth* re-turns in a misquotation about those long dead whose "joys and griefs must now be forgotten even by the very boards on which they strutted and postured and laughed and wept" (*AA*, p. 75). And in Mr. Comp-son's story we hear Quentin's desperate monologue from *The Sound and the Fury*; now we remember, recognize in the myriad repetitions of "Father said," that voice reported in the earlier novel.

Mr. Compson's interruption of Rosa initiates a shift from Thomas Sutpen, her primary focus, to Sutpen's black son, Charles Bon.

> He is the curious one to me. He came into that isolated puritan coun-
> try household almost like Sutpen himself came into Jefferson: apparently
> complete, without background or past or childhood. . . .
>
> (AA, p. 93)

Mr. Compson's rewriting of Rosa's description of Sutpen's abrupting
into the world of Jefferson furthers the general demystification of Sutpen that follows in the course of the novel. But the shift is itself curious;
Mr. Compson sets Bon against the classically tragic oedipal image of
his father. Bon is depicted in terms of fin-de-siècle decadence:

> this man whom Henry first saw riding perhaps through the grove at the
> University on one of the two horses which he kept there or perhaps cross-
> ing the campus on foot in the slightly Frenchified cloak and hat that he
> wore, or perhaps (I like to think this) presented formally to the man re-
> clining in a flowered, almost feminized gown, in a sunny window in his
> chambers—this man handsome and elegant and even catlike and too old
> to be where he was, too old not in years but in experience, with some
> tangible effluvium of knowledge, surfeit: of actions done and satiations
> plumbed and pleasures exhausted and even forgotten.
>
> (AA, p. 95)

Somewhat later in the narrative the references to Wilde and Beardsley
become explicit (AA, p. 193). Mr. Compson's story relates how Bon
seduced Henry in order to seduce Judith, but in terms of his own dramatic (formalist) model of action what his story lacks is logical motivation. The refrain of Mr. Compson's narration is "something is missing."
What is missing is truth, the foundation of narrative authority, the law
that explains all human motivations and desires. What is missing is a
phallic principle, and that lack raises the specter, dreaded and yet fascinating, of Bon as violation of oedipal difference, a feminized man.
Mr. Compson's "demon" resides in the image of southern defeat and
failure, in the collapse of both dramatic and social order. His demon
is the decadence of Bon, the inexplicable corruption of a tragic, heroic
Old South myth.

> It's just incredible. It just does not explain. Or perhaps that's it: they dont
> explain and we are not supposed to know. We have a few old mouth-to-
> mouth tales; we exhume from old trunks and boxes and drawers letters
> without salutation or signature, in which men and women who once lived
> and breathed are now merely initials or nicknames out of some incompre-
> hensible affection which sound to us like Sanskrit or Chocktaw; we see

dimly people, the people in whose living blood and seed we ourselves lay dormant and waiting, in this shadowy attenuation of time possessing now heroic proportions, performing their acts of simple passion and simple violence, impervious to time and inexplicable—Yes, Judith, Bon, Henry, Sutpen: all of them. They are there, yet something is missing; they are . . . just the words, the symbols, the shapes themselves, shadowy inscrutable and serene, against the turgid background of a horrible and bloody mischancing of human affairs.

(AA, pp. 100–101)

The reference to the Civil War as the "mischancing of human affairs" invokes the curtain speech of another tragedy, *Hamlet*. This, too, in a modern version: we would call it oedipal after early-twentieth-century Freudian work of dramatic interpretation. It is not that Faulkner read Ernest Jones but rather that Mr. Compson's narrative inevitably draws the past into a modern perspective; the point of view is from the decadence of the southern present, after the fall. Charles Bon represents that unspeakable contradiction within the traditional order of law (the Lost Cause) that the modern southerner recognizes with ambiguous loathing and fascination. It is Bon's and not Sutpen's motives and desires that are incomprehensible to Mr. Compson. Bon is the seductive/deconstructive "word," "symbol," "shape" that mars any formalist, Aristotelian, oedipal model of dramatic plotting. Bon is the sign of something missing that transgresses oedipal castration, for Bon can be resolved into neither masculine nor feminine. He is the transgression of transgression, another mysterious, fascinating, frightening figure of the threshold.

This, then, is the father's voice, a denying voice of "interdiction," a term Mr. Compson uses often in the context of social taboos such as incest, violations of the class (or caste) system, and cannibalism, to name a few (*AA*, pp. 98, 109, 247). The oedipal voice is another sort of interdiction; it interrupts minorities, represses the otherness of that "speaking between" the lines that Alice Jardine found so central to the voice of the feminist theorist. Mr. Compson is the voice of legitimation, the law; he is, appropriately, a lawyer. And he appropriates the word "interdict" for the law's use, as a synonym for "prohibit." Is this a misuse of the word which literally says to speak between, or is it an acknowledgment of the marginalization of the other to the threshold of all prohibition?

However we may answer this question, the father's voice is the dominant narrative in Quentin's consciousness, although Rosa's subversive version of Sutpen's story has a lasting effect. Quentin himself emerges as a primary narrator only belatedly, at the beginning of chapter 6 marking a shift in the place of narration from Jefferson, Mississippi, to Cambridge, Massachusetts. The immediate occasion of this narrative event is a letter from his father telling of Rosa's death; the reading of that letter is interrupted in mid-sentence and is not resumed until the next to the last page of the novel, a span of over two hundred pages. The letter frames the exchange between Quentin and his college room-mate, Shreve, but what we should note is the point of interruption: an expression from the father that death may bring no relief from suffering in life.

> *And if there can be either access of comfort or cessation of pain in the ultimate escape from a stubborn and amazed outrage which over a period of forty-three years has been companionship and bread and fire and all, I do not know that either—*
>
> (*AA*, p. 174)

When the letter resumes, this expression of doubt gives way to a peculiar hopefulness: that death brings fulfillment of one's deepest desires, for Rosa the revenge of confronting Sutpen once more.

> *—or perhaps there is. Surely it can harm no one to believe that perhaps she has escaped not at all the privilege of being outraged and amazed and of not forgiving but on the contrary has herself gained that place or bourne where the objects of the outrage and of the commiseration also are no longer ghosts but are actual people to be actual recipients of the hatred and the pity. It will do no harm to hope—You see I have written hope, not think.*
>
> (*AA*, p. 377)

What occurs between the reporting of these two sections of the father's letter is enabling for Quentin, as noted by the narrator's intrusive comment preceding the return to the letter at the novel's end: "Now he (Quentin) could read it, could finish it—" (*AA*, p. 377). We read in this transmission of his father's voice a chilling acceptance of what we know is Quentin's obsessive drive toward suicide, the "finish" of his monologue in *The Sound and the Fury*. We also hear in this the autobiographical echo of Faulkner's great-grandfather's cool acceptance of his son's murder at the hands of an outraged husband, the ultimate violence of the oedipal father toward his son. Within this interrupted reading of his father's letter, Quentin and Shreve engage in a dialogue of life and death, one that begins portentously with Quentin's defiance of his father's voice in an escape into a narration designed to wrest narrative authority from the father and challenge oedipal law. He will tell the story once more, and it will be his story.

> (Tell about the South. What's it like there. What do they do there. Why do they live there. Why do they live at all)—that very September evening when Mr. Compson stopped talking at last, he (Quentin) walked out of his father's talking at last . . . not because he had heard it all because he had not been listening, since he had something which he was unable to pass. . . .
>
> (AA, p. 174)

Walking "out of his father's talking," however, proves impossible, and Quentin, at this point, does not really seek this escape through suicide. In the continuation of this passage Hamlet is raised again, this time explicitly. Hamlet was also a son who could not walk out of his father's talking, haunted by ghosts, voices. So Quentin retells the same story, although it is never quite a simple repetition. He revises; under Shreve's careful ear for contradictions, Quentin asserts his authority. His father did not know certain details; Quentin provides his father with the truth, essentially: that the motive for Henry's killing of Bon was to prevent his incestuous marriage to Judith.

> "Your father," Shreve said. "He seems to have got an awful lot of delayed information awful quick, after having waited forty-five years. If he knew all of this, what was his reason for telling you that the trouble between Henry and Bon was the octoroon woman?"
> "He didn't know it then. Grandfather didn't tell him all of it either, like Sutpen never told Grandfather quite all of it."
> "Then who did tell him?"
> "I did."
>
> (AA, p. 266)

It is this passage that Cleanth Brooks uses to justify his argument that Quentin learned of Bon's relationship to Sutpen in his unreported conversation with Henry on the night of his visit to Sutpen's Hundred with Rosa. Yet it is precisely here that we must be most cautious. Nothing in the text prevents the reader from accepting Brooks's claim; it has a logic based on the juxtaposition of events: Quentin's revelation of the incest theme to his father following upon his meeting with

Henry. The consequence of accepting Brooks's reading, however, is to legitimize Quentin's narration, to displace other voices by establishing Quentin's neurotic thematics of oedipal law as a primary explanatory system. Quentin's obsession with the incest motive becomes not simply the expression of one voice in the collective dialogue but the authoritative perspective. There is much in the novel that militates against such a resolution of narrative conflict. One must wonder why Faulkner so deliberately omitted to tell us how Quentin knows about Bon if the legitimizing of Quentin's narrative was his goal. The very passage quoted above, so central to Brooks's argument, was a late revision in the manuscript; Faulkner was aware of the issue and chose not to resolve it. Brooks would reduce the novel to a monologue, to a mere repetition of Quentin's monologue in *The Sound and the Fury*, in the face of the reader's experience of *Absalom, Absalom!* as dialogue. These are profoundly different readings.

Repressing dialogue distorts the sense of southern history that Faulkner sought to represent in *Absalom, Absalom!* Faulkner represents history as the interpenetration of past and present; history is ongoing dialogue, quotation, revision, appropriation, and interpretation. Faulkner represents history against the complexities of community; history is a collective project. There is a difference between the "failed" monologues of *The Sound and the Fury* and the polyvocal narrations, interruptions, and echoes of *Absalom, Absalom!* The earlier novel attempts to locate narrative exclusively within individual consciousness as an existential/phenomenological project. Time and place, the central tropes of history, are muted; in Quentin's chapter time and place are raised to themes, presented as subjects of debate, concepts to be rejected. We dwell in Quentin's world, in his reality. In *The Sound and the Fury* Quentin's monologue is contained within the unholy trinity of Oedipus: what the father says, what the son hears, and what the seductive voice of the object of desire suggests.

When Quentin speaks to us again in *Absalom, Absalom!* his voice appears and fades among other voices, and these voices do not thematize time and place but evoke it, produce it. There is a Heideggerian magic in this calling forth of the ground of human action and thought: the world that is erected on the very solid earth of the modern South. It has become so real that Faulkner's readers imagine, as Howard Odum expressed it in the quote with which we began this reading of Faulkner, that they have been there or could visit this fictional Mississippi. And so they can, if they take with them into the topography of this southern state the thought, the discourse which produces our only sense of time and place. The whole force of *Absalom, Absalom!* breaks through Quentin's efforts to escape the place of his birth and the history that is the consciousness of that place. In Faulkner's narrative we cannot derive time and place from individual consciousness; we view the production of time and place which precedes individual consciousness, as if consciousness were an afterthought.

We cannot, however, draw from this the simplistic idea that history is determinative; it is so only for Quentin, whose sense of fatedness has become distorted out of history into myth. His narrative is not by chance obsessively repetitive, filled with laments at having to tell and hear the Sutpen story over and over again (*AA*, pp. 174, 207, 261, 277). John Irwin's clever exposition of the repetition in *Absalom, Absalom!* draws support largely from Quentin's consciousness.[9] As Irwin knows, Quentin's repetitions reflect what Freud called an "instinctual" action, a "compulsion with its hint of possession by some 'daemonic power.'"

> But how is the predicate of being "instinctual" related to the compulsion to repeat? At this point we cannot escape a suspicion that we may have come upon the track of a universal attribute of instincts and perhaps of organic life in general which has not hitherto been clearly recognized or at least not explicitly stressed. *It seems, then, that an instinct is an urge inherent in organic life to restore an earlier state of things* which the living entity has been obliged to abandon under the pressure of external disturbing forces; that is, it is a kind of organic elasticity, or, to put it another way, the expression of the inertia inherent in organic life.
>
> This view of instincts strikes us as strange because we have become used to see in them a factor impelling towards change and development, whereas we are now asked to recognize in them the precise contrary—an expression of the *conservative* nature of living substance.[10]

Quentin's demon, not his father's or Rosa's, expresses his resistance to time and the particularity of place, his expulsion of change and his reduction of community. Compulsive repetition familiarizes, moves toward the psychical effects of Addie Bundren's repetition of her husband's name: she forgets Anse, represses him in the emptiness of the signifier which names him.

What Freud in 1920 called the desire for the "quiescence of the inorganic world"[11] manifest in the repetition compulsion appears in Faulkner's southern narrative as Quentin's rejection of generation and, hence, genealogy, history, and narrative itself. It is the extreme of that Keatsian aesthetic ideal of lyric stasis which fascinated Faulkner, but which he always represented as flawed and located within his narrative as a theme or character trait and never outside it as a principle of composition. That Keatsian ideal is profoundly modern, echoed in Yeats's golden bird and Stevens' fictionalizing act of the mind, all of which echo the Freudian interpretation of repetition as that which ties the aesthetic to a radical denial of the body, of sexuality and engendering. The aesthetic displaces sexuality, and, as Nietzsche long ago wrote of the Kantian aesthetics of "disinterested interest," it establishes the utterly ridiculous concept that art triumphs over sensuality, over desire.[12] Quentin's retreat from sensuality contrasts directly with Rosa's drive toward it; for Rosa, thought and discourse incline toward "touch." Words hurt. For Quentin, words detach from the body of being-in-the-world, of being with other beings, and, therefore, all manifestations of presence must be denied: all change, time, history, narrative, touch, sex, orgasm, marriage—even listening.

Quentin's incest, his verbal construct of incest, is an oedipal challenge but is not really anti-oedipal, for it does not transgress oedipal law, as Bon's presence in Mr. Compson's narrative seems to do. Quentin seeks recognition of his violation of the primal taboo in order to be punished under the terms of Oedipus, to be expelled from human society, from the community. Quentin's speaking seeks the invoking of an interdiction, a prohibition, rather than asserts his own disruptive interdiction of oedipal authority. Thus he seeks affirmation of oedipal authority rather than negation of it, and we see that the desire for the quiescence of the inorganic is masochistic. Freud believed it to be essentially self-destructive,[13] and so it may be associated with a death instinct, with suicide. Quentin seems a calculated exemplum; we are tempted to read Faulkner's Quentin novels against Freud's radical texts. But on closer reading *Absalom, Absalom!* is a text that forestalls Quentin's suicide, retracts it for a time and space of dialogue.

Quentin's narrative in this novel's time and space has nothing about it of suicide, although Quentin is masochistic. His compulsion to repeat also forestalls suicide; his desire is regressive but cannot reach beyond consciousness itself, beyond talking. In the cold, darkened room at Harvard where Quentin and Shreve talk, the room that Faulkner repeatedly calls "tomblike," Quentin sits seemingly impervious to the freezing temperature. Numb to all sensual experience save the auditory, Quentin seems to exist solely as a voice. The novel carries the reader toward those seemingly climactic moments of narration when identities are lost in the autonomy of the narrative itself, in the fiction that designates no real presence. But Faulkner never allows these regressions beyond, below identity, into fiction or into the imaginary, to function climactically. Quentin's effort to reduce narrative to stasis represents the specific aesthetic and social limits that Faulkner as a southern novelist strives to break through.

Interestingly, it is Quentin who initiates a series of moves designed to produce a kind of narrative entropy, to disperse difference; he says of Shreve, "He sounds just like father," and then repeats this claim several times (*AA*, pp. 181, 207, 211). But Quentin *hears* his father; he does not *listen* to Shreve. He seeks from Shreve what he desired of his father: recognition of his sin and confirmation of the repetitive, timeless oedipal law. But there is a crucial distinction to be made, one Faulkner stumbled upon in the necessity of rejecting Quentin's Keatsian aesthetics and southern mythmaking. It is the distinction between Rosa's demonic Sutpen, whose implementation of oedipal law is sadistic, a violent imposition of oedipal family and social order on others, an arrangement of bodies according to his rigid design, and Quentin's Sutpen who functions as the symbol of symbols, the father of fathers, the Symbolic Father, a name. What Quentin resists is passing through the oedipal stage. Sutpen functions for Quentin's narrative in the manner of Michael Rogin's imaginary father, as a psychologically overdetermined signifier that generates the paternalistic myth of Old South heroism and masculine identity. So we may say that Quentin is Faulkner's other self, self-victimized by his legendary great-grandfather, but then we must also conclude that it is that victimized self that *Absalom, Absalom!* attempts to exorcize even though such an exorcism also does away with the very foundations of southern culture, the mythic glory of the southern past. That exorcism will not permit the narration to resolve itself simply into an authorial monologue, into some aesthetic version of a marriage of speaking and hearing.

Faulkner makes us critically, judgmentally aware of the fact that Quentin's regression affirms the oedipal. He does this through a de-biologized form of symbolic generation, the production of symbols out of symbols, names out of names, voices out of voices, a form of symbolic action that represses the body, represses the ground of the imagination in pre-oedipal intersections of surfaces (touch, connection, interpenetration), prohibits, interdicts the revelation of the thresholds of oedipal law and authority. So Shreve turns Quentin's "He sounds just like father" back on Quentin, rewriting "father" as "old man." The passage Faulkner gives to Quentin in response to Shreve's demystifying accusation here is extraordinary.

> "Dont say it's just me that sounds like your old man," Shreve said. "But go on. Sutpen's children. Go on."
>
> "Yes," Quentin said. "The two children" thinking *Yes. Maybe we are both Father. Maybe nothing ever happens once and is finished. Maybe happen is never once but like ripples maybe on water after the pebble sinks, the ripples moving on, spreading, the pool attached by a narrow umbilical water-cord to the next pool which the first pool feeds, has fed, did feed, let this second pool contain a different temperature of water, a different molecularity of having seen, felt, remembered, reflect in a different tone the infinite unchanging sky, it doesn't matter: that pebble's watery echo whose fall it did not even see moves across its surface too at the original ripple-space, to the old ineradicable rhythm* thinking *Yes, we are both Father. Or maybe Father and I are both Shreve, maybe it took Father and me both to make Shreve or Shreve and me both to make Father or maybe Thomas Sutpen to make all of us.*
>
> (*AA*, pp. 261–62)

I will merely suggest a reading of this dense passage. The conflict between Shreve and Quentin is manifest in Shreve's insistent "go on," a narrative impulse, and Quentin's inability to do so, his expansion and transformation of a central image that rests on an obsessive theme. The topic is "children," specifically Thomas Sutpen's "legitimate" children, Henry and Judith, who bear his name; Bon is excluded. The theme is repetition imaged in the water's ripples. Into this rather conventional metaphor Quentin intrudes the unlikely and even inappropriate "umbilical," transforming the image of repetitious events into a metaphor of generation and engendering, the pebble (masculinity, sperm) disturbing the quiet of the womblike pool, the source of nurture in gestation. He introduces the "second pool," the child, a principle of difference, yet all the differences of temperature, molecularity, sight, feeling, remembering, individual experience do not "matter." The second pool is never more than a "watery echo" of the engendering pebble, tracing its secondary being to an origin prior to memory and experience. The paternal remains detached, prior, outside experience; the paternal enters consciousness not via experience but through "the old ineradicable rhythm." Quentin's thoughts have made another almost imperceptible shift, intruding an image of writing (that which cannot

be erased, effaced) into the metaphor of the engendering pebble and
gestational pool. The ripples across the surface of the water are the
disturbances of inscription on the blank surface of the page, the nota-
tion of origin and paternal authority in the Sutpen story. Engendering,
"making," even talking, are forms of self-reproduction. Now "sounds
like father" is also rewritten as a principle of generation, composition:
father is "Father." Making is exclusively masculine, for the story of
Sutpen is reappropriated from Rosa. Narrative, the "go on" of Shreve's
impatient charge, displaces experience (Rosa's eyewitness authority) by
symbolic engendering guaranteed by the symbol of symbols, the Symbol of the Father: Thomas Sutpen. Quentin is firmly within the oedipal
model of social order; there incest is the only probable explanation
for Henry's killing of Bon, an act of exclusion. But it is precisely here
that we understand why Quentin does not articulate Faulkner's final
design in *Absalom, Absalom!* for Faulkner resisted symbolic engendering by the Name of the Father in his own symbolic act of rewriting
his family name. He made himself, much like Lucas Beauchamp in *Go
Down, Moses*, as man "by himself composed, himself selfprogenitive
and nominate" (*GDM*, p. 281).

Neither Brooks's legitimation of Quentin's voice nor the unfortunate
reading of Faulkner's dialogic play of voices in *Absalom, Absalom!* as
resolving into a marriage that reduces differences to the same voice reflects the careful, self-conscious style of Faulkner's narrative. Neither
Quentin nor Shreve sounds exactly like Mr. Compson, and Quentin's
rather pointed exclusion of Rosa from the generational production of
the Sutpen narrative fails to silence her voice. Much of our understanding of Faulkner's dialogic novel rests on our perception of Shreve, the
outsider to the community of Quentin's discursive identity who is, for
a time, allowed inside. Shreve is disruptive and disorienting, as a Cana-
dian deliberately beyond even the Old South dichotomy of Confederate
and Yankee. François Pitavy argues that Shreve's function is "analogous
to that of the reader" and cites Faulkner's own characterization of the
reader as having a fourteenth way of looking at the blackbird (the story
of Sutpen), which fourteenth way, Faulkner claimed, he "would like
to think is the truth."[14] Yet neither Shreve as the reader's reader nor
the reader herself can lay such claims to truth, for neither can resolve
contradictions that Faulkner leaves in his narrative to mark divisions
between narrative voices, to mark the intrusion and revision of dialogue. Shreve does not represent some reader's power to complete what

Faulkner made sure frustrated all of his narrators. If anything, Shreve is analogous with a potential not for truth but for revision:

> Shreve ceased again. It was just as well, since he had no listener. Perhaps he was aware of it. Then suddenly he had no talker either, though possibly he was not aware of this. Because now neither of them were there. They were both in Carolina and the time was forty-six years ago, and it was not even four now but compounded still further, since now both of them were Henry Sutpen and both of them were Bon, compounded each of both yet either neither, smelling the very smoke which had blown and faded away forty-six years ago from the *bivouac fires burning in a pine grove, the gaunt and ragged men sitting or lying about them, talking not about the war yet all curiously enough (or perhaps not curiously at all) facing the South where further on in the darkness the pickets stood....*
>
> (*AA,* p. 351)

The Faulknerian shift into italics signals here an alteration in the narrative mode. What follows is a direct reproduction of two crucial conversations, one between Henry and his father, the other between Henry and Bon. In the first, Henry learns that Bon is not only his half brother but also black. In the second, Bon identifies the true motive for Henry's act of fratricide: "*So it's the miscegenation, not the incest, which you cant bear*" (*AA,* p. 356). Yet this marvelous passage with its illusion of being unauthored, and hence unprejudiced, fades back into Shreve's narration:

> —*You will have to stop me, Henry.* "And he never slipped away," Shreve said. "He could have, but he never even tried. Jesus, maybe he even went to Henry and said, 'I'm going, Henry' and maybe they left together and rode side by side dodging Yankee patrols all the way back to Mississippi and right up to the gate; side by side and it was only then that one of them ever rode ahead or dropped behind and that only then Henry spurred ahead and turned his horse to face Bon and took out the pistol; and Judith and Clytie heard the shot...."
>
> (*AA,* p. 358)

Yet finally, I believe, we cannot, we must not, sort out a primary narrative, a true version that subsumes all others, dissolves dialogue into monologue, for Shreve's proposition that miscegenation was the essential motive in Henry's killing of Bon does not erase Quentin's focus on incest any more than it silences Rosa's demonology version and Mr. Compson's theory of tragic decadence. Shreve returns the

Sutpen discourse to the unavoidable social issue of race; he supplies the dimension missing from all the other narratives with their Lost Cause apologetics in order to trace the fall of the Old South ideal to the unadorned fact of slavery. There is in Shreve's telling the story a strategy aimed at jarring Quentin out of his oedipal obsession, of removing the southern guilt from the realm of private abstract, even romanticized sinfulness to the register of public action, policy, politics. But Quentin's resistance is too powerful for Shreve's tactic; his acquiescence to Shreve's narrative explanation is momentary, retracted almost immediately as the novel closes on Quentin's string of negative responses to Shreve's persistent pressing of his point of view. In this context Quentin's agonized cry that he does not hate the South expresses most forcefully his inability to break free of the oedipal constraints that he confuses with the glories of the Old South culture. He does not hate the South, and to prove it he will submit himself to its strict punishment for those who sin against it. It is as if by provoking the wrath of the Father he will return the father to his former power and glory.

Faulkner here pauses at a moment of unresolvable conflict. The answer is clear: Shreve has unmasked the repressed that southern myth-making repetitively sought to mystify. But Faulkner's journey in *Absalom, Absalom!* is one of discovery and not resolution; that latter task will remain for *Go Down, Moses*, wherein the unambiguous merging of the incest and miscegenation themes brings the deep-seated agony of the modern South to its only possible resolution, once more in the theme of love. The ambiguity of *Absalom, Absalom!* reveals Faulkner's sense of the personalization of communal guilt, the internalization of collective sin, that produces endless mythic mediations and delusions. Faulkner is no optimist about the future of the South, but neither can we read into his fear of the future a simplistic nostalgia for the old cavalier ways. That Quentin's narrative is no less an apology for the South than Mr. Compson's or Rosa's is not ambiguous. Each of the three southern narrators finds a strategy of reconciliation with Old South codes, and each sacrifices in order to do so. That Shreve fails to depersonalize and, therefore, demystify Quentin's oedipal mythology for Quentin does not mean that Faulkner has failed to demystify it for the reader.

Thus there is no confusion about the moral implications of these southern discursive practices any more than there is a lack of sophistication in Faulkner's representation of the embeddedness of narrative practice in collective discourse. The "rag-tag and bob-ends of old tales and talking" (*AA*, p. 303) compose the powerful residual hold of the what-was-thought-to-have-been over the what-is and the what-one-wishes-to-be. Quentin's tragic death as it was presented in *The Sound and the Fury* is in *Absalom, Absalom!* given infinite depth. The discursive, narrative reality of *Absalom, Absalom!* seems to produce a Quentin for the very purposes of self-destruction, as scapegoat. It is this scapegoating that is the source of Faulkner's sympathy and hatred for his South; his is not a mindless nostalgia for the heroic times of "better" men. This is, assuredly, a position that stymies action and inevitably issues in the "go slow" resistance to reform (change) that mars Faulkner's later civil rights activism. But in Shreve's bold and revolutionary "go on" Faulkner has also released a voice of revision that truly overpasses that resistance to change. That Faulkner here identifies what is right and what is wrong does not assure him of the necessary triumph of good over evil. In his sense of the deep resistance to civil rights reform, resistance not only in the South, Faulkner may have seen beyond the heady days of progress in the 1960s and 1970s to what in the 1980s appears to be a heinous retreat from revolution in matters of racial and sexual equality. Quentin's moral weakness yet remains an obstacle to going on, necessitating radical action based on a radical critique. Faulkner's project in *Absalom, Absalom!* initiates such a critique.

PART III

Reading Faulkner

CHAPTER 14

Representation and Racial Difference

WRITING SPECIFICALLY about Faulkner's black characters, Thadious Davis claims that "more than any other writer, Faulkner explored the richness and complexity of southern life in his fiction."[1] This should always be a given of Faulkner criticism, an initial assumption that grounds all interpretations of his novels, but Davis, whose critical allegiance is to American formalism, quickly abandons the exploration of this "richness and complexity of southern life" when it raises unwelcome issues. The embarrassing ambiguity of Faulkner's attitudes on race relations in the South is just such a sticking point. The formalist strategy in such a case divides the artist from the man, preserving the purity of the former while consigning the latter to a critical purgatory inhabited by critics who have failed courses in art appreciation. Davis argues that "as a southerner Faulkner may have become embroiled in the unending controversy regarding race in the South; nevertheless, as an artist committed to communicating his vision of life, he is not so interested in blacks as individual characters as he is in formulating his aesthetic image and sense of the 'Negro.'"[2]

Davis is ensnared in an old formalist dichotomy between the aesthetic and the real. The language she uses to express this separation trivializes that which she considers not aesthetic or artistic; she dismisses too easily "the unending controversy regarding race." She replaces "southern life," in this instance the heroic struggle in the twentieth century to bring about racial equality and justice, with what she calls Faulkner's "vision of life," an aesthetic world signaled by writing "Negro" in quotation marks. The term "Negro," therefore, must

221

be read metalinguistically, as referring to language itself rather than to anything real. Moreover, "Negro," for Davis, is an abstraction that blurs individuality in order to close off lines of contact between aesthetic images and real social beings. This strained argument is designed to avoid the critical question of whether or not Faulkner, a white male southern author, was successful, or just, or insightful in his representation of blacks. But surely Davis' tactic of abstracting and aestheticizing the "Negro" fails to accomplish this aim, for the reading of particular black figures as types of the Negro reinforces racist stereotyping and discrimination. A perspective that differentiates in kind between whites and blacks but indiscriminately cancels out all differences between black and black sees blacks as irreducibly "other" than whites. Davis does not intend this to be the consequence of her approach; the aestheticizing of black into "Negro" ought to forestall any intrusion of the complex social and political issues of racial difference into the fictional world of Faulkner's novels. But the aestheticization of narrative characterization rests on a semiotic play of differences; the "Negro" is not a monolithic category but a diacritical sign defined by its juxtaposition with other signs representing racial identity. As a result, the term "Negro" cannot be aestheticized beyond its social-historical context; it is not a fiction that provides the illusion of an escape from reference. In fact, "Negro," like "Yoknapatawpha," is aligned with a very real Mississippi, with a very real history of slavery and racist violence in the old and new South, with the singularity of the Civil War, with old and new South economies, old and new South social hegemonies, and, most important of all, old and new South traditions of storytelling.

Set against the background of southern social history, the representation of racial difference involves far more individualization, or, in both its positive and negative implications, far more discrimination, than Davis' monolithic generalization, the "Negro," can support. For example, in a novel like *Intruder in the Dust* the term "Negro" and paradigmatically related terms like "nigger," "black," and "Sambo" are carefully plotted in order to differentiate racial attitudes, identify prejudices, trace character growth, and, most important, represent the extraordinary pressure of familiar social, hegemonic discourse on the attitudes and perceptions of individual members of that discursive community. The central figure in this representation of a discursive community is a young boy, Charles ("Chick") Mallison. As a result of the arrest of Lucas Beauchamp for the murder of Vinson Gowrie, Chick awakens to the discursive functioning of language, to hegemony; this is, of course, the same as an awakening to the functioning of the symbolic order, the crossing of a threshold. What he hears is repetition, the same words in diverse contexts from diverse speakers. The subject of this repetition is a central mystery in the community: why, against all communal expectations, did the quite lawless Gowries not lynch Lucas on the spot for killing one of their kind? One explanation is that the burial of Vinson had to be accomplished first.

> "They're burying Vinson this afternoon and to burn a nigger right while the funeral's going on wouldn't be respectful to Vinson."
> "That's so. It'll probably be tonight."
> "On Sunday night?"
> "Is that the Gowries fault? Lucas ought to thought of that before he picked out Saturday to kill Vinson on."
>
> (*ID*, p. 40)

The conversation is horrifying and at the same time absurd. What is most important, however, is that Chick hears the crucial statement that "Lucas ought to thought of that before he picked out Saturday to kill Vinson" on three occasions. The result is that he suddenly becomes self-conscious about language, about communal discursive practices *and* the implications of these practices.

> Whereupon the man said almost exactly what the man in the barbershop had said this morning (and he remembered his uncle saying once how little of vocabulary man really needed to get comfortably and even efficiently through his life, how not only in the individual but within his whole type and race and kind a few simple clichés served his few simple passions and needs and lusts).
>
> (*ID*, pp. 47–48)

Chick's uncle, Gavin Stevens, has provided the young boy with a simple explanation of a simple phenomenon, but Chick, on the occasion of the third repetition, elaborates and revises Stevens' theory.

> Now he heard for the third time almost exactly what he had heard twice in twelve hours, and he marvelled again at the paucity, the really almost standardized meagerness not of individual vocabularies but of Vocabulary itself, by means of which even man can live in vast droves and herds in concrete warrens in comparative amity. . . .
>
> (*ID*, p. 80)

The expansion of Stevens' observation to a commentary on "Vocabulary," that is, on language, raises the discussion to something akin to a metalinguistic level, but the focus is still, as always for Faulkner, on discourse, on the social functioning of language. Its paucity or poverty is the very force of communal bonding, for it not only reduces language to a few phrases but, far more important, reduces familiar reality, what in this novel is called "fact" or "expectation," to comfortable predictability. Human behavior, the truth, are reduced to a "standardized meagerness."

There are other repeated phrases, even intertextual quotations, that seem to draw the community of Faulkner's South more tightly together, spanning even a century of history, tracing through a family's genealogy. Lucas explains why he asks Chick, a young boy, to help him establish his innocence and not Chick's uncle, a prominent white lawyer in the community.

> "Young folks and womens, they aint cluttered. They can listen. But a middle-year man like your paw and your uncle, they cant listen. They aint got time. They're too busy with facks. In fact, you mought bear this in yo mind; someday you mought need it. If you ever needs to get anything done outside the common run, dont wast yo time on the menfolks; get the women and children to working at it."
>
> (*ID*, pp. 71–72)

The intertextual reference again links *Intruder in the Dust* with *Go Down, Moses*; Lucas repeats the advice given by his father, "Tomy's Turl," to McCaslin Edmonds in the story "Was." But this genealogical link is submerged in the context of *Intruder in the Dust*, for it is not the direct quotation that is startling to Chick (he could not know of the earlier version); it is the repetition of Lucas' words by Miss Habersham, who does, as Lucas predicted, help Chick prove Lucas' innocence, that reminds him of the poverty of language. Only this time, he recognizes a critical division in discursive practice. What is defined by Miss Habersham's repetition is an alternative community consisting of blacks, women, and children; it is a community of minorities, marginalized on the threshold of the dominant community of adult, white men. Moreover, the minority discourse, also marked by its own special kind of poverty, articulates "truth" as opposed to the "facts" which blind men to the truth. The dominant race, gender, class cannot listen to anything outside the familiar expectations, cannot say anything not already said:

> now Miss Habersham in her turn repeating and paraphrasing and he thought how it was not really a paucity a meagerness of vocabulary, it

was in the first place because the deliberate violent blotting out obliteration of a human life was itself so simple and so final that the verbiage which surrounded it enclosed it insulated it intact into the chronicle of man had of necessity to be simple and uncomplex too, repetitive, almost monotonous even; and in the second place, vaster than that, adumbrating that, because what Miss Habersham paraphrased was simple truth, not even fact and so there was not needed a great deal of diversification and originality to express it. . . .

"Lucas knew it would take a child—or an old woman like me: someone not concerned with probability, with evidence. Men like your uncle and Mr Hampton have had to be men too long, busy too long. . . ."

(*ID*, pp. 89–90)

Once more Faulkner returns us to the powerful dilemma he articulated in *As I Lay Dying*. In response to Miss Habersham and Lucas, Chick raises the problem of the relationship between the symbolic and the real, between, as Addie Bundren put it, words and doing. The language of "facts," therefore, contrary to the commonsense definition, has nothing to do with the real world of human actions. That world, grounded in the essential dualism of life and death, is the world of the body-without-words, inarticulate, a world of presence, of experience, a world not merely reflected in language but defined by discursive poverty, arranged and ordered by discursive hegemonies. *Intruder in the Dust* tells again of bodies that cannot be buried, erased, repressed, of identities that cannot be exchanged, disguised, supplemented. Associated with the world of symbolic order are the violences on the body that put Lucas' life at risk "not because he was a murderer but because his skin was black" (*ID*, p. 72). And not simply because he is black but because blackness has been encoded as a fact of guilt. Here one cannot say that language makes no contact with life. And so, too, are Chick, Miss Habersham, and the young black boy Alec Sander put at risk in the struggle to break through "facts" and "expectations," through hegemonic discourse to the "truth" of concrete social conditions.

The representation of racial difference in *Intruder in the Dust* rests on a representation of discursive practices in the community. Phrases that define attitudes toward Lucas, even those seemingly approving of, legitimizing his death at the hands of the Gowries—"be a nigger," "make a nigger out of him," and "act like a nigger" (*ID*, pp. 22, 32, and 48)—also trace the evolution of Chick's socialization, his adaptation to the dominant discursive practice and his eventual rebellion against it. What is most interesting about Faulkner's black characters is that their various representational functions insist that we become embroiled in the very social controversy that Davis wishes to exclude from our read-ing of the novels. In turn, we cannot avoid judging Faulkner's handling of these basic human concerns. The representation of racial difference ranges between two extremes, between seeking to overcome difference and affirming it. However, neither extreme—neither the denial of dif-ference nor the assertion of it—is in itself either racist or egalitarian. One may desire or fear the absence of difference, exploit or welcome its facticity. To his credit, Faulkner does not try to avoid these complex variations in his repeated struggles to represent blacks; to the dismay of his many admirers, he is not always critically alert to the ethical implications of his characterizations.

Of course, we do not read Faulkner for accuracy, for the true his-tory of race relations in the South. His version of southern life—to use his own formula from *Absalom, Absalom!*—is "probably true enough" (*AA*, p. 335) in that his voice intersects a complex southern discourse, engages a vast rhetorical project comprising countless other voices all strategically rewriting southern history into southern myth. In this col-lective project racial identity and racial difference are the structural terms of a troubled mythology, and as such, the ongoing southern dis-course on racial difference comprises both form and content of Faulk-ner's narratives of the South.

In *The Rhetoric of Doubtful Authority* Ralph Flores reads *Absa-lom, Absalom!* in order to trace the semiotic play of difference. He begins, interestingly, by noting the critical unrest caused by Faulkner's representations of southern blacks. "Commentators," he says, "have often found themselves helpless . . . to extract a 'consistent' Faulkner-ian viewpoint on race."[3] From Flores' narrow deconstructionist per-spective, however, inconsistency is merely an inevitable consequence of reading racial difference as Derridian *différance,* as an endless de-ferring of authoritative narration and thus of any authorized (that is, Faulknerian) point of view. Flores illustrates this deconstructionist ap-proach through an analysis of the semiotic functioning of characters like Charles Bon, and particularly Bon's (and Sutpen's) heir Jim Bond. Both Bon and Bond are of racially mixed parentage and, therefore, lack clearly defined racial identities. Miscegenation, Flores rightly sug-gests, problematizes the semiotics of difference: "Neither something nor nothing, Bond both is and undoes the Sutpen design which in any origins or results had repeatedly 'vanished and left no trace, nothing,' 'coming down like it had been built out of smoke.'"[4] Consistent with other formalist readings of *Absalom, Absalom!* Flores conflates Sutpen's design with the form of the narrative of that design, thereby also equating the undoing of Sutpen's dynastic dream and the endless deferring of both narrative closure and any expression of a consistent authorial stance on the issue of race. Blending deconstruction with formalism, Flores argues that the Derridian quality of Faulkner's deferred authority "confounds conventional measures of social critique." [5]

Curiously, this reading of *Absalom, Absalom!* emerges as a rather traditional defense of Faulkner's inconsistency on the issue of race, one not unlike Davis' aestheticizing of Faulkner's black characters. Flores suggests that social commentary has no place in the language of a Derridian text. For almost all American deconstructionists, Derrida's analytical methodology tends to become prescriptive so that deferral bars social commitment. The semiotic play of (racial) difference deconstructs not only the text of Sutpen's authoritarian design but also the text of Faulkner's authorial voice; in dismissing any critical search for a consistent authorial viewpoint, Flores dismisses all viewpoints whatsoever. Faulkner is inconsistent on race, but Flores fails to see that an inconsistent viewpoint is nonetheless a viewpoint. His argument that the play of differences in *Absalom, Absalom!* confounds social critique, moreover, is overthrown by Carolyn Porter's ambitious and insightful reading of the novel. The undoing of Sutpen's design, by which Faulkner represents the problematical play of difference in the social theme of miscegenation, springs, Porter demonstrates, from a fundamental contradiction inscribed in the cavalier mythology of the Old South, a contradiction between a paternalistic social myth and entrepreneural capitalism. Porter asserts that "the fusion of family and marketplace values was fostered, ironically, by the same presence which ultimately exploded it—the black slave, whose imputed status as a member of the family was in conflict with his economic function as a part of the labor force." [6]

Porter's sociological equivalent of Flores' textual or rhetorical explanation of the undoing of Sutpen's design redirects our attention to the historical embeddedness of Faulkner's freeplay of (racial) difference, but with Faulkner we are not dealing with a naive realism or with a simplistic theory of recognition or presencing. Formalisms from Platonism to deconstruction have found easy prey in the problematics of establishing some direct connection between words and things, signifiers and signifieds. What Faulkner offers us, however, is a representation not of ontic reality but of real discursive practice. Representation as naive realism, Terry Eagleton claims, is restricted by the demands of noncontradiction; discursive reality, on the other hand, opens the possibility of what might be called a "contradictory representation," the possibility of a conflict of realities which forms the concrete ground of our familiar, lived experience.

> But one must speak cautiously, because one cannot represent a contradiction as one can a *thing*. Contradictions are not objects to be reflected, any more than differences are; one cannot observe a contradiction as one can observe a factory gate. The contradiction between labor and capital, or colonized and imperialist is a matter of *interests*, and thus belongs to the realm of discourse—without, of course, being any the less "real" or "objective" for that.[7]

The frequency with which Faulkner foregrounds characters like Joe Christmas, Charles Bon, and the black woman of "Delta Autumn," who do not "look" black, forces the reader to an awareness that racial difference is a function of discursive practice. Racial difference is invisible, but as such it is, for racism, even more menacing. Racism, therefore, clings to what is known or remembered, to what can be established according to the prescriptions of the social codes, to the mathematics of "blood," to genealogy and, therefore, to language. The southern conception of family acts as a guarantee of racial identity, at least insofar as a semiotic formula structures legitimacy of descent through the passing on of the name of the father. When the genealogical family intersects with the southern myth of paternalism, the semiotic play of racial difference uncovers a catastrophic contradiction at the heart of southern society. Flores rightly notes that in characters of mixed racial parentage Faulkner portrays a principle of difference that is also a Derridian deferral of identity. What he does not grasp is the link between the portrayal of that problematical difference and a fundamental contradiction in the South's self-definition. Miscegenation, as Faulkner powerfully portrays it, is a family affair. Racism is a system of classification within genealogy, and, therefore, racism is a mode of writing and rewriting history, of defining difference (and sameness) as descent, of transcending history in order to produce mythic narratives which justify, legitimize racist discrimination and guarantee the hegemony of the interests of the dominant white race. The southern narrators of Sutpen's story in *Absalom, Absalom!* engage the discursive practice of southern mythmaking as they revise the history of the Sutpen family into the mythic stasis of "Sutpen's design." Yet in Faulkner's narrative they do not in fact transcend history; they repeatedly uncover the complex and contradictory history of southern discursive practice. There is, then, a writing which unwrites what is written, which demystifies myth into social history; it is a writing that produces novels like *Absalom, Absalom!* and *Go Down, Moses* and *Intruder in the Dust.*

The inconsistency of attitudes expressed in Faulkner's various representations of blacks reflects a climate of distrust heightened by a destabilized social economy in the Depression era South. Moreover, a fear of the unknown and of change, arising from the lingering effects of Lost Causism, was focused more intensely than ever on the issue of race under the rapidly increasing pressure of civil rights activity in the thirties and forties. The traditional stability of small rural communities was also disrupted by the rapid development of modern transportation, by the vast improvement of roads, and by the increased numbers of migrant workers who moved in and out of communities seasonally. Origins and genealogies became confused; there was no reliable knowledge about the family histories of transients. Racial purity was difficult to establish, and this tended to stiffen the resolve to maintain segregated social institutions at all costs. This "reality" invaded Faulkner's career at its most productive phase and embedded the author's decisions to write in the discursive practices of his native region. Faulkner returned again and again to the problems of race relations in his novels, seemingly in an attempt to bring into his narratives a sense of racial difference which represented the deep divisions that troubled the South.

The narrative representation of racial difference raises several issues of mingled social and aesthetic interest. Primary among these is a definition of voice or voices. The fundamental issue for Faulkner is the delimitation of the authorial self: a white male Southerner undertaking to articulate his sense of racial difference. In traditional terms this is a matter of authorial distance, objectivity, or the establishing of the limits of aesthetic freedom and control. The ground of such aesthetic matters, however, is social and political; they are the expression of relations of authority and power. Representing racial difference involves the distribution of power or the submerging of the authoritative voice of monologue in a genuine portrayal of difference through dialogue. To whom and from what locus of authority do Faulkner's black characters speak? This is not to ask, however, whether Faulkner allows his black characters to speak for themselves. The focus is not on the aesthetic illusion of direct quotation, a kind of ventriloquist's trick, but on the sense of otherness or difference his black characters represent. The reader must ask of Faulkner, What is the difference of your difference? The answer is entangled in the speaking relationships between black characters and the authorial voice and between black characters and other characters. An issue of narrative and social authorization is represented in the dialogue of racial difference.

To adequately measure Faulkner's struggle to represent racial difference we must read at least three novels intertextually. *Absalom, Absalom!, Go Down, Moses,* and *Intruder in the Dust* span more than a decade of his career and reflect a period of extraordinary social change. The crucial movement in the narrative structure of *Absalom, Absalom!* is the gradual shift of focus from Sutpen to his children. The story Sutpen told Grandfather Compson of his motives for coming to Mississippi only incidentally concerns racial differences; Sutpen's desires are class oriented, slaves being merely one form of wealth necessary in his dream of dynastic power. The gradual refocusing of the narrative on Sutpen's children, however, transforms this dream into a family affair and allows for the introduction of the issue of racial difference into the family model. Charles Bon's racial identity is uncertain, and he intrudes that uncertainty into Sutpen's design. Whether or not Sutpen knows the truth about Bon is irrelevant. The primary narrators of Bon's interaction with Henry and Judith Sutpen do not know, and that absence of motive itself motivates the freeplay of Shreve's and Quentin's dialogue, their effort to determine why Henry killed Bon. What they construct is a discursive supplementation of the motives of incest and miscegenation which represents that "fusion of family and marketplace values" Porter insightfully defined as the underlying social and political meaning of the novel.

Incest and miscegenation, which are in supplemental play in *Absalom, Absalom!* are compressed into identity in *Go Down, Moses.* The result is a novel very different from *Absalom, Absalom!* in tone and narrative structure. Ike's discovery of the original family sin while reading the old ledgers of the McCaslin plantation unambiguously outlines the contradiction at the origins of the McCaslin family, and through an analogy frequently articulated in the novel, at the origins of the South. There is here a continuation of a theme first raised by Rosa in *Absalom, Absalom!*: that the fall of the South had its causes deep within the southern culture itself and could be blamed on no alien evil. And this version, too, can be traced to its predecessor text, to the first of Faulkner's fall-of-the-South novels, *Flags in the Dust,* with its central theme of Sartoris suicidal fatedness. *Go Down, Moses* is an extraordinary tangle of family and social structures, of displaced authority and power, of dispersed voices. It is, nevertheless, a novel sure of its social base structure, a narrative made possible by *Absalom, Absalom!* in that the associations of McCaslin genealogy and southern history, family identity and racial difference are assumed and not sought. Unlike *Absalom, Absalom!* however, there is in *Go Down, Moses* a sense of resignation. The voices of difference are muted by a tone of fatalism that would seem to stifle further dialogue and resist critique. As a result, the uncovering of the fundamental social contradiction in *Absalom, Absalom!* and its full and confident development in *Go Down, Moses* may leave the essential myth of southern racism unexamined.

Yet Faulkner never lapses into complacency; the fatalism, even resignation, of *Go Down, Moses* does not bar rewriting. The contradiction continues to motivate, to produce revisions, and even in a work like *Intruder in the Dust*, once roundly, and justly, condemned for its racist voices, there remains a tendency to disrupt monologic authoritarianism with the insistence of dialogue. Both *Absalom, Absalom!* in its historicizing of *The Sound and the Fury*, and *Go Down, Moses* rest the theme of racism on the primary myth of Oedipus; sins of racial violence are supplementations of the primal sin against the father, the violation of the prohibition of sexual union with the (m)other. Racism is a version of paternalism. But *Intruder in the Dust* is a representation of a post-oedipal consciousness. After all, the myth of original oedipal violence produces only lyric repetition; what is of crucial importance to Faulkner is the narrative consequence of that originary act and not the act itself. An obsession with the act of transgression is what marks Quentin's repetition compulsion, Quentin's death wish, and it is Shreve's function to attempt to penetrate that death wish with a revisionary spirit. Shreve would prevent endings even as Quentin insists upon them.

Faulkner, of course, is never centrally concerned with originary acts; his narratives of the Old South always slip toward the narration of such narratives. Originary oedipal violence, which comes to be contained in the incest prohibition and can be rewritten as a prohibition of miscegenation, may seem to be encoded in unambiguous and invariable (repetitive) law, but nevertheless remains mysterious and seductive. Accordingly, true narration of the origins of Faulkner's First Ancestors can begin only in the departure from the seductive mystery, in the revision of myth into history, in the dispersal of authoritative monologue into dialogue.

Intruder in the Dust suggests a rather extraordinary reading of the oedipal origin myth, one that brackets the originary violence of the Freudian family romance. Interest is focused instead on collective action, on a demystified, even pragmatic and rational exchange or dialogue that in truth needs no mysterious originary act as its motivation. The novel tells not of origins but of the form of narrative and of historical understanding. Freud narrates such a myth not so much to reveal the universality of the oedipus romance but to universalize the prohibition against fratricide as the foundation law of civilization. Nothing is solved in the primal horde's elimination of the tyrant father; something is learned.

> Sexual desires do not unite men but divide them. Though the brothers had banded together in order to overcome their father, they were one another's rivals in regard to the women. Each of them would have wished, like his father, to have all the women to himself. The new organization would have collapsed in a struggle of all against all, for none of them was of such overmastering strength as to be able to take on his father's part with success. Thus the brothers had no alternative, if they were to live together, but . . . to institute the law against incest by which they all alike renounced the women whom they desired and who had been their chief motive for dispatching their father. In this way they rescued the organization which had made them strong.

> It was not until long afterwards that the prohibition [against fratricide] ceased to be limited to members of the clan and assumed the simple form: "Thou shalt do no murder." The patriarchal horde was replaced in the first instance by the fraternal clan, whose existence was assured by the blood tie. Society was now based on complicity in the common crime; religion was based on the sense of guilt and the remorse attaching to it; while morality was based partly on the exigencies of this society and partly on the penance demanded by the sense of guilt.[8]

The notable gap in Freud's narrative of the establishing of a utopian society, of the founding of an essential law of equitable distribution of property, power, and wealth, is the transition from fraternal clan to "society." It is in that gap that *Intruder in the Dust* sets up its story, not to bridge the gap but to repeat the ideal.

There is a critical moment in the novel's plot. The mob gathered to witness the lynching of Lucas Beauchamp for the murder of Vinson Gowrie has quickly and quietly dispersed when the news that Vinson was killed by his brother Crawford is revealed. Chick Mallison's first thought is that the mob runs away in shame for wrongly accusing

Lucas. Gavin Stevens, as always, has his own theory. In effect, Stevens argues that the crime of fratricide is more heinous than the crime of lynching an innocent black man. The mob's dispersal, he argues, constitutes a far more violent action against the guilty Crawford than any lynching (be the victim the innocent Lucas or the guilty Crawford).

> "They didn't want to destroy Crawford Gowrie. They repudiated him. If they had lynched him they would have taken only his life. What they really did was worse: they deprived him to the full extent of their capacity of his citizenship in man."
>
> (*ID*, p. 202)

This rather astounding argument is in fact consistent with the terms of Freud's description of the institution of a clan law against fratricide. Chick provides an important moment of dialogic disruption in Stevens' overpowering monologue.

> "So for a lot of Gowries and Workitts to burn Lucas Beauchamp to death with gasoline for something he didn't even do is one thing but for a Gowrie to murder his brother is another."
> "Yes," his uncle said.
> "You cant say that," he said.
> "Yes," his uncle said. "*Thou shalt not kill* in precept and even when you do, precept still remains unblemished and scarless: *Thou shalt not kill* and who knows, perhaps next time you wont. But *Gowrie must not kill Gowrie's brother*: no maybe about it, no next time to maybe not Gowrie kill Gowrie because there must be no first time. And not just for Gowrie but for all: Stevens and Mallison and Edmonds and McCaslin too; if we are not to hold to the belief that that point not just shall not but must not and *can*not come at which Gowrie or Ingrum or Stevens or Mallison may shed Gowrie or Ingrum or Stevens or Mallison blood, how hope ever to reach that one where *Thou shalt not kill at all*, where Lucas Beauchamp's life will be secure not despite the fact that he is Lucas Beauchamp but because he is?"
>
> (*ID*, pp. 200–201)

We must not underestimate the force of Chick's brief objection, his assertion that Stevens "cant say that"; nor may we assume that Stevens' response to that objection is designed to obliterate Chick's objection, for it does not. Chick's actions on Lucas' behalf proved Lucas innocent and led to the uncovering of the real murderer. The plot of the novel, therefore, reinforces Chick's objection to Stevens' racist, "go slow" rationalizations. Why should the reader believe Stevens when he, too, merely assumed Lucas was guilty like almost all the rest of the community, like all of those gathered in the mob in front of the jail waiting to see the Gowries lynch Lucas? Whether Stevens or Chick has correctly identified the mob's motivations, of course, remains unknown to us and, therefore, insignificant. What is important is the nature of the explanation offered by Stevens, the sense of an arrested social development which leaves the utopian Freudian ideal of equal protection under the law somewhere in the future. We have heard the argument before. It opposed the Emancipation Proclamation, taking the form of an assertion that former slaves were simply not ready for freedom; in Faulkner's modern, segregated South it was expressed in the argument that blacks were not ready yet for full citizenship. The extension of human rights beyond the clan is far more problematical than Freud's narrative conveyed.

The "not yet ready argument," as a defense of "go slowism," was seductive to Southerners, and Faulkner was no exception. His public statements on the topic of civil rights repeat an argument no less repressive and immoral than Ike McCaslin's outraged response to the black woman of "Delta Autumn."

> "That's right. Go back North. Marry: a man in your own race. That's the only salvation for you—for a while yet, maybe a long while yet. We will have to wait."
>
> (GDM, p. 363)

Why is such an argument so seductive? From what fears and needs does it draw its motives? How can one who sees so clearly the self-destructive violence of racism yet always postpone its overthrow? The answers may lie in the escape from genealogy marked by the presence of Lucas Beauchamp in *Intruder in the Dust* and the absence of his McCaslin family connections, which are directly mentioned only once (*ID*, p. 19). This late novel is a self-conscious departure from the mystifying oedipal family romance of the earlier genealogical narratives, a departure from the themes of both incest and miscegenation. *Intruder in the Dust* is not a family story, and yet its link to those family stories ties it into Faulkner's revisionary narrative; it stands as a necessary commentary on those earlier narratives. In *Intruder in the Dust* Faulkner tells the same story, the story of modern southern society, but in a radically different way.

It is as if Faulkner's perspective had matured; the family was no longer the primary measure of all human actions. Perhaps Old W. C.

Falkner had finally been demystified. The subject of *Intruder in the Dust* is the community itself, society but not simply as the family writ large. Incest and miscegenation recede into variations on a central pattern of exclusion/inclusion, a logic of difference. The perspective is, once more, modernist. Difference is elemental, an "I" and a "Thou" that cannot be further broken down. There is, therefore, a deep suspicion of anything egalitarian, anything that erases difference. Without the authoritarian guarantees of difference, difference becomes more fragile, and more valuable. This is another way of saying that the uprootedness of modern southern society had deconstructed reliable, legitimizing markers of elemental difference. The family theme, the prohibition of miscegenation, was raised to a general, and modernist, principle of self-identity. The rhetorical force of such an argument rendered innocent that which was virulently discriminatory. Faulkner could not think beyond difference as exclusive/inclusive, as the struggle of master and slave, but how many modernists can? Who among us is not a modernist? It is the logic of difference that justifies (like a myth?) the "not yet ready" argument of modern racism; the argument is heard today, for the thinking of a truly egalitarian society is difficult. It would require a different kind of difference, a difference that did not mythologize itself in exclusive/inclusive oppositions.

We have no language for it; it is not Gavin Stevens alone who cannot say "that," cannot articulate racism. Society provides him with the words, with a discursive practice that makes easy the supplemental variations, the repetitions, of racism's repressive self-justifications. The problem is not that Gavin Stevens has no word for his prejudices but that Chick Mallison cannot articulate a different sense of difference. The problem is profound for the form of Faulkner's narrative in *Intruder in the Dust*, because the representation of the voice of the other seems pale beside the loud and dominant voice of a Gavin Stevens. Lucas Beauchamp is virtually silenced in the novel, bound almost exclusively to a marginal communication with other minorities, other blacks, women, and children. These are the outsiders, and, although their subversive power does achieve Lucas' last-minute rescue, the novel does not really seem to eliminate the word *difference* from the vocabulary of racism, classism, and sexism.

Racism's scare tactics are powerful; egalitarianism is rewritten as loss of difference, that is, as loss of the self. Difference is, therefore, grounded in the universal origins of human society, giving us an order, a law without which we are subject to savage violence. Segregation, slavery, racism diminish their own violence behind the myth of a greater one. Speaking specifically of racism in South African apartheid Derrida notes that all racisms tend "to pass segregation off as natural—and as the very law of origin." He argues further that

> there's no racism without a language. The point is not that acts of racial violence are only words but rather that they have to have a word. Even though it offers the excuse of blood, color, birth—or, rather, *because* it uses this naturalist and sometimes creationist discourse—racism always betrays the perversion of man, the "talking animal." It institutes, declares, writes, inscribes, prescribes. A system of marks, it outlines space in order to assign forced residence or to close off borders. It does not discern, it discriminates.[9]

He describes here a violence of language that accompanies, justifies, even encourages physical atrocities. He carefully notes that physical and verbal violence are not the same thing, yet herein lies the problem. Derrida describes "apartheid" as "racism's last word" and claims that it is not a final reality in the societies of human beings. Surely this is a utopian ideal that his own theory of supplementarity in language undermines. Ultimately we must ask: what are the social/discursive conditions under which a Gavin Stevens cannot say the racist word? Must we return to the Derridian "other" language of *Speech and Phenomena*, a speech of silence or nondifference (egalitarianism), or nondeferral (revolution), or nondiscrimination (love)?[10] This seems an alternative composed only of talk. It is nihilistic and, therefore, beyond narrative, beyond history. Reading Faulkner is a corrective to sanitized language games, for reading Faulkner uncovers the social and political dimensions of discursive practice. Racism's last word will come only with the alteration of the concrete social experience wherein racism's language finds its ultimate support. Like Chick Mallison, we must exhume the buried body, raise the repressed.

Origin myths narrate primal social laws, define human relations, discriminate identities. The movement from myth to discourse merges contradiction and difference, but difference here is both what is represented and the mode of representation. Eagleton explains this doubling of difference:

> Contradiction implies difference, but it is, so to speak, difference doubly articulated, difference differentiated, set in a context where its terms

can be grasped as antagonistic, as well as diacritical. Difference is itself already an articulation, an effect of discursive practice; but this articulation is then displaced and re-articulated within a "higher" discourse that transcodes its terms as mutually oppositional. (Not, of course, that the process is in reality as sequential as that.) If difference is already a dislocation of the object's ideological self-identity, contradiction redivides that initial dislocation by rearticulating it in a signifying context that reveals how certain differences will be indissociable from *struggle*.[11]

Eagleton speaks here of social struggle which exists on the level of unbinding difference from its perversion into a "higher" discourse of discrimination, of racism. Moreover, Eagleton also realizes that this struggle is not contained solely within the deconstruction of racism's words; it is contextualized by a particular social/historical discursive practice. That is, the higher discourse, the myth of origins, operates within the realm of real concrete human relations.

Thus the contradiction within southern society that enters into the foundations of southern discursive practice, that is, southern myth-making, is revealed through Lucas' confrontations with the codes of racial discrimination that he is compelled to test simply because he is a black McCaslin. Lucas *is* the southern contradiction, but he is also the vehicle for the representation of both a real psychological and a real social struggle of blacks in the South. The fear of the loss of difference in Faulkner is fundamentally racist, for its most articulate expression comes in the clear form of a threat hurled by Shreve at Quentin on the climactic final page of *Absalom, Absalom!*

> "Do you want to know what I think?"
> "No," Quentin said.
> "Then I'll tell you. I think that in time the Jim Bonds are going to conquer the western hemisphere. Of course it wont quite be in our time and of course as they spread towards the poles they will bleach out again like the rabbits and the birds do, so they wont show up so sharp against the snow. But it will still be Jim Bond; and so in a few thousand years, I who regard you will also have sprung from the loins of African kings. Now I want you to tell me just one thing more. Why do you hate the South?"

Quentin's ambiguous response affirms that which is by its own terms unsupportable because the alternative is, to him, unthinkable, unsayable.

"I dont hate it," Quentin said, quickly, at once, immediately; "I dont hate it," he said. *I dont hate it* he thought, panting in the cold air, the iron New England dark; *I dont. I dont! I dont hate it! I dont hate it!*

(*AA*, p. 378)

The dilemma Faulkner represents here is expressed as the hatred of hate, which is for Quentin, for the South, the impossibility of rejecting a heritage (that is the self) even while acknowledging its destructive evil. There is, certainly, no ambiguity in Faulkner's moral stance on this point, for the refusal to express the hatred of that hate is portrayed in Quentin as inevitably self-destructive. The reader, however, must read beyond this dilemma of either/or, for the representation of a dilemma of difference, the fear of the loss of the powers of discrimination, must itself be discriminated. Is there, beyond the mere hatred of hate, a community of love wherein discursive practice can differentiate without discrimination? These are the questions raised in reading Faulkner.

NOTES

Chapter 1. Representation: Theory and Practice

1 Quoted in Louis D. Rubin, Jr., and Robert D. Jacobs, eds., *Southern Renascence: The Literature of the Modern South* (Baltimore, 1953), p. 97.
2 Martin Heidegger, "The Origin of the Work of Art," *Poetry, Language, Thought*, trans. Albert Hofstadter (New York, 1971), p. 48.
3 Pierre Macherey, *A Theory of Literary Production*, trans. Geoffrey Wall (London, 1978), p. 78.

Chapter 2. Political Writing / Political Interpretation

1 Maxwell Geismar, *Writers in Crisis: The American Novel, 1925–1940* (New York, 1961), p. vii.
2 Warren Beck, *Faulkner* (Madison, 1976), p. 3.
3 Daniel Joseph Singal, *The War Within: From Victorian to Modernist Thought in the South, 1919–1945* (Chapel Hill, 1982), p. 156.
4 Richard H. King, *A Southern Renaissance: The Cultural Awakening of the American South, 1930–1955* (Oxford, 1980), p. 218.
5 William Faulkner, *As I Lay Dying* (New York, 1957), pp. 165–66. Hereafter in the text as *ALD*.
6 William Faulkner, *Absalom, Absalom!* (New York, 1964), p. 303. Hereafter in the text as *AA*.
7 Malcolm Cowley, *The Faulkner-Cowley File: Letters and Memories, 1944–1962* (New York, 1966), p. 114. See also Singal, *War Within*, p. 154.
8 Judith Bryant Wittenberg, *Faulkner: The Transfiguration of Biography* (Lincoln, 1979), pp. 105–6.
9 Robert Penn Warren, "Introduction. Faulkner: Past and Present," in *Faulkner: A Collection of Critical Essays*, ed. Robert Penn Warren (Englewood Cliffs, N.J., 1966), p. 17.
10 Frederick L. Gwynn and Joseph L. Blotner, *Faulkner in the University* (New York, 1959), p. 177.
11 Ibid.

12   Carvel Collins, "Faulkner and Mississippi," *University of Mississippi Studies in English*, 15(1978), 159.

13   John Bassett, *William Faulkner: The Critical Heritage* (London, 1975), p. 13.

14   Jean-Paul Sartre, "On *The Sound and the Fury*: Time in the Works of Faulkner," in Warren, *Faulkner*, p. 88.

15   William Faulkner, *Requiem for a Nun* (New York, 1951), p. 92.

16   Edmund Wilson, "William Faulkner's Reply to the Civil-Rights Program," in Warren, *Faulkner*, p. 220.

17   William Faulkner, Introduction, *Sanctuary* (New York, 1932), p. vii. See also a discussion of this issue in André Bleikasten, *Faulkner's As I Lay Dying*, trans. Roger Little (Bloomington, 1973), pp. 10–11, and a slightly different view in David Minter, *William Faulkner: His Life and Work* (Baltimore, 1980), pp. 119–20.

18   Minter, *William Faulkner*, p. 117.

19   Cleanth Brooks, "Faulkner and the Fugitive-Agrarians," in *Faulkner and the Southern Renaissance*, ed. Doreen Fowler and Ann J. Abadie (Jackson, Miss., 1982), p. 27.

20   Minter, *William Faulkner*, p. 118.

21   Bleikasten, *Faulkner's As I Lay Dying*, p. 17.

22   Sylvia Jenkins Cook, *From Tobacco Road to Route 66: The Southern Poor Whites in Fiction* (Chapel Hill, 1976), pp. 39–40.

23   William Faulkner, "Wash," *Collected Stories* (New York, 1976), pp. 546–47. Hereafter in the text as *CS*.

24   Louis D. Rubin, "Faulkner and the Southern Literary Renascence," in Fowler and Abadie, *Faulkner and the Southern Renaissance*, p. 90.

25   Richard King, "Memory and Tradition," in Fowler and Abadie, *Faulkner and the Southern Renaissance*, p. 155.

26   Macherey, *Theory of Literary Production*, p. 78.

27   Gwynn and Blotner, *Faulkner in the University*, pp. 245–46.

28   Walter Taylor, *Faulkner's Search for a South* (Urbana, 1983), pp. 166–67.

Chapter 3. Great Works, Late Works:
The Representation of the Present

1   Singal, *War Within*, p. 197. See also R. W. B. Lewis, "William Faulkner: The Hero in the New World," in Warren, *Faulkner*, p. 209.

2   Myra Jehlen, *Class and Character in Faulkner's South* (Secaucus, N. J., 1978), p. 55.

3   Ibid., p. 34.

4   Ibid., p. 151.

5   Ibid., p. 65.

6   Ibid., p. 73.

7   Ibid., p. 64.

8   Ibid., p. 83.

9   Ibid., p. 173.

10 Ibid., p. 134.

11 See for example her discussion of *Absalom, Absalom!* where the reading of Quentin's suicide in *The Sound and the Fury* against the ending of *Absalom, Absalom!* is presented as a break with traditional critical practice. Jehlen, *Class and Character*, p. 69. Jehlen cannot avoid this intertextual association, but she limits her cross-textual interpretation to the unavoidable.

Chapter 4. Roads and the Disintegrating Family

1   William Faulkner, *Intruder in the Dust* (New York, 1948), pp. 194–95. Hereafter in the text as *ID*.

2   Thomas D. Clark, *The Emerging South* (New York, 1961), p. 93.

3   Rembert W. Patrick, "The Deep South, Past and Present," in *The Deep South in Transformation*, ed. Robert B. Highshaw (Birmingham, Ala., 1964), pp. 114–15.

4   W. J. Cash, *The Mind of the South* (New York, 1941), p. 25.

5   William Faulkner, *Go Down, Moses* (New York, 1940), pp. 344–45 and 354. Hereafter in the text as *GDM*.

6   Philip Van Doren Stern, *Tin Lizzie* (New York, 1955).

7   W. T. Couch, Preface, *These Are Our Lives* (Kingsport, Tenn., 1969), p. xv.

8   Ibid., pp. 20–21.

9   Ibid., pp. 58–59.

10 Ibid., p. 82.

11 Ibid., pp. 55 and 56.

12 Ibid., pp. 89–90.

13 Ibid., p. 32.

14 Ibid., p. 31.

15 Ibid., p. 35.

16 Ibid., p. 36.

17 Ibid.

18 Wesley Morris, "The Irrepressible Real: Jacques Lacan and Poststructuralism," in *American Criticism in the Poststructuralist Age*, ed. Ira Konigsberg (Ann Arbor, 1981), pp. 116–34.

19 Clark, *Emerging South*, p. 177.

20 William Faulkner, *Flags in the Dust* (New York, 1973), p. 66. Hereafter in the text as *FD*.

21 This theme is explored at length by Eric J. Sundquist, *Faulkner: The House Divided* (Baltimore, 1983), particularly pp. 57–58.
22 Singal, *War Within*, p. 181.
23 Frank E. Vandiver, "The Confederate Myth," in *Myth and Southern History*, ed. Patrick Gerster and Nicholas Cords (Chicago, 1974), p. 152.

Chapter 5. Violence: Writing as Revision and Perversion

1 George B. Tindall, "Mythology: A New Frontier in Southern History," in *The Idea of the South: Pursuit of a Central Theme*, ed. Frank E. Vandiver (Chicago, 1978), p. 15.
2 Jack Temple Kirby, *Media-Made Dixie* (Baton Rouge, La., 1978), p. 38.
3 Singal, *War Within*, p. 66.
4 Vandiver, "Confederate Myth," p. 149.
5 Melton A. McLawrin, *The Knights of Labor in the South* (Westport, Conn., 1978), pp. 14–15.
6 Ibid., p. 14.
7 Singal, *War Within*, p. 280.
8 *These Are Our Lives*, p. 66.
9 George Brown Tindall, *The Emergence of the New South* (Baton Rouge, La., 1967), p. 410.
10 Singal, *War Within* pp. 70–71.
11 See Clifton Fadiman's review of *Absalom, Absalom!* in *New Yorker*, October 31, 1936, pp. 62–64.
12 See Bernard De Voto's review of *Absalom, Absalom!* in Bassett, *Faulkner*, p. 203.
13 Ibid., p. 202.
14 Claude Lévi-Strauss, "The Structural Study of Myth," *Structural Anthropology*, trans. Claire Jacobson and Brooke Grundfest Schoepf (New York, 1967), particularly p. 227 on "mediation."
15 Sundquist, *Faulkner*, pp. 56–59.
16 Clark, *Emerging South*, p. 22.
17 Ibid., p. 94.
18 Ibid., p. 97.
19 King, *Southern Renaissance*, p. 31.
20 See Singal's exceptional discussion of Odum, *War Within*, pp. 115–52, which leads into his discussion of Faulkner.
21 King, *Southern Renaissance*, pp. 15–16.
22 Quoted in William Faulkner, *Early Poetry and Prose*, ed. Carvel Collins (Boston, 1962), p. 72. See also King, *Southern Renaissance*, p. 98.
23 William Faulkner, *The Unvanquished* (New York, 1966), pp. 256–57. Hereafter in the text as *UV*.

24 John T. Irwin, *Doubling and Incest / Repetition and Revenge* (Baltimore, 1975), p. 58.
25 Jehlen, *Class and Character*, p. 51.
26 Joanne Creighton, *William Faulkner's Craft of Revision: The Snopes Trilogy, The Unvanquished, and Go Down, Moses* (Detroit, 1977), p. 77.
27 Singal, *War Within*, pp. 171–72.
28 William Faulkner, Introduction to *The Sound and the Fury, A Faulkner Miscellany*, ed. James B. Meriwether (Jackson, Miss., 1974), p. 159.
29 Ibid., pp. 160 and 161.

Chapter 6. "Art and Southern Life": Revision, Repression, Perversion

1   Faulkner, Introduction to *The Sound and the Fury*, pp. 158–59.
2   Ibid., p. 169.
3   Ibid., p. 156.
4   Singal, *War Within*, p. 200.
5   John L. Stewart, *The Burden of Time: The Fugitives and Agrarians* (Princeton, 1965), pp. 114–19, and Richard Gray, *The Literature of Memory: Modern Writers of the American South* (Baltimore, 1977), p. 41.
6   See particularly the discussion of Frank Owsley in King, *Southern Renaissance*, and in Carolyn Porter, *Seeing and Being: The Plight of the Participant Observer in Emerson, James, Adams, and Faulkner* (Middletown, Conn., 1981).
7   Singal, *War Within*, p. 201.
8   King, *Southern Renaissance*, p. 51.
9   Ibid., p. 34.
10 Singal, *War Within*, p. 166.
11 Joseph Blotner, *Faulkner: A Biography* (New York, 1974), 1: 690–91.
12 Cleanth Brooks, "Thomas Sutpen: A Representative Southern Planter?" *William Faulkner: Toward Yoknapatawpha and Beyond* (New Haven, 1978), p. 284.
13 Ibid., pp. 288–89.
14 Ibid., p. 293.
15 Ibid., p. 294.
16 Ibid., p. 294, italics by Brooks.
17 Porter, *Seeing and Being*, pp. 230 and 231.
18 Ibid., p. 219.
19 Rubin, "Faulkner and the Southern Literary Renascence," p. 90.
20 Peter Swiggart, *The Art of Faulkner's Novels* (Austin, 1962), pp. 323–24.
21 Walter Sullivan, *A Requiem for the Renascence: The Study of Fiction in the Modern South* (Athens, 1976), p. xix.
22 Ibid., p. 14.

23 Ibid., p. 23.
24 Robert Jacobs, "Faulkner's Tragedy of Isolation," in Rubin and Jacobs *Southern Renascence*, p. 190.
25 Ibid., p. 191.
26 Ibid., p. 173.
27 Ibid.
28 Olga Vickery, *The Novels of William Faulkner: A Critical Interpretation* (Baton Rouge, 1964), p. 250. See also *ID*, p. 150.
29 On Faulkner as a failed poet see André Bleikasten, *The Most Splendid Failure: Faulkner's The Sound and the Fury* (Bloomington, 1976); James Guetti, *The Limits of Metaphor: A Study of Melville, Conrad, and Faulkner* (Ithaca, 1967); Walter Slatoff, *Quest for Failure: A Study of William Faulkner* (Ithaca, 1960). See also Gwynn and Blother, *Faulkner in the University*, p. 22.
30 *Novels of William Faulkner*, p. 299. See also Gwynn and Blotner, *Faulkner in the University*, p. 202.
31 Vickery, *Novels of William Faulkner*, p. 299.
32 M. M. Bakhtin, *The Dialogic Imagination*, trans. Caryl Emerson and Michael Holquist (Austin, 1981).
33 David Minter, *The Interpreted Design as a Structural Principle in American Prose* (New Haven, 1969), p. 219.
34 Ibid.
35 Minter, *William Faulkner*, p. 157.
36 Ibid., p. 228.
37 Irwin, *Doubling and Incest*, p. 20.
38 Minter, *William Faulkner*, pp. 152–53.
39 Ibid., p. 153.
40 Ibid., p. 156.
41 Ibid., p. 250.
42 Irwin, *Doubling and Incest*, pp. 171–72.
43 Ibid., p. 161.
44 Ibid., p. 163.
45 Ibid., p. 159.
46 Minter, *William Faulkner*, p. 103.
47 Ibid., p. 250.
48 Irwin, *Doubling and Incest*, p. 170.
49 Quoted in Minter, *William Faulkner*, p. 103.
50 William Faulkner, "Essay on the Composition of *Sartoris*," ed. Joseph Blotner, *Yale University Library Gazette*, 47 (January 1973), 122–23.
51 William Faulkner, *Mosquitoes* (New York, 1927), p. 320. Hereafter in the text as *MO*.
52 Blotner, *Faulkner*, 1: 185.

Chapter 7. Genealogy and Writing

1   The biographical information on William Clark Falkner is drawn largely
    from Blotner, *Faulkner*; from Robert Coughlan, *The Private World of
    William Faulkner* (New York, 1954); from Robert Cantwell, "The Faulk-
    ners: Recollections of a Gifted Family," *New World Writing*, 2 (November
    1952), 300–315; and from Minter, *William Faulkner*. There is also a very
    interesting discussion of the Old Colonel's influence on his great-grandson
    in Wittenberg, *Faulkner*. See also Murry C. Falkner, *The Falkners of Mis-
    sissippi: A Memoir* (Baton Rouge, 1967).
2   Joseph L. Fant and Robert Ashley, *Faulkner at West Point* (New York,
    1969), p. 108: "he was a martinet."
3   Wittenberg, *Faulkner*, p. 9.
4   Blotner, *Faulkner*, 1: 9–10. See also Minter, *William Faulkner*, p. 4, and
    Wittenberg, *Faulkner*, p. 11.
5   *Falkners of Mississippi*, p. 7, and Wittenberg, *Faulkner*, p. 14.
6   Blotner, *Faulkner*, 1: 37. See also Coughlan, *Private World of William
    Faulkner*, p. 39n.
7   Blotner, *Faulkner*, 1: 22–23.
8   Cantwell, "Faulkners," p. 56. See also Blotner, *Faulkner*, 1: 46–47.
9   Edmund Leach, *Genesis as Myth and Other Essays* (London, 1969), pp.
    10–11.
10 Ibid., p. 15.
11 Lévi-Strauss, *Structural Anthropology*, p. 11.
12 Leach, *Genesis as Myth*, p. 21.
13 Gwynn and Blotner, *Faulkner in the University*, pp. 167, 285–86. See also
    pp. 50, 150, and especially p. 33 where Faulkner comments that "the Old
    Adam in man suggests to him to be a blackguard if he can get away with
    it," and p. 58 where he mentions the "conflict with conscience and the
    glands, the Old Adam."
14 Coughlan, *Private World of William Faulkner*, p. 38.
15 Minter, *William Faulkner*, pp. 3–4 and 23.
16 Falkner, *Falkners of Mississippi*, p. 6. See also Coughlan, *Private World
    of William Faulkner*, p. 43.
17 Falkner, *Falkners of Mississippi*, p. 6.
18 Eric J. Sundquist, *Home as Found: Authority and Genealogy in Nine-
    teenth-Century American Literature* (Baltimore, 1977), p. xii.
19 Jacques Derrida, *Of Grammatology*, trans. Gayatri Chakravorty Spivak
    (Baltimore, 1976), p. 255.
20 Ibid., p. 265. Derrida labels the incest prohibition the hinge (*brisure*)
    between nature and culture.
21 Claude Lévi-Strauss, *The Elementary Structures of Kinship*, trans. James
    Harle Bell, Jon Richard von Sturmer, and Rodney Needham (Boston,
    1969), p. 12.

22   Ibid., pp. 8–9. The italics are added.

23   Derrida, *Of Grammatology*, p. 267.

24   Edward Said, *Beginnings: Intention and Method* (New York, 1975), p. 146.

25   Ibid., p. 170.

26   Blotner, *Faulkner*, 1: 53. See also John Faulkner, *My Brother Bill: An Affectionate Reminiscence* (New York, 1963), p. 73. On J. W. T. Falkner see especially Wittenberg, *Faulkner*, pp. 14–15, and Falkner, *Falkners of Mississippi*, pp. 62–77.

27   John Faulkner, *My Brother Bill*, p. 11. See also Minter, *William Faulkner*, p. 8. On Murry Falkner see Falkner, *Falkners of Mississippi*, pp. 11–12; John Faulkner, *My Brother Bill*, p. 14; and Blotner, *Faulkner*, 1: 67–68. On Maud Butler Falkner see Falkner, *Falkners of Mississippi*, pp. 9–10. Especially insightful on Faulkner's relationship with his parents are Wittenberg, *Faulkner*, pp. 16–19, and Minter, *William Faulkner*, pp. 5–11 and 16–18.

28   Michael Paul Rogin, *Fathers and Sons: Andrew Jackson and the Subjugation of the American Indians* (New York, 1975), p. 53. See also Minter, *William Faulkner*, p. 10: the Faulkner boys all "felt their mother's strong domination," and all of them "feared and resented it."

29   Rogin, *Fathers and Sons*, p. 54. See also Minter, *William Faulkner*, p. 18: William started thinking of himself as the child of his great-grandfather."

30   Gwynn and Blotner, *Faulkner in the University*, p. 3.

31   Cantwell, "Faulkners," p. 56.

32   Ibid.

33   Fant and Ashley, *Faulkner at West Point*, p. 109.

34   Minter, *William Faulkner*, p. 3: Faulkner "came early to feel himself branded."

35   Said, *Beginnings*, p. 170.

36   See Minter, *William Faulkner*, pp. 65–66, for an interesting discussion of these passages in *Mosquitoes*.

37   Cowley, *Faulkner-Cowley File*, p. 14.

38   Blotner, *Faulkner*, 1: 701, 828, 830, and 832.

39   Minter, *William Faulkner*, p. 211. See also *Selected Letters of William Faulkner*, ed. Joseph Blotner (New York, 1977), p. 199.

Chapter 8. "They ain't my Sartorises . . . I just inherited 'em"

1   William Faulkner, "And Now What's to Do?" *Faulkner Miscellany*, pp. 145–48.

2   Ibid., p. 145.

3   Joseph Blotner, "The Falkners and the Fictional Families," *Georgia Review*, 30 (Fall 1976), 574.

4   Faulkner, "And Now What's to Do?" p. 146.

5   Faulkner, "Essay on the Composition of *Sartoris*," pp. 122–23.

6   Ibid., p. 123.

7   Blotner, *Faulkner*, 1: 532.

8   William Faulkner, *Sartoris* (New York, 1929), p. 79.

9   Gwynn and Blotner, *Faulkner in the University*, p. 251.

10 Blotner, "Falkners and the Fictional Families," p. 584.

11 Lawrence Thompson, Afterword, in the Signet Classic paperback edition of Sartoris (New York, 1964), p. 312.

12 Michel Foucault, *The History of Sexuality*, Vol. 1: *An Introduction*, trans. Robert Hurley (New York, 1978), particularly p. 108.

13 Susan Stuart, *On Longing: Narratives of the Miniature, the Gigantic, the Souvenir, the Collection* Baltimore, 1984), p. 135.

14 Ibid., pp. 22–23.

15 Lawrence Stone, "The Rise of the Nuclear Family in Early Modern England: The Patriarchal Stage," in *The Family in History*, ed. Charles E. Rosenberg (Pittsburg, 1975), p. 29.

16 Ibid., p. 13.

17 Ibid., p. 32.

18 Foucault, *History of Sexuality*, 1: 33–34.

19 The items Bayard examines are quite significant. Most are military in nature, recalling the various wars in which the Sartoris men served. The derringer is the weapon John Sartoris used to kill the as yet unnamed "Northerners" we later learn, in *Light in August*, to be the Burdens, and the dueling pistols are the weapons to avenge his father's death that Drucilla Sartoris, John's wife, offers Bayard in *The Unvanquished*.

20 Blotner, *Faulkner*, 1: 560.

Chapter 9. Narrative Voice: A Narrated within the Narrator

1   David Wyatt, *Prodigal Sons: A Study in Authorship and Authority* (Baltimore, 1980), p. 81.

2   See Irwin (*Doubling and Incest*) and Wittenberg (*Faulkner*) for parallel discussions of this issue.

3   Jean-François Lyotard, *The Postmodern Condition: A Report on Knowledge*, trans. Geoff Bennington and Brian Massumi (Minneapolis, 1984), p. 22.

4   Ibid., pp. 20–21.

5   See Harold Bloom, *The Anxiety of Influence: A Theory of Poetry* (London, 1973).

6   Peter Burger, *Theory of the Avant-garde*, trans. Michael Shaw (Minneapolis, 1984).

7   Wesley Morris, *Friday's Footprint: Structuralism and the Articulated Text* (Columbus, Ohio, 1979), pp. 21–24.
8   Jacques Derrida, *Speech and Phenomena: Other Essays on Husserl's Theory of Signs*, trans. D. B. Allison (Evanston, 1973), p. 104.
9   William Faulkner, *The Hamlet* (New York, 1940), p. 28. Hereafter in the text as *HAM*.
10 Andrea Domino, "Why Did the Snopeses Name Their Son 'Wallstreet Panic'?: Depression Humor in Faulkner's *The Hamlet*," *Studies in American Humor* (San Marcos, Tex.), 3 (Summer/Fall 1984), 159–60.
11 Ibid., p. 156.
12 Ibid., p. 168.
13 Ibid., p. 169.
14 Jehlen, *Class and Character*, p. 147.

Chapter 10. A Writing Lesson: The Recovery of Antigone

1   Said, *Beginnings*, pp. 83–84.
2   William Faulkner, *The Sound and the Fury* (New York, 1929), pp. 56–58. Hereafter in the text as *SF*.
3   Faulkner, *Selected Letters*, p. 285.
4   Alice A. Jardine, *Gynesis: Configurations of Woman and Modernity* (Ithaca, 1985), p. 76.
5   Ibid., p. 67.
6   Ibid., p. 73.
7   Jean-Paul Sartre, *The Words*, trans. Bernard Frechtman (New York, 1964), p. 16.
8   George Steiner, *Antigones* (Oxford, 1984), p. 18.
9   Bleikasten, *Most Splendid Failure*, p. 56.
10 Steiner, *Antigones*, pp. 17–18.

Chapter 11. A Writing Lesson: As I Lay Dying *as tour de force*

1   Jardine, *Gynesis*, p. 58.
2   Ibid., p. 61.
3   Bleikasten, *Faulkner's As I Lay Dying*, pp. 120–21.
4   Ibid., p. 121.
5   Ibid., p. 145.
6   Olga Vickery, "The Dimensions of Consciousness: *As I Lay Dying*," in *William Faulkner: Three Decades of Criticism*, ed. Frederick J. Hoffman and Olga Vickery (New York, 1960), p. 237.
7   Ibid., pp. 237–38.

8 Ibid., p. 238.
9 Jehlen, *Class and Character*, p. 64.

Chapter 12. The Narrative Scene: The Voice of the Body

1 J. L. Austin, *How to Do Things with Words* (New York, 1962).
2 David Carr, *Time, Narrative, and History* (Bloomington, 1984), pp. 164–68.
3 Barbara Hardy, "Towards a Poetics of Fiction: An Approach through Narrative," *Novel*, 2 (1968), 5.
4 Maurice Merleau-Ponty, *Consciousness and the Acquisition of Language*, trans. Hugh J. Silverman (Evanston, 1873), p. 18.
5 See a discussion of Burke's "dramatism" in Bernard Duffey, *A Poetry of Presence: The Writing of William Carlos Williams* (Madison, 1986).
6 Michel Foucault, *This Is Not a Pipe*, trans. James Harkness (Berkeley, 1982), particularly p. 44 on the difference between "series" and "resemblance."
7 John T. Matthews, *The Play of Faulkner's Language* (Ithaca, 1982), p. 153.
8 Ibid., pp. 156–57.
9 Ibid., p. 129.
10 Ibid., p. 156.
11 Ibid., p. 157.
12 Jacques Derrida, *Limited Inc. abc*, trans. Samuel Weber, *Glyph*, 2(1977), 172.
13 Perry Anderson, *In the Tracks of Historical Materialism* (Chicago, 1984), p. 39.
14 Matthews, *Play of Faulkner's Language*, p. 161.

Chapter 13. Dialogue

1 M. M. Bakhtin, *Problems of Dostoevsky's Poetics*, trans. Caryl Emerson (Minneapolis, 1984), p. 75.
2 Gilles Deleuze and Felix Guattari, *Kafka: Toward a Minority Literature*, trans. Dana Polan (Minneapolis, 1986).
3 Louis A. Renza, *"A White Heron" and the Question of Minor Literature* (Madison, 1984).
4 Ludwig Wittgenstein, *Philosophical Investigations*, trans. G. E. M. Anscombe (New York, 1958).
5 Richard Rorty, "The Contingency of Language," *London Review*, April 17, 1986, p. 6.

6 Ibid., May 8, 1986, p. 14.
7 Vernon Lee, *Music and Its Lovers* (New York, 1933), particularly pp. 30–34.
8 Eliseo Vivas, *The Artistic Transaction* (Columbus, 1963).
9 Irwin, *Doubling and Incest.*
10 Sigmund Freud, *Beyond the Pleasure Principle*, trans. James Strachey (New York, 1961), p. 30.
11 Ibid., p. 56.
12 Friedrich Nietzsche, *The Genealogy of Morals*, in *The Birth of Tragedy and The Genealogy of Morals*, trans. Francis Golffing (New York, 1956), particularly pp. 238–40 on "disinterested interest."
13 Freud, *Beyond the Pleasure Principle*, pp. 48–49. See also *Civilization and Its Discontents*, trans. James Strachey (New York, 1961), chap. 6.
14 François Pitavy, "The Narrative Voice and Function of Shreve: Remarks on the Production of Meaning in *Absalom, Absalom!*" *William Faulkner's Absalom, Absalom!: A Critical Casebook* (New York, 1984), p. 192.

Chapter 14. Representation and Racial Difference

1 Thaddious M. Davis, *Faulkner's "Negro": Art and the Southern Context* (Baton Rouge, 1983), p. 13.
2 Ibid., p. 17.
3 Ralph Flores, *The Rhetoric of Doubtful Authority* (Ithaca, 1984), p. 147.
4 Ibid., p. 168.
5 Ibid.
6 Porter, *Seeing and Being*, p. 231.
7 Terry Eagleton, "Text, Ideology, Realism," in *Literature and Society: Selected Papers from the English Institute*, ed. Edward Said (Baltimore, 1978), pp. 164–65.
8 Sigmund Freud, *Totem and Taboo*, trans. James Strachey (New York, 1950), pp. 144 and 146.
9 Jacques Derrida, "Racism's Last Word," *Race, Writing, and Difference*, ed. Henry Louis Gates, Jr., *Critical Inquiry*, 12 (Autumn 1985), 292.
10 Derrida, *Speech and Phenomena*, p. 108.
11 Eagleton, "Text, Ideology, Realism," p. 165.

INDEX

Aaron, Daniel, 66
"Abraham's Children," 100
Absalom, Absalom!, 9, 17, 20, 21–24,
  37, 38, 44, 46, 47, 48, 67, 68, 69, 70,
  71, 72, 76, 77, 78, 79, 84, 85, 86, 98,
  100, 118, 122, 141, 144, 145, 146,
  148, 166, 171, 176–96, 197, 198,
  201–18, 226, 227, 228, 229, 230, 237
aestheticism, 62, 63, 64, 154, 155, 198
Agee, James, 9
Agrarians, the, 40, 62, 64, 66, 69, 72, 74,
  79
Aiken, Conrad, 15
"And Now What's To Do?," 101–2, 190
Antigone. See Sophocles
Arendt, Hannah, 50
Aristotle, and formalism, 74, 75, 84, 122,
  162, 202, 207
Armstid, Henry, character in *The Hamlet*,
  130, 131
Armstid, Lula, character in *The Hamlet*
  and *As I Lay Dying*, 132, 159
Arnold, Matthew, 66, 79
As I Lay Dying, 9–10, 11–16 *passim*, 20,
  28–35, 37, 149, 150–75, 178, 179,
  225
Auden, W. H., 77
Austin, J. L., 180, 192–93

Bakhtin, Mikhail, 76, 197
"Barn Burning," 48
Bascomb, Maury, character in *The Sound
  and the Fury*, 136
Beardsley, Aubrey, 85, 206
Beauchamp, Hubert, character in *Go
  Down, Moses*, 123
Beauchamp, Lucas, character in *Go
  Down, Moses* and *Intruder in the Dust*,

97, 132, 144, 170, 215, 222, 223, 224,
  225, 232, 233, 234, 235, 237
Beauchamp, Molly, character in *Go
  Down Moses*, 149, 170–71, 172
Beauchamp, Sophonsiba, character in *Go
  Down Moses*, 123
Beck, Warren, 8
Benbow, Horace, character in *Flags in the
  Dust* and *Sanctuary*, 48, 59, 60, 61,
  73–74, 105
Benbow, Julia, character in *Flags in the
  Dust*, 105
Benbow, "Little Belle," character in
  Sanctuary, 59, 60, 105
Benbow, Narcissa, character in *Flags in
  the Dust*, 59, 60, 105
Black woman, character in "Delta
  Autumn," *Go Down, Moses*, 149, 170,
  228, 234
Bleikasten, André, 15, 146, 157–58, 159,
  160
Bloom, Harold, 5, 120
Blotner, Joseph, 67, 103, 104
Bon, Charles, character in *Absalom,
  Absalom!*, 37, 47, 85, 146, 172, 174,
  184, 191, 192, 193, 194, 204–16
  passim, 226, 228, 230
Bond, Jim, character in *Absalom, Absa-
  lom!*, 177, 193, 196, 226, 237
Brecht, Bertolt, 9
Brooks, Cleanth, 14–15, 59, 65, 66–69,
  73, 74, 75, 160, 195, 209, 210, 215
Browning, Robert, 62–63
Bunch, Byron, character in *Light in
  August*, 73
Bundren, Addie, character in *As I Lay
  Dying*, 9–10, 11, 31, 32, 33, 34–35,
  150, 151–61, 162, 163, 164, 166, 167,

253

The Wisconsin Project on American Writers

A series edited by Frank Lentricchia